An Activity-Based
Approach to Early Intervention

An Activity-Based Approach to Early Intervention
Second Edition

by

Diane Bricker, Ph.D.
Early Intervention Program
Center on Human Development
College of Education
University of Oregon, Eugene

with

Kristie Pretti-Frontczak, Ph.D.
Department of Educational Foundations and
    Special Services
Kent State University, Ohio

and

Natalya McComas, M.S.
Early Intervention Personnel Preparation Programs
College of Education
University of Oregon, Eugene

·P A U L·H·
BROOKES
PUBLISHING C?

Baltimore • London • Toronto • Sydney

Paul H. Brookes Publishing Co.
Post Office Box 10624
Baltimore, Maryland 21285

www.pbrookes.com

Typeset by Brushwood Graphics, Inc., Baltimore, Maryland.
Manufactured in the United States of America by
The Maple Press Co., York, Pennsylvania.

The photographs on the front and back covers are courtesy of the Paul H. Jones Child Development Center at Kent State University in Ohio; the photographs were taken by Mike Cardew.

The case studies and examples used in this book are based on real individuals. Identifying information has been changed to protect confidentiality.

Many figures in this book are reproduced with permission from Bricker, D. (Ed.). (1993). *Assessment, evaluation, and programming system for infants and children: Vol. 1. AEPS measurement for birth to three years.* Baltimore: Paul H. Brookes Publishing Co.; Bricker, D., & Pretti-Frontczak, K. (Eds.). (1996). *Assessment, evaluation, and programming system for infants and children: Vol. 3. AEPS measurement for three to six years.* Baltimore: Paul H. Brookes Publishing Co.; Bricker, D., & Waddell, M. (Eds.). (1996). *Assessment, evaluation, and programming system for infants and children: Vol. 4. AEPS curriculum for three to six years.* Baltimore: Paul H. Brookes Publishing Co.; and Cripe, J., Slentz, K., & Bricker, D. (Eds.). (1993). *Assessment, evaluation, and programming system for infants and children: Vol. 2. AEPS curriculum for birth to three years.* Baltimore: Paul H. Brookes Publishing Co.

Library of Congress Cataloging-in-Publication Data

Bricker, Diane D.
   An activity-based approach to early intervention / by Diane
Bricker with Kristie Pretti-Frontczak and Natalya McComas.—2nd
ed.
     p.   cm.
   Includes bibliographical references and index.
   ISBN 1-55766-351-3
   1. Handicapped children—Education (Preschool)—United States.
2. Education, Preschool—Activity programs—United States.   3. Child
development—United States.   I. Pretti-Frontczak, Kristie.
II. McComas, Natalya.   III. Title.
LC4019.2.B74   1998
371.990472—dc21
                                                     98-24852
                                                        CIP

British Library Cataloguing in Publication data are available from the British Library.

Contents

About the Authors

Diane Bricker, Ph.D., Associate Dean for Academic Programs, Director, Early Intervention Program, Center on Human Development, College of Education, 5253 University of Oregon, Eugene, Oregon 97403

Diane Bricker completed her undergraduate work at Ohio State University, her master's degree in special education at the University of Oregon, and her doctoral degree in special education at George Peabody College. Her initial work focused on improving the language skills of institutionalized children with severe disabilities. That work led to the development of one of the first community-based integrated early intervention programs in the early 1970s. Since then, her work has continued to address issues in the area of early intervention. Dr. Bricker has directed a number of national demonstration projects and research efforts focused on examining the efficacy of early intervention; the development of a linked assessment, intervention, and evaluation system; and the study of a comprehensive, parent-focused screening tool. Other research interests include the development of intervention strategies to enhance communication in infants and young children with disabilities. Dr. Bricker has also directed a graduate training program focused on preparing early interventionists. More than 300 students have received their master's or doctoral degree from this program and have gone on to practice in the field.

with

Kristie Pretti-Frontczak, Ph.D., Assistant Professor, Department of Educational Foundations and Special Services, 405 White Hall, Kent State University, Kent, Ohio 44242

Kristie Pretti-Frontczak received her doctoral degree in early intervention from the University of Oregon in 1996. In 1997, she became an assistant professor in the Department of Educational Foundations and Special Services at Kent State University and the director of the Early Childhood Intervention Specialist Program, Family Child Learning Center. In collaboration with the Family Child Learning Center, Dr. Pretti-Frontczak coordinates several federally funded projects designed to examine the effects of activity-based intervention on young children and their families. Dr. Pretti-Frontczak frequently provides training and technical assistance to programs across the United States interested in an activity-based approach.

Natalya McComas, M.S., Instructor/Field Placement Coordinator, Early Intervention Personnel Preparation Programs, College of Education, 5253 University of Oregon, Eugene, Oregon 97403

Natalya McComas completed her master's degree in early intervention special education at the University of Oregon in 1990. She then served as the lead interventionist in a 5-year, federally funded program that developed a model demonstration of the activity-based intervention approach. She is an instructor and field placement coordinator for the Early Intervention Personnel Preparation Programs, College of Education, University of Oregon. In addition, Ms. McComas consults with a number of Head Start and other community-based early intervention programs on the implementation of activity-based intervention. Together with Jennifer Olson, she has developed a self-directed training manual entitled *An Activity-Based Approach to Learning.*

Foreword

When the first edition of *An Activity-Based Approach to Early Intervention* was published in 1992, it represented the cumulation of more than three decades of theory and research that had steadily driven the field of early intervention toward truly effective methods. *Activity-based intervention* (ABI) was defined as a "child-directed, transactional approach that embeds intervention on children's individual goals and objectives in routine, planned, or child-initiated activities, and uses logically occurring antecedents and consequences to develop functional and generative skills" (Bricker & Cripe, 1992, p. 40). For the first time in a single volume, the authors had integrated a wide range of theories, research, techniques, and procedures into a remarkably congruent, intuitively appealing framework. Not surprising, the first edition was quickly adopted by the field as one of a small handful of books that describes both how intervention should be conducted and why the approach prescribed should be effective.

Since publication of the first edition, both the theoretical and empirical bases for activity-based teaching have grown on many fronts, and there has been widespread acceptance of ABI principles and practices. Nevertheless, one senses a great struggle just below the surface in the well-intended efforts of practitioners to embed ABI into the actual day-to-day practices of child care centers and preschool classrooms. ABI may be theoretically, empirically, and intuitively appealing, but it is not easy to do well and cannot be implemented using a "cookbook approach."

The authors of the second edition, Bricker, Pretti-Frontczak, and McComas, are clearly aware of the challenges of implementing and maintaining effective activity-based intervention. The second edition reflects the authors' dedication to enhancing the effectiveness of ABI by further refining the protocols and procedures necessary to implement it. They are fully cognizant that practitioners must often modify ABI to make it work under the unique constraints faced in daily practice. The second edition offers numerous insights into how to modify the approach without losing its essence. Indeed, readers already thoroughly familiar with the theoretical and empirical roots of ABI may wish to devote most of their attention to the first section of the book, which describes and explains how to apply ABI. Most readers, however, would be ill advised to skip the second section, which contains five chapters that address the uses of ABI and similar naturalistic early intervention approaches. As I noted, ABI is not a cookbook approach. Its effective use will always depend on practitioners' having a deep grasp of its conceptual bases. A great cook can successfully modify a recipe only because he or she understands how all of the ingredients can be made to work together to achieve the desired outcome. The same is inherently true for great practitioners.

The second edition of *An Activity-Based Approach to Early Intervention* is by no means the last word on this approach. It is instead an important step on the journey toward increasingly effective early intervention practices. When we look back to the practices in use in the 1970s, the truly revolutionary nature of the ABI approach is starkly apparent. Yet for all of the progress it represents, we remain some distance from achieving optimal early intervention approaches, in practice if not in theory. Still, this volume will likely move us much closer to achieving exactly the outcomes we desire for all children.

Steven F. Warren, Ph.D.
Professor of Special Education and Psychology
Peabody College, Vanderbilt University
Nashville, Tennessee

Acknowledgments

Historically, a number of professional colleagues have helped shape the conceptual development of activity-based intervention. William Bricker sparked Diane's thinking toward the development of an approach that would produce better outcomes in young children with severe disabilities. Gisela Chatelanat introduced Piaget and the importance of blending intervention techniques with the developmental process. The Schoggens, Phil and Dikkie, made clear through conversations over the years the importance of environmental context to children's learning. Bob and MaryLynn Cantrell assisted in moving that thinking to intervention efforts with children. Repeated debates with John Filler, Roger Smith, Lizbeth Vincent, and Rick Brinker were also critical in the development of the underlying conceptual framework from which activity-based intervention has evolved.

Since its formal inception in the early 1980s, we have profited from the feedback provided by the many students and interventionists who have used activity-based intervention and who have pointed out what elements and procedures of the approach worked and in which areas change was necessary. In respect to this volume, we would like to acknowledge Head Start of Lane County in Oregon for their cooperation, support, and collaboration with the University of Oregon Early Intervention Program in using activity-based intervention in their home- and center-based programs. We were also richly rewarded from collaboration with the Florence PACE Program in Florence, Oregon, whose staff explored the use of activity-based intervention in rural settings. Directors, teachers, assistants, and support staff from these programs dedicated time and effort toward training and subsequent implementation of activity-based intervention with the children and families they served.

During the 1980s and 1990s, doctoral students who participated in the University of Oregon Early Intervention Leadership Training Program provided careful analysis of activity-based intervention that has resulted in the development of more comprehensive and effective procedures. We would also like to express our appreciation to Early Intervention faculty who have read and provided valuable feedback on previous versions of this volume.

Juliann J. Woods Cripe is due special recognition for her contribution to the first edition of this book. Juliann assisted in getting the activity-based approach into a cohesive package that could be used by early intervention personnel throughout the nation. Her contributions clearly helped broaden and balance the approach.

Steven F. Warren has consistently encouraged us to clarify issues associated with activity-based intervention and has led us to exciting work addressing aspects of naturalistic intervention with children that we had not considered. We appreciate his encouragement over the years.

This volume did not spring forth full-blown. Rather, the process has been a set of iterative revisions that have been cheerfully typed and retyped by Karen Lawrence. Karen has also quietly and competently completed a myriad of other important tasks associated with the development of a book manuscript. Hill Walker's leadership style continues to encourage all of us associated with the Center on Human Development. Personnel at Brookes Publishing have been flexible and supportive as we have trudged through the details necessary for creating a defensible piece of work. Finally, our families, Clint, Sierra, Mike, and Lonnie, have supported our individual and collective efforts to produce this book.

To this long list we must add our thanks to the hundreds of children and families who participated and supported the evolution of activity-based intervention. In repayment, we hope that this participation has enhanced the quality of their lives.

To the many students and professionals who have used the activity-based intervention approach and who have offered feedback that has been vital in the development and refinement of this approach

An Activity-Based
Approach to Early Intervention

Chapter 1

Introduction

Activity-based intervention is an early intervention approach that was described in 1992 in the forerunner to this edition. During the ensuing years, activity-based intervention has been well received by the early intervention community. This approach, as with other "naturalistic" strategies, has been seen by many as an important step forward in assisting young children who have or who are at risk for disabilities to acquire and generalize developmental and educational goals. We like to think that the first edition of this book was instrumental in the adoption of so-called "naturalistic" approaches by early intervention programs throughout the United States and internationally. Other disciplines are exploring the usefulness of activity-based intervention (e.g., Block & Davis, 1996), and a variety of curricula have been developed using the approach (e.g., *Assessment, Evaluation, and Programming System* [Bricker, 1993]; *Activity-Based Approach to Learning* [McComas & Olson, 1997]). However, considerable work remains to make activity-based and other similar approaches maximally effective with a broad range of infants, toddlers, and young children. Since the publication of the first edition, the study, refinement, and expansion of the activity-based approach to early intervention has moved forward at a steady pace. The information gathered since 1992 has been examined, synthesized, and incorporated into this volume. This volume offers an expanded context for understanding child-directed approaches in general and activity-based intervention in particular.

The content and organization of this volume has changed significantly from the first edition. The book has been organized into two sections following this brief introductory chapter. Section I contains six chapters that describe and explain in detail how to apply activity-based intervention. Chapter 2 presents the definition and elements of the approach and offers several examples of the approach. Chapter 3 discusses a linked systems approach that provides a broad framework for activity-based intervention. Chapter 4 contains material on teams and the use of activity-based intervention by teams. Chapters 5 and 6 present the underlying structure of the approach and its application to individual children and groups of children, respectively. Chapter 7, the final chapter in Section I, discusses the importance of evaluation and evaluation strategies that can be used with activity-based intervention.

Section II contains five chapters that address the uses of activity-based intervention and other similar child-directed approaches. Chapter 8 presents a discussion of naturalistic teaching approaches and the essential features that constitute these approaches. Chapters 9 and 10 describe the historical and conceptual bases of activity-based intervention. Chapter 11 addresses the issues associated with the approach, and Chapter 12 offers a brief summary of future directions for early intervention, early childhood special education, early childhood education, and activity-based intervention.

The changes in this volume are based on our considerable experience in assisting teachers, therapists, interventionists, aides, and caregivers in learning and using activity-based intervention. These professionals have shown us clearly what was understandable and easy to grasp and which parts of the approach were problematic for them to understand and implement. We have attempted to remedy the latter through improving descriptions, adding illustrations, and reformatting pieces of the structural framework. We believe that the changes introduced in this volume will enable readers and users of activity-based intervention to grasp the underlying conceptual framework of activity-based intervention and effectively use the approach in a variety of settings with a range of children and families.

PURPOSE AND AUDIENCE

As indicated previously, the purpose of this volume is to describe activity-based intervention and provide the necessary structure to enable interventionists to use the approach. Although no set of words can be entirely satisfactory when attempting to learn and employ new information, strategies, and skills, the hope is that the detailed descriptions provided will permit most readers to 1) understand the major assumptions that underlie the approach; 2) grasp the necessary assessment processes, goal setting, and environmental arrangements that provide the guiding structure; and 3) incorporate into their teaching repertoires the essential elements that define activity-based intervention.

We believe that the individuals for whom this book is intended will vary in their ability to reach these three goals of understanding, grasping, and incorporating for a variety of reasons. Some will be experienced in using child-directed techniques and find adoption of the approach relatively straightforward. Other caregivers, interventionists, and therapists may have been educated in adult-directed approaches and will find it challenging to learn to become observers of, and responders to, children. Often, ingrained habits are difficult to relinquish even with the intent to do so. Adults who direct children through individual activities as well as through the entire school/home day may find it difficult to permit children to engage primarily in self-directed activities or may find it perplexing to use routines and daily activities as teaching vehicles.

We have also noted that many interventionists, teachers, therapists, and caregivers are eager to learn the concrete elements of an approach and are less interested in the conceptual base and underlying structure of the approach. These individuals may be tempted to focus on Section I of this volume and not read Section II. We believe the material in Sections I *and* II is essential to the effective and generalized application of activity-based intervention. When we observe a teacher, therapist, interventionist, or caregiver having significant problems in applying the approach, we find that these individuals often have a limited appreciation of the conceptual base of the approach or have little or no knowledge about the framework and structure that underlie the approach. As with so much of life, understanding the fundamentals of something is essential to effective application and absolutely vital to diagnosing and remedying problems.

DEFINITION OF TERMS AND CONCEPTS

We believe that to help ensure clarity of the material presented in this volume it is useful to define and briefly discuss the parameters that surround several terms that appear throughout the chapters. The terms *early intervention* and *early intervention/early childhood special education* are used interchangeably. These terms refer to a field of study and a method of intervention focused on children who have or who are at risk for disabilities from birth through 5 years of age and their families. Early intervention or early intervention/early childhood special education programs refer to a formal system of services, content, and procedures that are delivered under the direction of trained professionals.

The term *young children who have or who are at risk for disabilities* refers to children who range in age from birth through 5 years of age. In addition, these children either have a documented disability or have a documented medical or environmental condition, or both, that significantly raises their risk of developing a disability in the future.

The term *interventionist* is used to represent the array of professionals and paraprofessionals who deliver services to young children who participate in early intervention programs. We find the term *teacher* to be overly limiting when, in fact, the team of professionals who work in early intervention programs often includes speech-language pathologists, occupational therapists, physical therapists, psychologists, and medical personnel as well as other individuals. The term *interventionist* is intended to include all of the professionals and paraprofessionals associated with early intervention programs.

We agree with the federal mandate that most children with disabilities and their families require a team of professionals to offer the array of needed services specified in the individualized education program/individualized family service plan. We, therefore, use the term *team* to refer to the group of professionals, paraprofessionals, and parents/caregivers who work together to deliver the needed services. In addition, we use the terms *interventionists* and *teams* interchangeably throughout the volume.

REFERENCES

Block, M., & Davis, T. (1996). An activity-based approach to physical education for preschool children with disabilities. *Adapted Physical Activity Quarterly, 13,* 230–246.

Bricker, D. (Ed.). (1993). *Assessment, evaluation, and programming system for infants and children: Vol. 1. AEPS measurement for birth to three years.* Baltimore: Paul H. Brookes Publishing Co.

McComas, N., & Olson, J. (1997). *Activity-based approach to learning (Building Effective Successful Teams Module 2).* Moscow: University of Idaho, Idaho Center of Developmental Disabilities.

How to Use
Activity-Based Intervention

Chapter 2

A Description of Activity-Based Intervention

While turning the pages in a book, Tobia stops and says, "Horsie!" Tobia's mother, who is busy dusting furniture, turns to her 3-year-old and asks, "What?" Tobia says again, "Horsie." "Oh, where do you see a horsie?" asks her mother. Tobia looks at the picture and says, "Here. . . lookie." Then Tobia looks up at her mother. Tobia's mother sits down next to her and says, "Oh, I see the horse. It's brown." Tobia responds, "Brown?" "Yes," her mother answers. "The horse is brown. The horse also has a brown mane and brown tail." Tobia repeats, "Mane?" "Yes," her mother replies. "The hair on the horse's neck is called a mane. Do you see the horse's mane?" Tobia touches the horse's mane and says, "Mane." Tobia's mother smiles and lays her hand on Tobia's head asking, "Do you have a mane?" Tobia laughs and says, "No, I have hair." Tobia's mother smiles and says, "You're right. Horses have manes, and people have hair. Your hair is brown like the horse's mane." Tobia grins, "I have brown hair!"

Joel, who is 12 months old, is side-stepping down the length of the couch when he notices a favorite ball that is just beyond his reach. The baby points to the ball and asks, "Ba?" His father passes by, and Joel looks at him and then back to the ball, again pointing and asking, "Ba?" The father stops, leans over the infant, and says, "Ball. You want the ball?" Joel says, "Ba," and his father responds, "Do you want to play with the ball?" Joel first looks at his father, then at the ball, and then back to his father and says, "Ba." The father picks up the ball and places it on the couch beside Joel. The baby reaches to pick up the ball. The father holds out his hands and says, "Throw the ball to me." Joel releases the ball, laughs, and waves his arms. His father laughs and picks up the ball and holds it

7

out to Joel. "Do you want the ball? Come and get it." Joel says, "Ba," and takes several steps to his father. The father, still holding out the ball, says, "Here's the ball. Such a big boy."

Five-month-old Marta is in an infant seat on the kitchen counter while her mother puts away some groceries. The baby waves her arms and coos. Her mother leans toward the infant and imitates the cooing sound. The mother then picks up a paper bag to discard it, and the crackling paper attracts the infant's attention. Marta looks intently at the paper and waves her arms again. Her mother shakes the paper bag for the infant who immediately quiets and stares at the paper bag. Her mother then places the paper bag within easy reach of the infant. Marta reaches for the paper bag, grasps it, and moves it to her mouth. Her mother says, "That's a noisy paper bag." She then guides the infants hand away from her mouth and moves the baby's arm to shake the paper bag. As the bag moves, the crackling sound occurs, and the infant stops her activity. After a few seconds, the mother gently shakes the infant's arm again, causing the paper to make the crackling noise. Marta pauses but soon shakes her arm independently to produce the crackling noise.

Jae Hyung comes into his house in tears. His mother asks the 5-year-old what happened. Jae Hyung sniffles that his playmate, who is visiting, took his toy truck. His mother comforts him and then asks, "What should we do about it?" The child shakes his head. His mother says, "Could you ask Billy to share the truck? Or, could we find another truck for you?" Jae Hyung runs to his bedroom but soon yells to his mother, "I can't find a truck." His mother replies, "Where did you look?" "I looked in my toy box," says Jae Hyung. "Where else can you look?" asks his mother. In a few minutes, Jae Hyung stands before his mother with a red fire truck in his hands and explains, "It was under my bed."

Such transactions, which occur frequently for most children, appear to provide much of the information and feedback necessary for children to learn how to negotiate their social and physical environment. Several interesting features of the child–parent transactions described previously should be noted. First, the transactions were at least equally initiated and directed by the child. The parents followed their children's leads and provided the information and feedback that appeared to meet their children's needs. Second, the transactions were a meaningful sequence of reciprocal exchanges that were appropriate to the child's level of development. Third, the interventions may each have some novel characteristic; for example, Joel may have never before found the ball on the couch. Fourth, if both partners are responsive, then the interaction is somewhat obligatory yet positive.

Compare the preceding child–parent transactions with the following vignettes:

> Lori, a 16-month-old child with Down syndrome, is crawling toward a toy on the floor. Her mother intercedes, picks up the child, and seats her in a small chair at a table. The mother sits across the table and says, "Come on, Lori, let's find the toys." The mother goes on to explain that it's Lori's job to find hidden objects today. To begin, the mother holds a small rattle for Lori to see. Lori looks at the rattle and then reaches for it. Without letting the child touch the rattle, the mother removes the rattle and, while Lori is watching, places it under a small cloth and says, "Lori, find the rattle." Lori looks away and the mother prompts a response by shaking the cloth. Lori looks at the cloth and picks it up. The child shakes the cloth and places it on her head to play Peekaboo. The mother says, "Lori, look at the rattle," and removes the cloth from the child's head. Lori sweeps the rattle on the floor with her arm.
>
> Tomaselo's father has placed him in his lap. The 5-year-old has spina bifida and developmental delays. His father says, "Hey, it's time to work on naming colors." The father has a set of small cards, each containing a swatch of color. He shows Tomaselo the first card and asks, "What color is this?" The child looks at the card and says, "Red." "Great," says his father, "that's right." Turning the next card, his father asks again, "What color is this?" "Red," says Tomaselo. "No," says his father, "this is green. Say green." "Green," says the child as he looks at his dog across the room. "Okay," says his father. As he turns the next card, he asks, "What color is this?" Tomaselo looks at his father and, without conviction, says, "Green."

Not many people would question the motivation and concern of these parents for their children or the concern and commitment of the early intervention personnel who suggested the intervention activities. Repeated observation of such transactions, however, raises questions about the effectiveness of intervention activities that do not appear to recognize the child's motivation or the relevance of the activities for the child. The interactions of the first four children described were rich in comparison to the transactions between Lori and Tomaselo and their parents. Tobia, Joel, Marta, and Jae Hyung were permitted to initiate and lead the activities. The sequence of events was logical and continuous, and the interaction was meaningful to both partners in each situation.

The examples offered previously describe interactions between individual children and their parents. Transactions that occur between groups of children and their caregivers/interventionists can also be either child initiated and directed or adult initiated and directed.

> At opening group time at the Morehead Kindergarten class for children with disabilities, the interventionist asks the children, "What songs shall we sing today?" The children voice a number of requests. The interventionist says, "How shall we decide which songs to sing?" The children and interventionist discuss the problem and decide to write the names of the requested songs on the flipchart. Because there are too many songs for one day, the children then decide which songs to sing on Monday and the rest of the days of the week. This activity provides the children with an opportunity to address goals in early literacy, to learn the names and days of the week, and to practice problem-solving and linguistic skills.

> The Pleasant Hill Kindergarten uses an adult-directed approach, and group time begins with the interventionist indicating the need for the children to sit quietly in their assigned places. Once accomplished, the interventionist tells the children which activities will occur. First, the children are asked to indicate the day of the week and the day's weather. A specific child is asked to select the correct "day" card and place it on the board. Another child is asked to select the correct "weather" card and do likewise. Then the interventionist indicates that she would like everyone to sing a song about rainy weather. During the interventionist-selected and interventionist-directed activities, the children have little opportunity to indicate their interests.

These two vignettes are offered to make clear the distinction between situations in which children's interests are followed and shaped into important learning opportunities and situations in which the adult selects and directs the activity. Our observations suggest that much of the intervention work conducted with children who have or who are at risk for disabilities is largely adult selected and/or adult directed. One is likely to see scenarios such as those portrayed for Lori and Tomaselo and the Pleasant Hill Kindergarten. The approach described in this book was developed as an alternative to these scenarios.

Activity-based intervention was designed to capture the essence of the type of transaction that occurred between Tobia, Joel, Marta, and Jae Hyung and their parents and the children and interventionist at the Morehead Kindergarten. This approach capitalizes on children's motivation and the use of activities that have meaning and relevance to children.

DEFINITION AND ELEMENTS OF ACTIVITY-BASED INTERVENTION

The activity-based intervention approach described in this book is designed to take advantage, in an objective and measurable way, of the various aspects of daily transactions that occur between most parents and adults and their infants and young children. Activity-based intervention is a child-directed, transactional approach that embeds children's individual goals and objectives in routine, planned, or child-initiated activities and uses logically occurring antecedents and consequences to develop functional and generative skills. A schematic of this approach is contained in Figure 2.1. The definition of *activity-based intervention* contains four major elements:

1. Uses child-initiated transactions
2. Embeds children's goals and objectives in routine, planned, or child-initiated activities
3. Uses logically occurring antecedents and consequences
4. Develops functional and generative skills

Child-Initiated Transactions

The first major element of the activity-based intervention approach is the attention given to the children's interests and actions. This is done primarily by encouraging children to initiate activities. Rather than the caregiver or interventionist selecting activities, as in the examples of Lori, Tomaselo, and the Pleasant Hill Kindergarten, the child's (or children's) interests are identified. Then, if possible, the adult joins the child in the activity of interest (Bricker, 1989; MacDonald, 1989). The premise is that activity and actions initiated by children are more likely to engage and maintain their attention and involvement than activity and actions initiated by adults (a notion discussed by John Dewey, see Chapter 10).

Although it is important to attend to children's interests, caregivers and interventionists are not required to always follow children's leads. There may be times when it is appropriate and useful to direct or redirect children's activities, and there

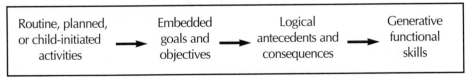

Figure 2.1.   Schematic of the activity-based intervention approach.

are many times when adults can and often should guide and/or expand children's initiations. Marta's mother, for example, used the baby's interest in a crackling paper bag to guide her exploration of the bag. Tobia's mother, too, used her child's interest in the picture of the horse to introduce a color name and new vocabulary item.

In addition to encouraging child initiation, activity-based intervention is designed to follow the child's lead in directing activities whenever possible. For example, Lori's mother could have followed her child's lead by playing Peekaboo rather than directing Lori to find the rattle. Lori's mother could have also taken turns playing Peekaboo and hiding the cloth (e.g., under the table, in back of Lori, under her shirt) because it was the focus of the child's attention. The goal of working on object constancy would be maintained, but the object and activities would be changed to match the child's interests.

By capitalizing on children's motivations, the need for using reinforcers apart from the activity is reduced (Bricker, 1989; Goetz, Gee, & Sailor, 1983). Lori's attainment of an object of interest likely is enough reinforcement to maintain her searching behavior, and, thus, tangible or secondary rewards (e.g., adult saying, "Good looking"; use of stickers) are unnecessary. In the Morehead Kindergarten example, the children's selection of the songs to be sung may be adequate to maintain their interest and participation.

Another important aspect of directing attention to the child's interests and actions is the transactional nature of the child's responses. That is, as the child behaves, the social and physical environment responds in a reciprocal manner (Bricker & Carlson, 1980). For example, if the child vocalizes, the caregiver or interventionist vocalizes in return. In general, adults will respond to the nature of the child's vocalization if it is interpretable; if not, they will request clarification. For example, if the child points to a picture and says, "Dat?" with rising inflection, the caregiver may respond in several appropriate ways to maintain the interaction and encourage the child to continue responding. The caregiver might say, "Yes, that's your truck. Do you want to play with your truck?"; ask, "Oh?" "What do you see?" or "That's a flower. Can you say flower?"; or simply make eye contact with the child. Such exchanges or transactions provide the child with feedback that is informational (e.g., labeling the object), that indicates the social environment's responsiveness (e.g., caregiver responds to the child's communicative attempts), and that assists the child in learning the communication game (e.g., speakers and listeners take turns).

Transactions such as those described for Joel and Marta are useful to children if they initiate the action and the caregiver follows their leads. Such transactions take advantage of the child's motivation. Using the child's motivation or interest has been shown to enhance learning in a variety of populations and settings (Goetz et al., 1983; Mahoney & Weller, 1980; Stremel-Campbell & Campbell, 1985); however, it is important to note that the transactional element of activity-based intervention can be used even when planned activities are introduced to children. As shown in the Morehead Kindergarten vignette, during opening group time children can be encouraged to initiate actions in a variety of ways. Children can suggest songs to sing, actions to accompany the songs, and variations on how the group responds. In addition, interventionists can introduce variations in planned activities that encourage children to initiate different actions. For example, if the record player suddenly stops working, the interventionist can use this opportunity to encourage the children to ask questions and suggest solutions to the problem, such as playing rhythm instruments instead of records.

Embedding Children's Goals and Objectives

The second element of activity-based intervention has two important parameters: 1) embedding goals in activities and 2) the type of activities available for embedding individualized education program (IEP)/individualized family service plan (IFSP) goals and objectives. Embedding is a critical concept to activity-based intervention. We define *embedding* as a procedure in which children's goals or objectives are included in an activity or event in a manner that expands, modifies, or is integral to the activity/event in a meaningful way. The introduction of a goal or objective should be done in a manner that captures the meaningfulness of the activity/event and the interest of the child. For example, if a child's IFSP motor goal is "Pull to stand," the caregiver might embed this goal by moving a desired block from the floor to the couch, thus requiring the child to pull to stand to retrieve the block. Or, while crawling, the child might be encouraged to move to the kneeling adult and pull to stand to play Pat-a-cake. Or, as in the Morehead Kindergarten example, the goal of learning weekday names was embedded into the group singing activity. The frequent embedding of children's goals and objectives into ongoing activities provides multiple and varied opportunities for children to acquire, practice, and generalize important skills.

The second parameter of this element of activity-based intervention is the type of activities that can be used to embed children's goals and objectives. Three types of activities are targeted in this intervention approach: routine, planned, and child initiated.

Routine Activities

Routine activities refer to events that occur on a predictable or regular basis, such as meals, diapering and dressing, snacks, clean-up, and arrival and departure at center-based programs. Often, these activities can be used or refocused to provide children opportunities to learn new skills or practice skills being acquired.

Planned Activities

Planned activities refer to designed events that ordinarily do not happen without adult guidance. Planned activities should interest children and be developed in ways that children find appealing as opposed to being designed exclusively to practice a targeted skill. Examples include planting seeds, acting out a song, or playing circus.

Child-Initiated Activities

Activities selected by the child are referred to as *child-initiated activities.* If children introduce and persist in an activity, the actions and events associated with the activity likely are appealing to them. Activities that are inherently interesting to children require little external support or reward. For example, reaching and grasping a desired object likely is its own reward.

These three types of activities can be, and often are, combined. That is, children can initiate some action or activity within a planned or routine activity. In fact, caregivers or interventionists should encourage child initiation within activities. Planned or routine activities may be changed or modified by children if the changes provide them with opportunities to develop and practice important skills targeted in their IEP/IFSP goals and objectives. The activity itself is less important than providing children the opportunities to practice targeted skills and to allow for meaningful participation in developmentally appropriate activities. Providing multiple practice opportunities requires that caregivers or interventionists be flexible in their use of routine and planned activities and that they be able to incorporate opportunities for practicing targeted skills in a variety of activities.

Routine, planned, and child-initiated activities have important commonalities. First, activities should make sense to children. For example, labeling pictures from a photograph file to increase vocabulary may not be as functional for a child as labeling objects that he or she is using to obtain a certain outcome (e.g., objects gathered for water play). Asking children to perform behaviors different from their usual context may be confusing and result in slower skill attainment (Warren & Bambara, 1989). Second, activities should be interesting to children. As indicated previously, this often reduces or precludes the use of artificial rewards. Children can be engaged in preferred activities that provide the frequent repetition necessary for learning. Third, activities should be gauged to children's developmental capabilities and require children to expand their repertoire to the next level of developmental sophistication. Children should learn new skills and new uses for acquired skills by building on their current developmental repertoires. Finally, activities should involve social interactions and physical contexts that are familiar to children. Using the people and places meaningful to children helps ensure practical utility.

As a child's day unfolds at school or at home, a variety of daily or routine activities occur as well as multiple opportunities for child-initiated activities. The activity-based intervention approach promotes the use of such activities for the embedding of children's IEP/IFSP goals and objectives as frequently as possible. Enhancement of communication skills occurs when children communicate a need or message as they negotiate daily activities. For example, targeting verbal requests should occur when children want to go outside, want juice in their cups, or want hats to play dress-up. Using such meaningful and relevant occurrences makes the communication genuine in that the child expresses a need (e.g., getting a coat), and the communication relates directly to the IEP/IFSP target of improving expressive language through verbal requesting. It seems likely that expressing needs under meaningful and relevant conditions leads to effective and efficient learning by children.

Although we believe that many IEP/IFSP goals and objectives can be targeted during child-initiated and routine activities, planned activities can also be beneficially employed. Such activities should be viewed by infants and young children as fun and interesting as opposed to forced training endeavors. For example, if working on improving eye–hand coordination, problem solving, and communication, an interventionist might introduce a water play activity. To begin, the children would help to assemble necessary materials such as bowls, small toys that float and sink, and aprons. Setting up the activity provides the opportunity to practice problem-solving skills (e.g., determining what is needed for the activity), communication skills (e.g., asking questions and making statements about retrieving materials), motor skills (e.g., obtaining, carrying, and arranging materials), and social skills (e.g., taking turns getting materials and sharing materials). Once set up, this activity provides children many opportunities to retrieve small toys that float and sink. While retrieving toys and pouring water, many opportunities present themselves for working on communication skills (e.g., requests, labeling objects and actions, exclamations of delight) and problem-solving skills (e.g., how to balance toys, how to obtain toys out of reach). The activity ends with the children putting away the toys and cleaning up. The clean-up period also provides the children with practice in problem-solving skills (e.g., putting materials back together, returning items to shelves), communication skills (e.g., practicing new words or word combinations), adaptive and motor skills (e.g., drying and rearranging items), and social skills (e.g., determining who will do what, discussing the activity). Including the children in the assembling and dismantling of the activity provides a clearly defined logical sequence, offers many opportunities for child initiation and intervention on targeted skills, and establishes a consistent framework that allows children to gain independence. The water play activity provides a richer context for children to learn a variety of functional skills than working on eye–hand coordination by sitting at a table and picking up pegs to insert in a board.

Logically Occurring Antecedents and Consequences

Simply having a child participate in routine, planned, or child-initiated activities will not necessarily produce desired changes. Such activities should provide a rich and meaningful context for intervention, but additional safeguards are necessary to ensure that children develop important skills. In an activity-based approach, multiple opportunities to practice targeted skills are ensured through the systematic use of appropriate antecedents and consequences that occur as logical initiators and outcomes of actions or activities. Logically occurring antecedents are those events that occur or are chosen to elicit a target response and are consistent with or meaningfully related to the child's response. For example, to elicit a grasp response from a child, the adult might place an object within the child's reach. Logically occurring consequences are outcomes or reactions that follow a child's response and are connected to the response in a meaningful way. For example, the logical consequence of grasping is obtaining a desired object.

Permitting children to engage in water play may or may not result in changes in behavior, depending on the caregiver's or interventionist's use of the activity. Prior to initiation of an activity or use of a routine activity, the caregiver or interventionist must know the participating children's goals and objectives. If improving pincer grasp, wrist rotation, and release of objects into defined spaces are targeted objectives, then the interventionist must ensure that antecedents appropriate to eliciting these motor skills occur frequently during the activity, that children have adequate opportunity to practice the target response, and that environmental feedback is adequate to acquire and maintain the response. Children's response repertoires will not necessarily expand and become more sophisticated by simply engaging in fun activities. The interventionist must provide the necessary materials, events, models, and assistance as needed to maintain engagement and to practice the targeted skill. In activity-based intervention, children are not "left to play" with the hope that learning will occur; the caregiver or interventionist assumes an active partnership role, following and leading, arranging and waiting, asking and answering, and showing and guiding. Antecedents (e.g., materials, questions, delays, comments, models, physical assistance) must be carefully analyzed to meet each child's individual needs to ensure that learning occurs.

During child-initiated, routine, or planned activities, it is essential to measure the number and type of antecedents offered, the type and frequency of children's responses, and the nature of the consequences. Only through careful documentation of antecedents, responses, and consequences can the impact of intervention be determined.

In the activity-based intervention approach, it should be emphasized that, for the most part, consequences are seen as an integral part of the action or activity; that is, consequences are generally inherent in the activity or a logical outcome of an action or activity. For example, if a toddler sees a bottle of juice (antecedent) and requests a drink (response), the relevant consequence is getting to drink the juice. If the child is learning to climb the steps of a slide, the logical outcome is getting to slide down. If a child desires an adult's attention, the consequence for calling out to the adult is that his or her attention is obtained. Using this approach requires minimal use of artificial consequences for producing desired responses.

Functional and Generative Skills

Early intervention personnel should target skills for infants and young children that are functional and generative. *Functional skills* refer to skills that permit children to negotiate their physical and social environment in an independent and satisfying manner to themselves and others. For example, it is generally more functional to assist children in learning how to open and close doors, turn on faucets, and flush toilets than to focus on helping them learn to stack blocks or complete puzzles. It likely is more useful for children to learn to initiate interactions with peers than to walk on a balance beam.

Children with disabilities and, often, children at risk for disabilities have developmental delays that set them apart from their typically developing peers. These children experience difficulties that require some form of compensatory intervention. Their developmental needs require that caregivers and interventionists be judicious in the selection of intervention targets. Targets should assist the caregiver(s) and interventionist(s) in building children's functional repertoires so that the developmental discrepancies between them and their typically developing peers are minimized and independence is enhanced.

Equally important to acquiring functional skills is the need to help children acquire generative skills that will assist children's independent functioning in a variety of settings. The concept of *generative* refers to a child's ability to use information or a skill appropriately across people, events, objectives, and settings. In addition, *generative* refers to the child's ability to make minor modifications in response to similar, but changing, conditions. For example, learning to assign the label of "car" to all appropriate vehicles as opposed to only the family car or learning to remove lids from all types of jars and bottles as opposed to only those used in training assists children in acquiring independence. Activity-based intervention provides caregivers and interventionists with a framework for providing multiple opportunities to target functional skills in a way that will encourage the generalization of the response to other appropriate conditions.

A primary goal of activity-based intervention is to assist infants and young children in efficiently acquiring functional and generative skills. This approach does not focus on teaching children to respond to specific cues under specific conditions, but rather it focuses on developing generalized motor, social, adaptive, communication, and problem-solving skills that permit independent functioning. This approach attempts to develop associations between classes of antecedents and classes of responses rather than establishing one-to-one correspondences. More traditional approaches might begin intervention with single words by showing a child a set of objects or pictures (e.g., spoon, car, ball). Often, specific cues (antecedents) are used to elicit responses (e.g., "Tell me what this is. This is a _____"). As the child learns the association between specific antecedents and responses, variations in the antecedents are introduced until a response is generalized across appropriate antecedents.

Activity-based intervention uses a different approach. A variety of antecedents are associated with the response, and response variation is encouraged. In this approach, antecedents are seen as classes of similar stimuli or events that should be associated with classes of similar responses, as shown in Figure 2.2.

To assist a child in learning to label objects, an interventionist using the activity-based approach would introduce pictures of cars as well as a variety of toy cars, real cars, and symbols for cars (e.g., words) to ensure that the child understands that the label "car" can and does stand for all of these examples. Offering children multiple examples helps ensure that the response "car" generalizes to all appropriate examples, making the word a functional part of the child's language repertoire.

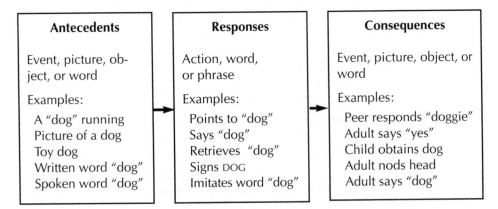

Antecedents	Responses	Consequences
Event, picture, object, or word	Action, word, or phrase	Event, picture, object, or word
Examples:	Examples:	Examples:
A "dog" running Picture of a dog Toy dog Written word "dog" Spoken word "dog"	Points to "dog" Says "dog" Retrieves "dog" Signs DOG Imitates word "dog"	Peer responds "doggie" Adult says "yes" Child obtains dog Adult nods head Adult says "dog"

Figure 2.2.   Examples of classes of antecedents, responses, and associated consequences.

SUMMARY

The four elements of activity-based intervention—child-directed transactions; embedding goals and objectives in routine, planned, and child-initiated activities; systematic use of logically occurring antecedents and consequences; and functional and generative skills—blend together to create an approach that can be used in a variety of settings (e.g., home, school, store, playground) and under a variety of conditions. Interventionists and caregivers can learn to use the approach, and its flexibility permits a broad application to infants and young children who have or who are at risk for mild, moderate, or severe disabilities.

Not only can activity-based intervention be successfully used with groups of children whose developmental levels vary, this approach is also appropriate for use across children and families with diverse economic backgrounds, experiences, values, and cultures. This approach uses child-initiated, routine, and planned activities that are not predetermined but rather instigated by the children and caregivers in particular environments. The importance assigned to child-initiated activities allows the child to engage in activities that are familiar and engaging and likely reflect the family's values (e.g., the types of toys and books available to the child in the home). So, too, the use of routine activities lends itself well to the incorporation of the child's learning into activities the family members have chosen as essential parts of their lives. Finally, the types of planned activities can also be chosen or designed to reflect family experiences, cultures, and values. The introduction of a zoo activity might make little sense to young children who have never visited a zoo, whereas planning an activity focused on domestic animals may be meaningful. Fundamental to the successful implementation of activity-based intervention is the tailoring of training activities to the children and their goals that, in turn, permit respect for diversity.

The examples presented in this chapter focus on interactions between children and their parents or an interventionist. As we note in Chapter 1, the terms *interventionist* and *team* are used interchangeably as most early intervention programs have on staff a variety of personnel (e.g., aide, teacher, communication specialist, occupational therapist) who deliver services to young children and their families. Although teams may vary considerably across programs and agencies, the important notion is that participating children and families require support from professionals with different expertise. Activity-based intervention lends itself well to an integrated team approach. Children's goals and objectives are to be addressed throughout the day whether the children are engaged in, for example, motor activities (e.g., physical therapy) or language activities (e.g., speech-language therapy). Parents and other team members work together to select goals and then identify and plan times and activities when these goals can be addressed in child-initiated, routine, and planned activities. The use of activity-based intervention by teams is addressed in detail in Chapter 4.

REFERENCES

Bricker, D. (1989). *Early intervention for at-risk and handicapped infants, toddlers and preschool children.* Palo Alto, CA: VORT Corp.

Bricker, D., & Carlson, L. (1980). An intervention approach for communicatively handicapped infants and young children. In D. Bricker (Ed.), *Language intervention with children* (pp. 477–515). San Francisco: Jossey-Bass.

Goetz, L., Gee, K., & Sailor, W. (1983). Using a behavior chain interruption strategy to teach communication skills to students with severe disabilities. *Journal of The Association for Persons with Severe Handicaps, 10*(1), 21–30.

MacDonald, J. (1989). *Becoming partners with children.* San Antonio, TX: Special Press, Inc.

Mahoney, G., & Weller, E. (1980). An ecological approach to language intervention. In D. Bricker (Ed.), *Language resource book* (pp. 17–32). San Francisco: Jossey-Bass.

Stremel-Campbell, K., & Campbell, R. (1985). Training techniques that may facilitate generalization. In S. Warren & A. Rogers-Warren (Eds.), *Teaching functional language* (pp. 251–285). Baltimore: University Park Press.

Warren, S., & Bambara, L. (1989). An experimental analysis of milieu language intervention: Teaching the action-object form. *Journal of Speech and Hearing Disorders, 54,* 448–461.

Chapter 3

A Linked Systems Approach

Chapter 2 provides a definition of activity-based intervention and describes the four elements that compose the approach. Equally important to understanding the elements of an activity-based approach is understanding the broad framework that provides its foundation. Activity-based intervention is part of a larger system consisting of a total early intervention/early childhood special education (EI/ECSE) program. The major components of a program should include assessment, goal development, intervention, and evaluation. As a part of this larger systems framework, activity-based intervention is interrelated to the other major program components as shown in Figure 3.1. This type of linked systems framework permits the direct use of information collected during *assessment* for the development of appropriate *goals* and subsequent *intervention* content. The *evaluation* that is conducted following intervention is also linked to the assessment, targeted goals and objectives, and intervention so that teams can make direct and relevant comparisons of child and family progress.

The purpose of this chapter is to 1) discuss a linked systems framework, 2) review the role of assessment in EI/ECSE, 3) explain the fundamental importance of assessment/evaluation tools for developing appropriate goals and objectives and for intervention content, 4) describe one assessment/evaluation tool's

Figure 3.1. The four major program components of a linked systems framework.

features that permit direct linking of assessment efforts to activity-based intervention, and 5) discuss a five-step process for developing appropriate goals and objectives for the successful implementation of an activity-based approach.

Several examples of a linked systems framework have been described in the EI/ECSE literature (e.g., Bagnato & Neisworth 1991; Bagnato, Neisworth, & Munson, 1997; Bricker, 1989, 1993, 1996a, 1996b). These descriptions stress the importance of conceptualizing program components as a series of related activities. The interrelatedness of program components permits an efficient and focused approach that maximizes the probability that children and their families will acquire targeted skills.

As shown in Figure 3.2, an analogy to a tree's annual life cycle is used to illustrate the four components of the linked systems framework including assessment, goal development, intervention, and evaluation. The first component, *assessment*, is "an ongoing collaborative process of systematic observations and analysis" (Greenspan & Meisels, 1995, p. 23). The assessment component is represented by the roots of a tree, for as roots give a tree vital nutrients and life, assessment provides interventionists and caregivers with essential information regarding children's development.

The second component of a linked systems framework, *goal development*, is analogous to the tree's trunk and branches, which serve as the major supports or guides for intervention. In practice, goals and objectives should be "fed" by the assessment process in order to serve as the foundation for children's future growth and development during intervention. *Intervention* is the third component of a linked systems framework. Intervention comprises many different teaching methods, strategies, activities, and events and can, therefore, be equated to the different leaves, flowers, or fruit that sprout from the tree's branches. Selecting and implementing different intervention methods and activities should be done using assessment results and children's targeted goals and objectives as a guide.

Evaluation is the fourth component of a linked systems framework and refers to an ongoing process in which children's previous performance in an area is compared with a later performance. Evaluation is represented by the falling leaves in Figure 3.2, for as falling leaves continue the life cycle of the tree by protecting and feeding the roots, evaluation continues the cycle of services by providing ongoing feedback to other program components. Evaluation data can be used to monitor and alter assessment procedures, targeted goals, and intervention efforts to better meet the needs of children, families, and programs.

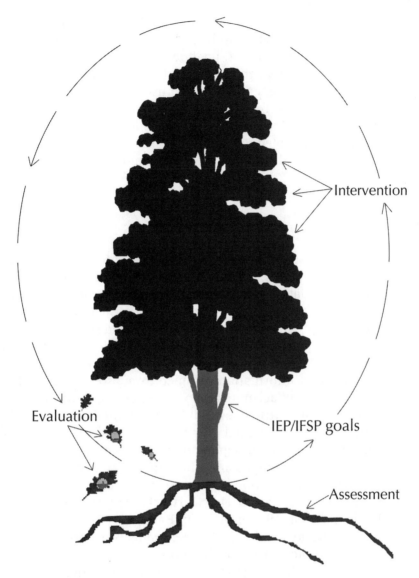

Intervention

Evaluation

IEP/IFSP goals

Assessment

Figure 3.2. Illustration of a linked systems framework.

The link among assessment, goal development, intervention, and evaluation begins with a child's entry into a program and should continue in a cyclical process as shown in Figure 3.2. Employing a linked systems framework allows for 1) efficiency of effort and use of resources, 2) accountability in terms of program impact over time, and 3) individualization through the design of programs specific to the needs of children and their families. Furthermore, the linked systems framework described previously provides a foundation for the implementation of activity-based intervention. It is important to recognize that although the activity-based approach focuses directly on the intervention component of a linked systems framework, the approach cannot be appropriately or fully implemented without attention to assessment, goal development, and evaluation efforts. In particular, the successful application of activity-based intervention is dependent on the use of an assessment tool that yields outcomes that easily translate into appropriate goals and objectives for children. The approach is dependent on developing goals and objectives that are based on a child's interest, are meaningful and functional for the child, and are a priority for the team.

TYPES OF ASSESSMENT/EVALUATION TOOLS

Comprehensive assessment/evaluation information should be collected regarding a child/family and should be used to formulate appropriate outcomes and intervention content. Outcomes for young children and their families are listed on individualized education programs (IEPs) or individualized family service plans (IFSPs). The outcomes (i.e., goals and objectives) from IEPs/ IFSPs should drive the entire intervention effort. It is, therefore, essential that information obtained from assessment/evaluation tools provide an accurate and comprehensive profile of the child and/or family. Outcomes that are functional, meaningful, and accurate can be obtained only from assessment/evaluation tools that are specifically designed to yield such outcomes. A number of authors have emphasized the importance of matching assessment/evaluation tools to the purpose for which they were developed (Bagnato & Neisworth, 1991; Bagnato et al., 1997; Bricker, 1996a, 1996b; McLean, Bailey, & Wolery, 1996). Many of the tools available to EI/ECSE teams were not developed to meet multiple purposes; therefore, understanding and appreciating the differences between tools and their purposes is important.

In general, assessment/evaluation tools developed for young children can be used to screen, determine diagnosis or eligibility for services, provide programmatic/intervention content, or evaluate child outcomes/progress. These four types of assessment/evaluation tools and their purpose, associated criteria, and outcomes are shown in Table 3.1. When assessment/ evaluation tools are used indiscriminately (i.e., used for the wrong purpose), problems may arise.

The first type of assessment/evaluation tool, screening tools, was designed to assign large groups of children into two categories: those whose development appears okay and those

Table 3.1. Types of assessment/evaluation tools and their purpose, criteria, and outcomes

Type/example(s)	Purpose	Criteria	Outcome(s)
Screening tools			
• Denver II (Frankenburg & Dodds, 1992) • Ages & Stages Questionnaires (ASQ) (Bricker, Squires, Mounts, Potter, Nickel, & Farrell, 1995)	To identify children in need of further testing	• Standardized • Norm referenced • Quick to administer • Inexpensive	Determine if further testing is necessary
Diagnostic tools			
• Bayley Scales of Infant Development—II (Bayley, 1993) • Battelle Developmental Inventory (Newborg, Stock, Wnek, Guidubaldi, & Svinicki, 1988)	To identify problems and delays in comparison with a normative group, and to establish eligibility for services	• Standardized • Norm referenced • Trained examiner	Determine eligibility for services
Programmatic tools			
• Hawaii Early Learning Profile (HELP) (VORT Corp., 1995) • Transdisciplinary Play-Based Assessment (TPBA) Linder, 1993) • Assessment, Evaluation, and Programming System (AEPS) (Bricker, 1993; Bricker & Pretti-Frontczak, 1996)	To identify IEP/IFSP goals and objectives and develop intervention content	• Criterion referenced • Curriculum based • Comprehensive (covers major domains of development)	Determine current skill level; select intervention goals, plan intervention activities/events

(continued)

Table 3.1. *(continued)*

Type/example(s)	Purpose	Criteria	Outcome(s)
Evaluation tools			
• Assessment, Evaluation, and Programming System (AEPS) (Bricker, 1993; Bricker & Pretti-Frontczak, 1996) • Battelle Developmental Inventory (Newborg, Stock, Wnek, Guidubaldi, & Svinicki, 1988)	To measure effects of intervention	• Criterion referenced • Curriculum based	Determine progress on IEP/IFSP goals and overall progress; evaluate program effects

whose development is suspect. This purpose requires that screening tools be administered quickly and economically and that they make relatively gross discriminations about children (i.e., further testing is or is not needed).

The second type of assessment/evaluation tools are those tools that assist in determining children's eligibility for EI/ECSE services. These diagnostic tools are usually standardized and used by teams to determine a child's performance in relation to a normative sample. Diagnostic tools are typically administered by trained professionals (e.g., speech-language pathologists, occupational therapists, psychologists), often under controlled conditions using standardized materials and procedures. Results from diagnostic tools often provide a summary of children's development in one or more areas.

The third type of assessment/evaluation tools are those from a genre of tools referred to as programmatic (i.e., criterion referenced, curriculum based, curriculum embedded, or curriculum compatible). Unlike diagnostic tools, programmatic tools compare a child's performance with a criterion and can be administered using nonstandardized procedures. Programmatic assessment/evaluation tools often encourage family involvement and are specifically designed to assist teams in describing a child's level of functioning; selecting, prioritizing, and writing appropriate goals; designing appropriate intervention content; and monitoring children's progress.

The fourth type of assessment/evaluation tools are those that serve an evaluative function. Evaluation activities can provide comparative data at weekly, quarterly, or annual intervals. Depending on the evaluative purpose, either a norm-referenced or programmatic assessment/evaluation tool or both can be used to measure child and/or family progress.

As indicated previously, problems can arise when tools are used inappropriately or are used for purposes other than those for which they were designed (Bagnato & Neisworth, 1991; Bagnato et al., 1997; Bricker, 1989). For example, screening tools and other standardized norm-referenced developmental tests (e.g., Bayley Scales of Infant Development—II [Bayley, 1993]; Denver II [Frankenburg & Dodds, 1992]) are generally not appropriate for determining intervention content because these tools 1) often contain items that have little relevance to intervention, 2) use standardized procedures that may be inappropriate for children with disabilities, 3) are often administered over brief time periods by unfamiliar adults, and/or 4) produce results that may not be useful for IEP/IFSP development or intervention planning.

The use of inappropriate tools to generate intervention content is unfortunate because this practice likely widens the gap between assessment, goal development, intervention, and evaluation rather than linking these major program components (Bagnato et al., 1997). Furthermore, the use of assessment/evaluation tools that do not yield intervention-relevant content can lead to the development of IEP/IFSP goals and objectives that are fragmented, too broad, too narrow, or developmentally inappropriate (Bricker & Pretti-Frontczak, 1998; Notari & Bricker, 1990; Notari & Drinkwater, 1991).

The following section of this chapter describes curriculum-based assessment/evaluation (CBA/E) tools that have gained increasing support for use in the development of IEP/IFSP goals and objectives and intervention content. In particular, the Assessment, Evaluation, and Programming System (AEPS) (Bricker, 1993; Bricker & Pretti-Frontczak, 1996) is described as an example of a CBA/E tool. The AEPS was designed to develop functional and generalizable goals and objectives that are critical to linking assessment/evaluation results with intervention and is specifically for use with activity-based intervention.

CURRICULUM-BASED ASSESSMENT/EVALUATION TOOLS

Increasingly, EI/ECSE teams are being encouraged to use CBA/E tools for making decisions regarding 1) children's present levels of functioning, 2) selection of goals and objectives, 3) intervention focus, and 4) determination of child progress (McLean et al., 1996). CBA/E tools are defined as "a form of criterion-referenced measurement wherein curricular objectives act as the criteria for the identification of instructional targets and for the assessment of status and progress" (Bagnato & Neisworth, 1991, p. 97). Curriculum-based and criterion-referenced tools both fall under the larger classification of programmatic tools (see Table 3.1).

CBA/E tools have several advantages over the use of standardized norm-referenced assessments in linking major program components and in the application of activity-based intervention: 1) they allow teams to gather information across settings, time, materials, and people; 2) they are commonly composed of functional skills that are appropriate targets for children's IEP/IFSPs; 3) they are comprehensive; and 4) they can be modified in order to assist in designing individualized curricula. CBA/E tools are designed to generate comprehensive and detailed information about children's development and to be used for developing goals and objectives as well as associated intervention content (Bagnato et al., 1997; Notari, Slentz, & Bricker, 1990). A critical role that CBA/E tools play in EI/ECSE is the development of IEP/IFSP goals and objectives, thus providing a direct link between assessment and intervention; however, the selection and writing of appropriate goals and objectives is predicated on the use of a tool that generates comprehensive and relevant information.

The AEPS is a CBA/E tool that generates comprehensive and relevant information and was specifically developed to link the components of assessment, goal development, intervention, and evaluation (Bricker, 1993). The appendix at the end of this chapter provides a case study of how results from the AEPS Test can be used to link assessment results, goal development, and intervention content. It is important to note that other CBA/E tools exist that can assist teams in developing goals and planning intervention. For a review of other CBA/E tools, see Bagnato et al. (1997) and McLean et al. (1996). The AEPS is used in this chapter to illustrate the linkage between assessment outcomes and goal development because it "exemplif[ies] the new direction in curricular assessment and intervention toward more authentic, functional, treatment-linked, developmentally appropriate practices" (Bagnato et al., 1997, p. 84).

Assessment, Evaluation, and Programming System (AEPS)

The AEPS is divided into two developmental levels: an assessment and associated curriculum for the developmental range from birth to three years and one for those from three to six years (*AEPS Measurement for Birth to Three Years* [Bricker, 1993], and *AEPS Curriculum for Birth to Three Years* [Cripe, Slentz, & Bricker, 1993]; *AEPS Measurement for Three to Six Years* [Bricker & Pretti-Frontczak, 1996], and *AEPS Curriculum for Three to Six Years* [Bricker & Waddell, 1996]). The AEPS was developed for use by direct service personnel (e.g., classroom interventionists, home visitors) and specialists (e.g., speech-language pathologists, occupational therapists, physical therapists, psychologists) to assess and evaluate the skills of infants and young children who have or who are at risk for disabilities.

Outcomes from the AEPS can be used directly to formulate IEP/IFSP goals and objectives and intervention content and can be used to measure or evaluate the effectiveness or impact of intervention on participating children (Bagnato et al., 1997). The AEPS Test can be used in conjunction with the AEPS Curriculum or other similar curricula (e.g., *The Carolina Curricu-*

lum for Infants and Toddlers with Special Needs, Second Edition, [Johnson-Martin, Jens, Attermeier, & Hacker, 1991]; *The Creative Curriculum for Early Childhood* [Dodge & Cokler, 1992]).

In addition to the AEPS Tests, the system has accompanying materials that are designed to enhance its utility. These materials include 1) a set of IEP/IFSP goals and objectives tied directly to test items, 2) AEPS Data Recording Forms, 3) associated AEPS curricula that link directly to the child's performance level, 4) assessment/evaluation forms for family members to assess their child(ren) (AEPS Family Report), 5) an assessment of family interests (AEPS Family Interest Survey), and 6) a child progress monitoring form (AEPS Child Progress Record).

Both the birth to 3 years and the 3 to 6 years developmental levels of the AEPS cover six broad curricular domains: fine motor, gross motor, adaptive, cognitive, social-communication, and social. Each domain encompasses a particular set of skills that consist of related developmental phenomena. Each domain is then divided into strands that organize related groups of behavior under a common category. Each strand contains a series of test items (goals and objectives). The number of strands, goals, and objectives varies across domains. Items on the AEPS Tests are sequenced to facilitate the assessment/evaluation of a child's ability to perform particular skills. The strands and goals are arranged from easier or developmentally earlier skills to more difficult or developmentally advanced skills. The objectives are arranged under each goal in descending order (most difficult to easiest). Figure 3.3 contains an illustration of the developmental organization of the AEPS Tests.

The AEPS Tests recommend three methods of collecting assessment and evaluation information: observation, direct test, and report. Observation is the preferred method. While observing children across settings and conditions, team members complete the AEPS Data Recording Forms. A sample of a portion of the gross motor domain Data Recording Form for the AEPS Test Birth to Three Years is shown in Figure 3.4. Children's responses can be scored as "2," which indicates that the criteria for the item were met; "1," which indicates that the child performed the item inconsistently or partially; or "0," which indicates that the child did not meet the stated criteria after several opportunities to do so.

The AEPS Tests were designed for use by professional staff, while the AEPS Family Reports were designed for use by family members. AEPS Family Report items parallel items on the AEPS

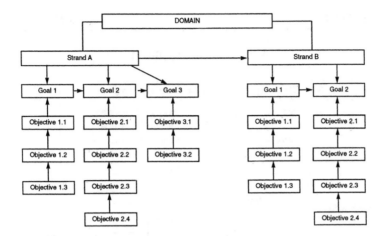

Figure 3.3. Developmental organization of the AEPS Tests.

Tests but are written in language at fourth- to sixth-grade reading levels. Caregivers/parents complete the AEPS Family Report as they observe their child across routine settings and activities.

The AEPS has several advantages for interventionists interested in linking assessment outcomes and intervention content. These advantages are summarized as features of the AEPS Tests in Figure 3.5. In addition to these advantages, AEPS Tests' features promote a link between assessment/evaluation and the successful application of an activity-based approach. Table 3.2 shows the link between the four elements of activity-based intervention and the AEPS Tests' features.

As indicated previously, the successful application of activity-based intervention is highly dependent on the targeting and embedding of functional goals and objectives. Highlighted in the following section is how CBA/E tools are designed to help teams develop appropriate goals and objectives that can then be targeted during intervention. A five-step process for developing appropriate goals and objectives from CBA/E results is described in the remainder of this chapter.

Goal Development

Interventionists and caregivers who do not use children's goals and objectives to direct their intervention efforts are *not* employing activity-based intervention. Fundamental to the appropriate application of this approach is that children's IEP/IFSP goals and objectives provide direction for the selection of activities. In other words, a primary method of ensuring a wise choice of specific intervention activities is through the careful development of individual goals and objectives for children. If

Gross Motor Domain

S = Scoring Key	Q = Qualifying Notes
2 = Pass consistently	A = Assistance provided
1 = Inconsistent	B = Behavior interfered
performance	R = Reported assessment
0 = Does not pass	M = Modification/adaptation
	D = Direct test

Name: _Susy Smith_

Test Period: –
Test Date: 10-97
Examiner: DB

	IEP	S	Q	S	Q	S	Q	S	Q
A. Movement and locomotion in supine and prone position									
1. Moves body parts independently of each other		2	R						
1.1 Turns head past 45°		2	R						
1.2 Kicks legs		2	R						
1.3 Waves arms		2	R						
2. Rolls by turning segmentally		2							
2.1 Rolls: back to stomach		2							
2.2 Rolls: stomach to back		2							
3. Creeps forward using alternating arm and leg movements	✓	0							
3.1 Rocks in creeping position	✓	0							
3.2 Assumes creeping position		2							
3.3 Crawls forward on stomach		2							
3.4 Pivots on stomach		2							
3.5 Bears weight while reaching		2							
3.6 Lifts head/chest off surface		2							
B. Balance in sitting									
1. Assumes balanced sitting position	✓	0							
1.1 Assumes hands and knees position from sitting		0							
1.2 Regains balanced sitting after reaching		0							
1.3 Regains balanced sitting after leaning		0							
1.4 Sits balanced without support	✓	1							

Figure 3.4. An example of a portion of the AEPS Gross Motor Domain Data Recording Form.

AEPS Tests' Features

- Relies on observations of children's performances during daily routines and play
- Contains a set of associated IEP/IFSP goals and objectives
- Targets functional and generalizable skills
- Covers six essential domains of development
- Contains items that are arranged hierarchically from simple to increasingly complex
- Permits adaptations and modifications for a range of disabling conditions
- Contains an associated curriculum that is compatible with an activity-based approach to intervention
- Is designed to be administered quarterly to monitor child progress
- Promotes family involvement and decision making

Figure 3.5.   AEPS Tests' features.

intervention targets for children are well chosen and operationally defined, then intervention efforts become clear, and the selection of activities or routines as well as the reinforcement of child-initiated activities become straightforward. Without appropriate and functional goals, interventionists and caregivers cannot select with confidence activities that will enhance learning. Direction cannot be offered if children's goals and objectives are developmentally inappropriate, poorly written, too general, or too narrow. Therefore, the development of a well-written, comprehensive set of IEP/IFSP goals and objectives is critical to the successful application of activity-based intervention and can be conceptualized as a five-step process: 1) *administration* of a CBA/E tool, 2) *summarization* of results, 3) *selection* of meaningful skills, 4) *prioritization* of skills, and 5) *writing* the goals and objectives to be understandable and measurable.

The first step in developing appropriate goals and objectives is the administration of a CBA/E tool. The assessment/evaluation tool used at this step should produce comprehensive information on a child's current behavioral repertoire and should provide direction in determining the next developmentally appropriate skills from across important developmental domains.

The second step in developing appropriate goals and objectives is for team members to summarize the results from the assessment/evaluation process. A summary of children's levels of functioning should include a description of their skills across domains and should describe specific skills that are beginning to emerge. Summarization of results should focus on a particular

Table 3.2. Activity-based intervention elements linked to AEPS Tests' features

Elements of activity-based intervention (ABI)	AEPS Tests' features
1. ABI is a child-directed transactional approach.	• Children's interactions during daily activities (e.g., play, dressing, meals, outside time) and across settings (e.g., home, school, community) are observed. • Interactions in social and physical environments are observed. • Items that build on children's interests and allow interventionists and caregivers to follow children's lead can be targeted.
2. ABI embeds goals and objectives in routine, planned, and child-initiated activities.	• AEPS Test items (goals and objectives) are educationally relevant and, therefore, can be embedded into a range of meaningful activities. • AEPS Test items can be targeted in a variety of settings by parents, interventionists, and/or consultants.
3. ABI uses logical antecedents and consequences.	• AEPS Test items are observed during routine, planned, and child-initiated activities that ensure the occurrence of logical antecedents and consequences.
4. ABI targets functional and generalizable skills.	• AEPS Test items are functional and generalizable. • AEPS Test items represent broad response classes rather than discrete skills.

child's strengths and interests rather than on numerical scores or limitations. Knowing about children's interests is critical to developing appropriate goals and objectives and implementing an activity-based approach. Consideration should be given to a particular child's interest at each step of the goal/objective development process.

Once a child's interests, strengths, and areas of need are identified, the third step in developing appropriate goals and objectives is to target skills that are important for the child to attain, master, and generalize. Targeted skills should meet four criteria. The skills should be 1) functional for the child; 2) usable across settings, people, and materials (i.e., generalizable); 3) observable and measurable so that team members can monitor and evaluate child progress; and 4) addressable within the child's daily environment (e.g., at home, in the park, at preschool). Table 3.3 reviews the four criteria for selecting appropriate skills.

The fourth step in developing appropriate goals and objectives, prioritization, occurs after the team identifies developmental skills targeted for intervention. Children with disabilities may show delays in all or many developmental areas, and addressing several skills from each area may not be possible or productive; therefore, it may be necessary for the team to prioritize targeted skills. In other words, caregivers and interventionists may become overwhelmed if they attempt to intervene and monitor change across 15–20 targeted skills. An alternative is to prioritize skills and then to select two to four that are the highest priority.

When prioritizing, teams should select skills that are not likely to develop without intervention, that will significantly enhance a child's behavioral repertoire, and that match a child's developmental level of functioning. For example, learning to request a variety of objects has the potential of enhancing a child's behavioral repertoire more than learning to label pictures in a book. By learning to request objects, children are able to get their needs met, interact with adults and peers, and engage in age-appropriate activities and play; whereas labeling pictures in a book is limited to a single activity that is not as likely to promote independence and problem solving.

Furthermore, teams should not select skills that are addressed as a part of the existing EI/ECSE curriculum or that will be frequently addressed during daily interactions. For example, EI/ECSE curricula commonly address skills such as playing cooperatively with peers or participating in group activities that

Table 3.3. Four criteria and their associated definitions for selecting appropriate skills

Criteria	Definition
Functional	Attainment of the skill(s) allows children to be independent within their daily environment. Functional skills allow children to perform actions or activities that would otherwise have to be completed by others.
Generalizable	Generalizable refers to skills and information that can be appropriately used across settings, events, activities, people, and materials. Furthermore, generalizable refers to skills that can be modified or adapted for a variety of disabling conditions.
Observable and measurable	Skill(s) can be seen or heard and, therefore, counted in terms of frequency, latency, or duration. Team members should be able to agree that the skill did or did not meet the stated criterion.
Addressable	Skills that can be easily targeted within children's daily routines (e.g., in the grocery store, during car rides, during art activities, while eating snack) by teachers, therapists, and caregivers should be selected.

may not need to be identified as a specific child's goal. In addition, skills such as labeling colors, shapes, numbers, and letters that are routinely addressed through daily interactions may not need to be selected as IEP/IFSP goals. For example, interventionists frequently ask children if they want the *green* cup or if they have a *big* ball or ask children to find the helper card with their name. At home, caregivers may routinely ask children to get their *pink* slippers or to count the number of plates on the table. When interventionists/caregivers routinely and frequently address skills as a part of the existing curriculum or as a part of daily interactions, targeting them as IEP/IFSP goals may not be necessary.

In addition, prioritizing becomes less difficult if team members select goals and objectives that target multiple skills across developmental domains. For a child with adaptive, language, motor, and social delays/needs, a goal that addresses all areas can offer great efficiency. For example, learning to self-feed (an adaptive behavior) can also provide opportunities for a child to work on motor, social, and communication skills—picking up pieces of food requires eye–hand coordination; biting and chewing addresses motor coordination of the tongue and lips; gaining attention is a social behavior; and if an individual "wants more" or "wants something different," then communication is necessary.

After prioritizing skills, team members are ready to address the fifth step, which is to write targeted skills so that they are observable, measurable, and understandable to team members. A simple, straightforward method for writing goals and objectives involves the use of the ABC formula in which *A* represents an antecedent, *B* stands for behavior or response, and *C* represents the criterion or level of acceptable performance. This formula is compatible with legal mandates and also allows teams to write goals and objectives in an understandable and usable manner. Table 3.4 presents definitions and examples of antecedents, behaviors, and criteria for acceptable performance. It is important for the team to remember that arranging logical antecedents, defining observable and measurable behaviors/ responses, and comparing performance to a specified criterion occur as a synergistic relationship—each element affecting the other.

This five-step process is designed to assist team members in developing appropriate goals and objectives that should guide intervention efforts. The reader is encouraged to review the case study in the appendix at the end of this chapter. The case

Table 3.4.   Definitions and examples of antecedents, behavior, and criteria

Component	Definition	Example
Antecedent	The conditions or context in which the child's behavior is to occur or the level of assistance	Showing the child objects to encourage naming; putting a snack out of reach; helping a child put on his or her coat
Behavior	The observable skill or response the child is to perform	Walks, names objects, opens door, puts on coat
Criteria	The quality, frequency, accuracy, duration, or fluency the child's behavior is to attain	Will name 10 objects; will drink from a cup without spilling; will put on coat independently

study illustrates the five-step process of developing appropriate goals and objectives from assessment/evaluation results, a necessary predecessor to the successful application of activity-based intervention.

SUMMARY

In this chapter, five major topics are addressed: 1) a linked assessment, goal development, intervention, and evaluation systems framework; 2) the purposes of assessment/evaluation tools; 3) the fundamental importance of CBA/E tools for developing appropriate goals and objectives and for developing intervention content; 4) the AEPS and how it promotes a linked systems approach; and, finally, 5) a five-step process for developing appropriate goals and objectives, particularly for the successful application of an activity-based approach to intervention. Chapters 5 and 6 provide a detailed description of how to employ activity-based intervention with an individual child and with groups of children.

REFERENCES

Bagnato, S., & Neisworth, J. (1991). *Assessment for early intervention: Best practices for professionals.* New York: Guilford Press.

Bagnato, S.J., Neisworth, J.T., & Munson, S.M. (1997). *LINKing assessment and early intervention: An authentic curriculum-based approach.* Baltimore: Paul H. Brookes Publishing Co.

Bayley, N. (1993). *Bayley Scales of Infant Development—Second Edition manual.* San Antonio, TX: The Psychological Corporation.

Bricker, D. (1989). *Early intervention for at-risk and handicapped infants, toddlers, and preschool children.* Palo Alto, CA: VORT Corp.

Bricker, D. (Ed.). (1993). *Assessment, evaluation, and programming system for infants and children: Vol. 1. AEPS measurement for birth to three years.* Baltimore: Paul H. Brookes Publishing Co.

Bricker, D. (1996a). Assessment for IFSP development and intervention planning. In S. Meisels & E. Fenichel (Eds.), *New visions for the developmental assessment of infants and toddlers* (pp. 169–192). Washington, DC: National Center for Clinical Infant Programs.

Bricker, D. (1996b). Using assessment outcomes for intervention planning: A necessary relationship. In M. Brambring, H. Rauh, & A. Beelmann (Eds.), *Early childhood intervention theory, evaluation, and practice* (pp. 305–328). Berlin/New York: Aldine de Gruyter.

Bricker, D., & Pretti-Frontczak, K. (Eds.). (1996). *Assessment, evaluation, and programming system for infants and young children: Vol. 3. AEPS measurement for three to six years.* Baltimore: Paul H. Brookes Publishing Co.

Bricker, D., & Pretti-Frontczak, K. (1998). *A study of the psychometric properties of the Assessment, Evaluation, and Programming Test for Three to Six Years: Final report for U.S. Department of Education* (NIDRR Grant No. H133G40147). Eugene: University of Oregon, Center on Human Development.

Bricker, D., Squires, J., Mounts, L., Potter, L., Nickel, R., & Farrell, J. (1995). *Ages & stages questionnaires: A parent-completed, child-monitoring system.* Baltimore: Paul H. Brookes Publishing Co.

Bricker, D., & Waddell, M. (Eds.). (1996). *Assessment, evaluation, and programming system for infants and young children: Vol. 4. AEPS curriculum for three to six years.* Baltimore: Paul H. Brookes Publishing Co.

Cripe, J., Slentz, K., & Bricker, D. (Eds.). (1993). *Assessment, evaluation, and programming system for infants and young children: Vol. 2. AEPS curriculum for birth to three years.* Baltimore: Paul H. Brookes Publishing Co.

Dodge, D., & Cokler, L. (1992). *The Creative Curriculum for Early Childhood* (3rd ed.). Washington, DC: Teaching Strategies, Inc.

Frankenburg, W.K., & Dodds, J.B. (1990). *Denver II training manual.* Denver: Denver Developmental Materials.

Greenspan, S., & Meisels, S. (1995). A new vision for the assessment of young children. *Exceptional Parent, 25*(2), 23–25.

Johnson-Martin, N., Jens, K., Attermeier, S., & Hacker, B. (1991). *The Carolina Curriculum for infants and toddlers with special needs* (2nd ed.). Baltimore: Paul H. Brookes Publishing Co.

Linder, T. (1993). *Transdisciplinary play-based assessment: A functional approach to working with young children* (Rev. ed.). Baltimore: Paul H. Brookes Publishing Co.

McLean, M., Bailey, D., & Wolery, M. (1996). *Assessing infants and preschoolers with special needs.* Columbus, OH: Charles E. Merrill.

Newborg, J., Stock, J., Wnek, J., Guidubaldi, J., & Svinicki, J. (1988). *Battelle Developmental Inventory.* Chicago, IL: Riverside Publishing.

Notari, A., & Bricker, D. (1990). The utility of a curriculum-based assessment instrument in the development of individualized education plans for infants and young children. *Journal of Early Intervention, 14*(2), 117–132.

Notari, A., & Drinkwater, S. (1991). Best practices for writing child outcomes: An evaluation of two methods. *Topics in Early Childhood Special Education, 11*(3), 92–106.

Notari, A., Slentz, K., & Bricker, D. (1990). Assessment-curriculum systems of early childhood/special education. In R. Brown & D. Mitchell (Eds.), *Early intervention for disabled and at-risk infants* (pp. 160–205). London: Croom-Helm.

VORT Corp. (1995). *Hawaii Early Learning Profile (HELP): HELP for preschoolers (3–6).* Palo Alto, CA: Author.

Appendix

Goal Development
A Case Study

Appropriate goals and objectives are critical to the successful implementation of activity-based intervention. Without appropriate goals and objectives, the application of an activity-based approach will likely not be effective. The purpose of this case study is to assist the reader in understanding how to develop appropriate goals and objectives from assessment/evaluation results using the five-step process discussed in this chapter. The five-step process for developing goals and objectives is illustrated using a 3-year-old girl named Jody.

Jody has been diagnosed with cerebral palsy and attends an inclusive preschool four mornings a week. Jody also receives occupational therapy once a week when a therapist visits her classroom. After Jody attends preschool in the morning, Jody's father takes her to a neighborhood child care center. Jody's individualized education program (IEP) team is composed of her father, grandmother, occupational therapist, classroom teacher, and child care provider.

STEP ONE: ADMINISTERING AN ASSESSMENT/EVALUATION TOOL

Prior to Jody's placement in the preschool classroom, her individualized family service plan (IFSP) team conducted an assessment of her current skills across important areas of development. Results from the assessment/evaluation tool were used to develop goals and objectives that address Jody's strengths, interests, and areas of need. The team was also interested in monitoring Jody's progress across the year. The team administered

43

the Assessment, Evaluation, and Programming System (AEPS) Measurement for Three to Six Years (Bricker, & Pretti-Frontczak, 1996) because it 1) contains a family component allowing for information to be collected from Jody's father and grandmother, 2) encourages observations of Jody across daily activities, 3) covers the six essential developmental domains, 4) addresses functional and generalizable skills, and 5) can be used to monitor Jody's progress.

The classroom teacher and other staff assessed Jody's skills in the cognitive and social domains using the AEPS by observing Jody playing and interacting with others in the classroom. The occupational therapist and classroom staff observed Jody during arrival, outside time, snacktime, and art to assess her adaptive, fine motor, and gross motor skills. For purposes of this example, only results from the Gross Motor Domain are used and are shown on the AEPS Data Recording Form contained in Figure A.1.

When administering the AEPS Test, all items are scored with a "2," "1," or "0." A score of "2" indicates that the skill was performed independently, consistently, and met criteria. A score of "1" indicates that the skill was performed with assistance, inconsistently, and/or met partial criteria. A score of "0" indicates that the skill was not performed or did not meet criteria. Jody did not meet criteria for items on Strand A or B in the Gross Motor Domain in the AEPS Measurement for Three to Six Years; therefore, the AEPS Measurement for Birth to Three Years was used for this domain. Results indicate that Jody met criteria for items in Strands A and B and met criteria for most items in Strand C (balance and mobility in standing and walking) but did not meet criteria for any item in Strand D (play skills).

Jody's father and grandmother completed the AEPS Family Report and asked the child care provider for her input on the Fine and Gross Motor Domains. When completing the AEPS Family Report, caregivers can indicate "Y" if the child can do the item, "S" if the child can sometimes do the item, and "N" if the child is not yet able to do the item. A completed AEPS Family Report for the Gross Motor Domain is shown in Figure A.2. Jody's father and grandmother indicated that Jody could do items 1–5 and 7, sometimes could do items 6 and 8, and could not yet perform items 9–11.

STEP TWO: SUMMARIZING ASSESSMENT/EVALUATION RESULTS

Following the administration and scoring of the AEPS Test and AEPS Family Report, the results were summarized. AEPS Test

Gross Motor Domain

S = Scoring Key	Q = Qualifying Notes
2 = Pass consistently	A = Assistance provided
1 = Inconsistent	B = Behavior interfered
performance	R = Reported assessment
0 = Does not pass	M = Modification/adaptation
	D = Direct test

Name: _Jody_

	Test Period:	–							
	Test Date:	8-98		–		–		–	
	Examiner:	TB,SW							
	IEP	S	Q	S	Q	S	Q	S	Q
A. Movement and locomotion in supine and prone position									
1. Moves body parts independently of each other		2	R						
1.1 Turns head past 45°		2	R						
1.2 Kicks legs		2	R						
1.3 Waves arms		2	R						
2. Rolls by turning segmentally		2	R						
2.1 Rolls: back to stomach		2	R						
2.2 Rolls: stomach to back		2	R						
3. Creeps forward using alternating arm and leg movements		2	R						
3.1 Rocks in creeping position		2	R						
3.2 Assumes creeping position		2	R						
3.3 Crawls forward on stomach		2	R						
3.4 Pivots on stomach		2	R						
3.5 Bears weight while reaching		2	R						
3.6 Lifts head/chest off surface		2	R						
B. Balance in sitting									
1. Assumes balanced sitting position		2	R						
1.1 Assumes hands and knees position from sitting		2	R						
1.2 Regains balanced sitting after reaching		2	R						
1.3 Regains balanced sitting after leaning		2	R						
1.4 Sits balanced without support		2	R						

(continued)

Figure A.1. A completed AEPS Recording Form in the Gross Motor Domain for Jody.

Figure A.1. (*continued*)

Name: **Jody**

Test Period: —
Test Date: **8-98**
Examiner: **TB, SW**

	IEP	S	Q	S	Q	S	Q	S	Q
1.5 Sits balanced using hands for support		2	R						
1.6 Holds head in midline when in supported sitting position		2	R						
2. Sits down in and gets out of chair		2							
2.1 Sits down in chair		2							
2.2 Maintains a sitting position in chair		2							
C. Balance and mobility in standing and walking									
1. Walks avoiding obstacles	✓	1	A						
1.1 Walks without support		1	A						
1.2 Walks with one-hand support		2							
1.3 Walks with two-hand support		2							
1.4 Stands unsupported		2							
1.5 Cruises		2							
2. Stoops/recovers without support		2							
2.1 Rises from sitting to standing		2							
2.2 Pulls to standing		2							
2.3 Pulls to kneeling		2							
3. Walks up and down stairs		0							
3.1 Walks up and down stairs with two-hand support		1	R						
3.2 Moves up and down stairs		1	R						
3.3 Gets up and down from low structure		2							
D. Play skills									
1. Jumps forward		0							
1.1 Jumps up		0							
1.2 Jumps from low structure		0							
2. Pedals and steers tricycle		0							
2.1 Pushes riding toy with feet while steering		0							
2.2 Sits on riding toy while adult pushes	✓	1	M						

(*continued*)

Figure A.1. (*continued*)

_____**AEPS**_____ Gross Motor Domain

	IEP	S	Q	S	Q	S	Q	S	Q
Name: Jody Test Period: — Test Date: 8-98 Examiner: TB, SW				—		—		—	
3. Runs avoiding obstacles		0							
3.1 Runs		0							
3.2 Walks fast		0							
4. Catches/kicks/throws/rolls ball		0							
4.1 Catches ball		0	D						
4.2 Kicks ball		0	D						
4.3 Throws ball		1	A						
4.4 Rolls ball at target		1	A						
5. Climbs up and down play equipment		0							
5.1 Moves up and down inclines		0							
5.2 Moves under/over/through obstacle		1	A						

A raw score can be computed for the domain by adding all the 2 and 1 scores entered in the S column for a specific test period. To determine the total percent score divide the total score by the total score possible.

RESULTS

Test Date	8-98			
Total Score Possible	110	110	110	110
Total Score	74			
Total Percent Score	67%			

results can be summarized through numerical tabulations, visual representations, and/or descriptive narratives. Jody's team used all three types of summaries. Total scores were obtained for each domain of the AEPS Test by adding together all scores of "2" and "1." This sum was then divided by the total number possible for a given domain and multiplied by 100 to obtain a Total Percent Score. (Refer to the end of Figure A.1.) Visual representations were obtained by taking Total Percent Scores and plotting them on a graph. Finally, a narrative summary of Jody's strengths, interests, and areas of needs was generated

AEPS   Gross Motor Domain

Gross Motor Domain

1. Does your child move arms, legs, and head sepa-
    rately while lying on his or her back? For exam-
    ple, your child waves both arms without kicking,
    or turns his or her head to the side without waving
    arms or kicking legs. (A1)

2. Does your child roll over from back to stomach
    and stomach to back, getting both arms out from
    under the body? (A2)

3. Does your child crawl forward at least 2 feet by
    alternating arms and legs? For example, your
    child will move one arm and opposite leg, then
    the other arm and opposite leg. (A3)

4. Does your child get to a sitting position on the
    floor from any position (e.g., standing, lying down,
    hands and knees) without help? (B1)

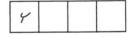

5. Does your child get into and out of a child-size
    chair without help? (B2)

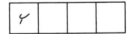

6. Without help, does your child *walk* around large
    toys, furniture, or people without bumping into
    them? (C1)

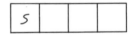

Y = Yes; S = Sometimes; N = Not Yet.

(continued)

Figure A.2. A completed AEPS Family Report Form in the Gross Motor Domain for Jody.

Figure A.2. (*continued*)

_____AEPS_____   Gross Motor Domain _____

7. Does your child bend over at the waist or bend at the knees to reach an object on the floor, and then stand back up without sitting down or leaning on something? (C2)

8. Does your child walk up and down stairs without help? He or she may walk with one or two feet on each stair and may or may not hold onto the railing with one hand. (C3)

9. Does your child jump forward with feet together? (D1)

10. Does your child pedal with both feet while steering a tricycle forward at least 5 feet? (D2)

11. Without help, does your child *run* around large toys, furniture, or people without bumping into them? (D3)

from assessment/evaluation results as shown in Figure A.3. The AEPS Family Report findings can be combined with the AEPS Test results or summarized separately.

Because the team administered a comprehensive assessment/ evaluation tool, they were able to learn about toys of interest,

Jody is able to get in and out of child-size chairs including the chairs at the snack table in the preschool classroom, chairs in the book corner at the child care center, and chairs around a small table in Jody's bedroom. Jody is beginning to walk up and down stairs by holding onto the railing and when holding the hands of an adult. Dad reports that Jody is able to walk up a flight of four stairs at her grandmother's house using only one hand for support. Jody often plays on the floor, building with Legos and putting puzzles together. She is able to pull to stand and stoop, pick up toys, and return to a standing position. Jody enjoys playing at the discovery table at the preschool and will stand unsupported during the entire activity. Jody is also able to wait in line and go on walks to the park with her family each weekend. Jody's grandmother says that Jody is beginning to walk without support but needs help walking across uneven surfaces such as grass.

Figure A.3. Narrative summary of Jody's current level of functioning in the Gross Motor Domain.

types of activities Jody enjoys, and skills she has mastered. In addition, by conducting a comprehensive assessment such as the AEPS, team members obtained information regarding Jody's performance across important developmental areas and gained an overall picture of her functioning. Summarization of this type of information should serve as a foundation for teaching Jody new skills and is critical to developing appropriate goals and objectives and to implementing activity-based intervention.

Table A.1 includes a summary of Jody's strengths, interests, and areas of need based on the team's observations and Jody's performance on the AEPS Test and Family Report. Jody's strengths were identified and summarized by determining which AEPS Test items were scored as "2" and which AEPS Family Report items were scored as "Y." These items indicate that Jody has mastered the skill and should serve as her strengths or as a foundation for learning new skills. Jody's interests are generated and summarized through observations by team members during the administration of the AEPS Test and Family Report. Areas of need are generated and summarized by examining which items on the AEPS Test and Family Report were scored "1" or "S." These items indicate that Jody is beginning to learn a particular skill or that the skill is emerging and with continued practice, intervention, and support, she will likely master and generalize the skill. Items scored with a "0" or an "N" may also serve as current or future goals.

STEP THREE: SELECTING MEANINGFUL SKILLS

Following the summarization of Jody's strengths, interests, and areas of need (based on assessment results), team members se-

Table A.1.   Jody's strengths, interests, and areas of need

Strengths	Interests	Areas of need
• Plays cooperatively with other children • Uses a variety of modified writing instruments to copy shapes, sizes, letters • Follows directions and routines • Feeds self • Uses the toilet when needed	• Enjoys activities in which she can get messy (e.g., shaving cream, water play) • Often plays with Mark and Sherry at child care • When given a choice, will choose the discovery table or the dress-up area at school and child care • At home, likes to take baths and play on the swing set	• Increase the frequency of manipulating small objects in both hands and using non-modified writing instruments • Improve frequency and quality of walking without assistance and walking to avoid obstacles • Learn to express likes and dislikes and needs to peers • Label one or two shapes, sizes, colors, and qualitative concepts

lected skills that were emerging and that were important for Jody to learn. The team used four criteria to evaluate whether the skills they selected were appropriate for Jody. Skills are considered appropriate when they 1) are functional, 2) are generalizable, 3) are measurable and observable, and 4) can be embedded into daily activities. Items on the AEPS Test were designed to meet these criteria. For example, an AEPS Test item such as learning to walk without support 1) allows a child to become more independent (functional); 2) is usable across settings (generalizable); 3) is measurable and observable; and 4) can be embedded in home, child care, and school activities. The team concluded that the skills identified as areas of need met these criteria and were, therefore, important targets for Jody.

STEP FOUR: PRIORITIZING SKILLS

Based on assessment results, 10 skills were selected as potential goals; however, because of the team's resources, targeting this many skills did not appear feasible. Therefore, team members targeted *walking without assistance* and *manipulating small objects in both hands* as the priority goals. It was decided that remaining goals would be addressed as time and resources permitted. For example, based on assessment results, team members believed that encouraging Jody's interests in messy activities and playing with her friends Sherry and Mark during outdoor play time would build on her interests and provide her with opportunities to improve performance on nontarget skills (e.g., labeling sizes and shapes, expressing likes and dislikes to peers). In addition, the discovery table (one of Jody's favorite activities) would provide multiple opportunities for Jody to work on the targeted fine motor goal while addressing nontargeted goals (e.g., labeling qualitative concepts). Finally, team members believed that nontargeted goals (e.g., using nonmodified writing instruments) would be addressed as part of existing classroom curricula and interactions (i.e., during daily art activities).

STEP FIVE: WRITING MEANINGFUL AND UNDERSTANDABLE GOALS AND OBJECTIVES

Once goals are prioritized, they need to be written in terms that are meaningful and understandable to team members. To assist in goal writing, the AEPS Tests contain an appendix in which test items are written as IEP/IFSP goals and objectives. Figure A.4 shows a sample of IEP/IFSP goals and objectives from the Gross Motor Domain of the *AEPS Measurement for Birth to Three Years*.

When goals and objectives from the AEPS Test are used, team members may have to modify them by using the simple ABC formula discussed previously in this chapter to accommodate the individual needs of children. Figure A.5 contains Jody's two priority goals. The Gross Motor goal was taken from *AEPS Measurement for Birth to Three Years* (Volume 1), Appendix B (Bricker, 1993), and the Fine Motor goal was taken from *AEPS Measurement for Three to Six Years* (Volume 3), Appendix B (Bricker & Pretti-Frontczak, 1996). Figure A.5 also indicates how these objectives and goals were modified using the ABC formula, resulting in IEP/IFSP goals and objectives that are meaningful, understandable, and individualized for Jody.

SUMMARY

The case study presented in this appendix illustrates how early intervention/early childhood special education teams can use assessment/evaluation results to develop appropriate IEP/IFSP goals and objectives. As stated previously, implementation of an activity-based approach is dependent on the development of appropriate goals and objectives. Thus, team members are encouraged to follow the five-step process shown in this case study; however, they are also encouraged to modify the process as necessary given their unique configuration and responsibilities. Furthermore, teams are reminded that many curriculum-based

IEP/IFSP
Goals and Objectives

GROSS MOTOR DOMAIN

Strand C: Balance and Mobility in Standing and Walking

G1 When walking unsupported, the child will move to avoid obstacles (e.g., toys, furniture, people).

1.1 The child will walk without support for at least 6 feet.

1.2 The child will walk when holding onto support with one hand for at least 15 feet.

1.3 The child will walk when holding onto support with two hands for at least 15 feet.

1.4 The child will stand alone for at least 30 seconds with back straight and head in midline.

1.5 The child will cruise (i.e., side-step to the left and to the right) while holding onto a stable support (e.g., couch, coffee table, wall) for at least 3 feet.

G2 The child will stoop by bending at waist or squat by bending knees to reach an object and will stand back up without support.

2.1 From a sitting position on the floor, the child will stand up without support.

2.2 From a sitting, kneeling, and/or creeping position, the child will pull to a standing position using a support (e.g., low table, chair).

2.3 From a sitting and/or creeping position, the child will pull to a kneeling position using a support (e.g., low table, chair).

G3 The child will walk up and down stairs. (The child may or may not use one-hand support and may or may not alternate feet.)

3.1 The child will walk up and down stairs using two-hand support (e.g., railings, adult's hands). (Child may or may not alternate feet.)

3.2 The child will move up and down stairs by creeping, crawling, and/or scooting on buttocks.

3.3 The child will climb onto and off of a low, stable structure (e.g., low step, raised platform).

Figure A.4. Sample of IEP/IFSP goals and objectives from the AEPS Test Gross Motor Domain.

assessment/evaluation tools exist and should be selected based on several key variables including but not limited to 1) the purpose for administering the assessment/evaluation; 2) the team's philosophy; 3) the flexibility of the tool for meeting the needs of children with disabilities; 4) the reliability, validity, and utility of the tool; and 5) the type of skills targeted within the tool (i.e., are the skills functional and generalizable). Once appropriate goals and objectives are written, the team is ready to begin designing and implementing activities that will provide children multiple opportunities to address targeted skills.

IEP/IFSP goals as written in the AEPS Test, Appendix B	Jody's IFSP goals as revised using the ABC formula
Gross Motor Domain, Strand C, Goal 1 (Vol. 1)	
Objective 1.1. The child will walk without support for at least 6 steps.	Jody will walk across a variety of surfaces/locations (e.g., grass, pavement, dirt, home, grocery store) without support for at least six steps once a day for 2 weeks.
Fine Motor Domain, Strand A (Vol. 3)	
Goal 1. The child will manipulate two small objects at the same time (e.g., string small beads, build with blocks or Tinkertoys).	During at least two activities at the preschool and home (e.g., art, choice time, the building corner, playing with grandma), Jody will manipulate two small objects at the same time (e.g., string small beads; build with blocks, Tinkertoys, or pieces of playdough) at least twice a day for 2 weeks.

Figure A.5.   Comparison of IEP/IFSP goals and objectives taken directly from the AEPS Tests and those modified using the ABC formula.

REFERENCES

Bricker, D. (Ed.). (1993). *Assessment, evaluation, and programming system for infants and children: Vol. 1. AEPS measurement for birth to three years.* Baltimore: Paul H. Brookes Publishing Co.

Bricker, D., & Pretti-Frontczak, K. (Eds.). (1996). *Assessment, evaluation, and programming system for infants and children: Vol. 3. AEPS measurement for three to six years.* Baltimore: Paul H. Brookes Publishing Co.

Chapter 4

Activity-Based
Intervention and the Team

As we have indicated throughout this volume, acceptable developmental progress for most children who have or who are at risk for disabilities requires the contribution and involvement of a range of professionals, paraprofessionals, and family members. We have referred to this range of individuals as the child's team. Furthermore, we have emphasized the necessity of including family members as partners on the team.

THE TEAM

The composition of early intervention/early childhood special education (EI/ECSE) teams varies across programs and agencies. That is, one program may have a team composed of a special educator, occupational therapist, and speech-language pathologist, whereas another agency may have a team composed of an early interventionist, physical therapist, and service coordinator. The variability in team composition occurs for several reasons: local/state requirements, availability of personnel, agency resources, and program/agency philosophy. Even with this variability, teams should ideally be composed of three constituencies: direct service delivery personnel, consultants, and family members.

Direct service delivery personnel are those people who provide the daily/weekly "hands on" interventions to the child and/or the family. Direct service delivery personnel can be teachers, child care workers, home visitors, aides, or early interventionists. Direct service delivery personnel can have their preliminary training as communication specialists, motor specialists, special educators, early childhood educators, psychologists, or medical specialists (e.g., nurses), but increasingly these personnel are being required to have additional training and licensure specific to EI/ECSE (Bricker & Widerstrom, 1996; Klein & Campbell, 1990). In addition, many disciplines are developing formal training programs that permit preservice students to focus on early intervention or are providing supplemental training that permits specialization in early intervention (Bricker & Widerstrom, 1996).

The second constituency group that should be represented on a team is consultants. These individuals have special disciplinary training that culminates with a professional licensure and include occupational therapists, physical therapists, physicians, nurses, communication specialists, psychologists, social workers, child development specialists, nutritionists, mobility specialists, and family therapists. As made clear in the Education of the Handicapped Act Amendments of 1986, PL 99-457, teams should include the expertise and perspectives from the range of disciplines necessary to address child and family needs (Johnson, McGonigel, & Kaufmann, 1989). It is well documented that many children and families who participate in EI/ECSE programs have multiple challenges requiring assistance from a range of specialists (Bricker & Veltman, 1990; Guralnick, 1997). Complex human needs require thoughtful solutions that can be derived only by examining the numerous facets of the problem and by developing effective and implementable procedures. This process can best be ensured through the active cooperation and collaboration of a range of consultants.

The final constituency group that should be represented on teams is family members, including parents; grandparents; other relatives; foster parents; and, in some cases, friends. The inclusion of family members on the team is critical to the successful application of activity-based intervention. The fundamental tenets of the approach—choosing functional goals, embedding target goals in daily activities, using logically occurring antecedents and consequences, learning from social interactions—require that family members be involved in the selection of goals and assist in shaping intervention content and activities. Without the integral participation of family members, professionals will find it difficult to identify family values and priorities and to transform daily home activities and transactions into learning opportunities.

Ideally, teams should be formed with representatives from these three constituency groups; however, this is only the first step to ensure a balanced and effective team. Little empirical information is available concerning the functioning of EI/ECSE teams; therefore, the majority of our knowledge about teams has been derived from experience. Our experience suggests that effective teams have members with skills that enable them to fill critical roles.

Having the necessary skills to fill critical roles is of fundamental importance; however, we also believe that it is equally important that team members have a shared attitude about how children learn and how to best facilitate that learning. Going through the motions of an approach in a mechanical, non-enthusiastic manner is likely to lead to little change in children. The reverse is also true; that is, any approach may be effective if delivered with commitment and enthusiasm (Cole, Dale, & Mills, 1991). To maximize children's progress, it seems best to adopt the approach with the greatest likelihood of success and then to employ this approach with genuine enthusiasm and the belief that it will be effective.

Not only is it important to be enthusiastic about the chosen approach, but it is also important that team members bring with them an attitude that fosters collaboration with and respect for other team members. The field of EI/ECSE has acknowledged for some time that no single person, discipline, and, in many cases, agency/program can meet the needs of diverse families and their children who have or who are at risk for disabilities (Bricker & Widerstrom, 1996). Children may show an array of problems or needs that require the expertise of motor, communication, psychological, medical, or nutritional specialists. Their families may need an equally comprehensive range of services, including legal, educational, and therapeutic, or may need assistance in day-to-day survival. EI/ECSE teams are necessary to address the many needs of children and families who are eligible for services. To maximize the services rendered to children and families, team members should convey to each other their mutual interdependence. Holding attitudes that foster respect and collaboration would seem to be an essential underpinning of effective team functioning.

In addition to displaying respect for professional expertise, team members should nurture similar attitudes toward family members. Specifically, the participation of caregivers who interact and affect children's lives is essential to a successful team. The inclusion of caregivers as team members should not be pro forma but be a genuine extension of equal partnership rights. The information and perspectives that family members bring to a team are essential in creating an accurate picture of the child's performance repertoire. In addition, without family member participation, the determination of family values and priorities is an educated guess at best.

If an attitude of respect and collaboration is established and maintained, then the chances of creating services that will maximize progress toward child and family outcomes are improved; however, having the "right" attitude is not sufficient for successful intervention. The remainder of this chapter addresses the roles of direct service delivery personnel, consultants, and family members that appear necessary for the successful application of activity-based intervention.

Direct Service Delivery Personnel's Roles

We prefer the nondisciplinary term *early interventionists* when referring to professionals who are direct service delivery personnel because these individuals often have diverse training backgrounds (e.g., early childhood, special education, elementary education, speech-language pathology, occupational therapy, physical therapy, nursing) that preclude associating them with only one discipline or profession. Although there may be some disagreement on what to call direct service delivery personnel, relative agreement exists on the core competencies that should be possessed by early interventionists. The core competencies include the knowledge of atypical and typical child development, the ability to conduct valid assessments and evaluations and summarize results, program development and maintenance skills, the ability to develop appropriate goals and program plans, intervention skills, family involvement and education skills, behavior management and environmental arrangement skills, and team participation skills (Bricker & LaCroix, 1996; Bricker & Slentz, 1988; Geik, Gilkerson, & Sponseller, 1982; McCollum & Catlett, 1997).

The knowledge and skills encompassed in these competencies are likely necessary for an effective early interventionist. In addition, the interventionists who employ activity-based intervention must have other skills consistent with the elements that constitute the approach. "When education is based upon experience and educative experience is seen to be a social process, the situation changes radically. The teacher loses the position of external boss or dictator but takes on that of leader of group activities" (Dewey, 1976, p. 59). This quote helps capture the fundamental role required for an interventionist to successfully employ activity-based intervention. In addition to guiding children's activities in nonintrusive ways, the interventionist is also responsible for arranging other aspects of children's daily environments to promote new and developmentally advanced skills. In essence, the role of the interventionist is to design the environment in such a way as to maximize children's and families' progress toward targeted outcomes. Within the activity-based intervention approach, however, the environmental engineering needs to be accomplished in ways that permit children to initiate and direct their activities whenever appropriate.

Interventionists should design and encourage activities that are or that replicate authentic practice (Brown, Collins, & Duguid, 1989). For example, language acquisition should be mapped onto the authentic need of children to communicate. Likewise, motor targets should encompass functional activities—for example, to work on mobility skills when a child needs to move from the snack to the play area or when a child wants to retrieve a desired toy. Rather than introduce a variety of activities that are artificial and perhaps of little interest to children, the interventionist using activity-based intervention must identify and use routine and child-initiated activities as training opportunities. Clearly, it may not always be possible to follow child initiations; therefore, interventionists should not be reluctant to introduce planned activities as long as these activities are of interest to and have meaning for children. Planned activities that meet these criteria require that interventionists be familiar with children's goals and objectives and be sensitive observers of children's behavior. The success of activity-based intervention is dependent on the interventionist's ability to use child-initiated, routine, and planned activities that are relevant and appealing to children and that also provide ample opportunity for children to gain and refine skills.

Other writers have encouraged the use of approaches similar to activity-based intervention, particularly in regard to language intervention. Jones and Warren referred to enhancing engagement because they suggested that "when the rate and quality of engagement are high, other processes critical for language development function more optimally" (1991, p. 48). These authors also suggested that children's attention is generally better when the focus is on objects and events that they choose rather than those chosen by an adult. Peck (1989) referred to this issue as adult versus child control of environmental variables. He argued that effective intervention is predicated on a balance between adult and child control, and we agree. Children should not be allowed to direct activities in ways that are unproductive; however, we find that personnel using activity-based intervention tend to err by being overly directive as opposed to permitting children to exercise control.

Activities that appeal to children should be designed, or the children's initiations should be followed. The interventionist, however, must constantly assess whether a child's engagement is leading to the acquisition of targeted objectives. Reduction of child engagement is likely to occur when interventionists or caregivers ask too many questions or give too many instructions (Peck, 1989). The goal is to subtly guide children's behavior into more complex, independent, and useful responses. The following comparative examples are offered to clarify this point.

A group of 3- and 4-year-old children are assembled at the classroom door and are guided by an interventionist to an outdoor play area. Each of the children has individualized education program (IEP) goals for improving his or her gross motor, social-communication, and social skills; therefore, the outdoor play time is particularly directed to improving the children's motor, communication, and social-interaction skills. Once outside, the interventionist directs the children to various play equipment: "Sally, you climb up and slide first; Jerry, you are second; and Mary, you are third." While waiting to slide, the children are reminded to "Take your turn." Children who do not participate in the prescribed manner are prompted by the interventionist (e.g., "Sally, it's Mary's turn now"). Although the children appear to enjoy their stair climbing and sliding, they initiate little activity that is not specified by the interventionist. In addition, when they talk, their comments are directed primarily to the interventionist.

Using an activity-based approach, the same group of children move to the outdoor play area as they request their jackets and assistance in opening the door (communication skills). The interventionist suggests that each child needs a buddy before going outside, requiring the children to negotiate with each other (social-interaction skills). Once outside, the children are allowed to choose an activity. One child discovers a flower, and the interventionist and other children join the child and talk about the flower (communication skills). The children decide not to pick the flower but to construct a rock wall to protect it (communication, social-interaction, and motor skills). Once the wall is completed, the interventionist suggests that the children may want to get seeds in order to grow more flowers. The children then discuss how they might obtain more seeds (communication and social-interaction skills).

In the first example, the interventionist planned and orchestrated the activities for the children. In this scenario, the children had little need to problem-solve, initiate, or even communicate. In the second example, the interventionist maintained control but permitted the children to initiate a variety of activities. The children's activities were used to provide opportunities to practice targeted social-communication, motor, and social-interaction skills. In addition, the interventionist guided some of the children's activities through her actions (e.g., select a buddy).

Consultants' Roles

Contributions from a variety of professionals with specialized training are often essential to the delivery of quality services to infants and young children who have or who are at risk for disabilities and their families. Beginning with assessment for determining program eligibility and referral for placement, specialists from many disciplines may need to be involved. In activity-based intervention, the general role that specialists play is that of consultant to the direct service delivery personnel and family members. Consultants need to fill two specific roles: 1) purveyors of knowledge and skills in their area of expertise and 2) coordinators and integrators of intervention content.

By definition, consultants have a specialized area of expertise (e.g., communication specialists, mobility specialists), and one of their primary roles is to share their expertise in ways that are useful to other members of the team. Consultants are expected to have the necessary knowledge and skills for assessing children, the necessary information and experience for formulating appropriate goals and intervention plans in specific areas or domains of behavior, and the necessary background to monitor change in these areas over time. Consultants are assigned to teams and programs because they have specialized training and experience that permits them to effectively address specific child/family disabilities or problems. In other words, they bring to the table information and skills not usually available to those who are not experts in that particular area.

A second major role for consultants is the coordination and integration of their area of expertise into a cohesive program of intervention for children and families. Without sensible integration of intervention activities, quality services cannot be delivered to children and families. The coordination of services should occur at screening, assessment, goal development, intervention, and evaluation meetings. Activity-based intervention is designed to facilitate the integration of services offered by consultants. A focus of activity-based intervention is on embedding training into familiar and meaningful activities for children. Therefore, the introduction of specific training regimens conducted apart from daily routines and play runs counter to the approach. Indeed, following children's leads and introducing a variety of planned activities, which are the essence of the approach, offers many opportunities for consultants to integrate specific training into activities that children choose and activities that occur on a regular basis.

Except in rare cases, activity-based intervention requires that special therapy or training be integrated into the child's and family's daily activities. Integrating therapy or special training into children's daily activities requires that the direct service provider and the consultants become synthesizers (Bricker, 1976). Synthesizers seek input from all personnel involved with the child and coordinate that input into a cohesive program for the child and family. For example, in cohesive and coordinated interventions, children are generally not removed from the classroom or the home to work on motor and adaptive skills. Furthermore, children are not asked to engage in drills or activities that lack meaning or that are not connected to functional activities. Rather, the occupational therapy consultant works closely with the interventionist and family members. Together, plans are made for addressing the child's motor and adaptive goals. Opportunities for enhancing adaptive skills during routine and planned activities are identified, and procedures for using these opportunities are devised.

Family Members' Roles

Family members have one primary role on the team—to participate as partners. The form of that participation, however, may vary according to the caregiver's values, availability, comfort level, experience, education, and background. The form of participation should, to the extent possible, be specified by the family member. It is likely that if more than one family member is involved, then participation may vary across members. For example, both of Suni's parents are members of the team; however, his mother has a job that offers flexible work hours, whereas his father does not. Consequently, Suni's mother is able to attend meetings more frequently than his father, but both parents spend time at home engaging in play activities with Suni. It is also important to point out that a family member's participation may change over time. For example, it is possible that Suni's mother could change jobs, which would require the nature of her participation to change.

As a team member, a caregiver can make a number of critical contributions. First, the caregiver is likely to have information about the child's performance repertoire that is essential in order to provide an accurate picture of his or her strengths and areas of need. Second, the caregiver can make clear the family's values and priorities that may significantly affect the goals that are chosen and the intervention content. Third, the caregiver can provide valuable information about children's likes, dislikes, and preferred activities. Fourth, the caregiver can provide important information about child progress in the home and other settings.

The Team's Role

Federal law and recommended practice require that children's assessment/evaluation and delivery of services be conducted by a team composed of professionals and family members. We recommend that teams be composed of direct service personnel (i.e., interventionists), consultants, and family members. Each of these constituency groups has specific but often overlapping roles thought to be necessary for an efficient and effective team. We believe that there are several guidelines for ensuring a coordinated and collaborative team approach:

1. Involved professionals, paraprofessionals, and caregivers should be committed to a team approach.
2. Team members need to respect each member's contributions.
3. Team members need to agree on the approach to be used.
4. Roles should be delineated and assigned.
5. Information, observations, and perspectives of team members should be integrated into a cohesive and coordinated plan of action.

Attention to developing models of team collaboration is growing by necessity, and an underlying theme of these models is that professionals and family members must coordinate their efforts (Bricker & Widerstrom, 1996; McCollum & Hughes, 1988; Woodruff & McGonigel, 1988). Once such models are adopted, the next stage is to prepare individuals to use them. Discussing strategies to prepare individuals to be effective team members is beyond the scope of this book; however, the following section presents a discussion of training team members in the use of activity-based intervention.

TRAINING TEAM MEMBERS TO USE ACTIVITY-BASED INTERVENTION

The background and training of many caregivers, interventionists, and consultants did not prepare them to use child-directed approaches such as activity-based intervention. In working with a sizable number of paraprofessionals, professionals, and caregivers, we have derived six principles that appear essential to the application of activity-based intervention.

The *first principle* is the need for team members to understand and be committed to the approach. In previous sections of this chapter, we have addressed the importance of appropriate attitude and enthusiasm for the approach of choice. Team members should be willing to fulfill the roles necessary for the implementation of activity-based intervention. Individuals who are skeptical about the approach (as well as team collaboration) will likely not gain the skills necessary for successful application of activity-based intervention.

The *second principle* that underlies the effective use of activity-based intervention is the need for reliable observation skills. Observing children's behavioral repertoires and determining under which conditions responses occur are fundamental to the successful use of activity-based intervention. Team members should be comfortable with the process of observing and not feel compelled to constantly respond or direct children's activities. To be efficient and useful, observation needs to be focused and yield objective findings. Team members should be able to discriminate between observable behavior (e.g., "Luis cried for 10 minutes following his mother's departure from the classroom") and inferences (e.g., "Because Luis was frightened, he cried when his mother left the classroom"). The use of videotapes may be useful in improving the observational skills of team members by helping them learn to distinguish observable behavior (e.g., crying) from inferences about behavior (e.g., "Luis was frightened").

The *third principle* in the application of activity-based intervention is learning how to follow or respond to children's leads (Warren, 1991). Team members may see their roles as organizers of children's days by planning a series of activities. Although such planning is required to ensure the necessary infrastructure for activity-based intervention, the structure should not be used to direct activities but rather to ensure that opportunities are provided for children to practice targeted goals and objectives—an essential distinction. Following children's leads requires observation of children by team members. Children may provide a rich array of behavior from which the team can select the response(s) that will potentially yield the most productive outcome for the child. Other children may initiate infrequently, or their behavioral cues may be extremely subtle. For these children, careful observation may be essential if the team is to follow their initiations. The use of videotapes may be a valuable training tool for team members to learn about children's interest and to detect minimal cues.

Learning how to shape either child-initiated or planned activities in directions that will yield desired outcomes is the *fourth principle* that underlies a team's use of activity-based intervention. Again, the use of videotaped demonstrations may be useful in assisting team members to see missed opportunities as well as successes. Through the careful use of antecedents and consequences, team members can become adept at designing and selecting activities that retain children's interest and involvement. For example, a caregiver can place specific items within a child's reach (e.g., crayons) to encourage practicing targeted fine motor skills or use attention and comments to encourage the continuation of an activity that promotes interaction with a peer. Once basic intervention skills are acquired, other specific techniques, such as time-delay prompting, can be used (Warren, 1991). The use of more directed and intrusive teaching strategies, such as the mand-model, can be used to augment child-initiated activities for those children whose progress is not satisfactory and who respond well to such strategies.

The *fifth principle* necessary for the successful application of activity-based intervention is that adequate numbers of opportunities be presented to children to practice targeted goals and objectives. Our observations of center- and home-visiting programs suggests that family members, direct service delivery personnel, and consultants do not recognize many opportunities that could be vehicles for acquiring and practicing targeted goals and objectives. Often one type of activity has been selected to address a child's particular problem and other potential opportunities are disregarded. Again, careful observation may lead to appreciating children's interests and the environmental opportunities that may capture those interests, which, in turn, may significantly increase the number of available training opportunities that occur across a child's day. Team members need to learn to observe children's interests and offer activities that will maximize their participation. Some children initiate action frequently and flourish in environments arranged with materials to facilitate learning in targeted areas; other children need frequent repetition and modification of activities to acquire targeted objectives more effectively within routine activities dispersed across the day. Most children thrive in programs that provide some balance among child-initiated, planned, and routine activities. The appropriate balance among the types of activities employed can be reached only through systematic monitoring of child progress, which is the *sixth principle*.

Use of approaches that embed goals and objectives into routine, planned, and child-initiated activities requires careful monitoring of child progress. Given that training is integrated into functional daily events and activities, team members need to devise and use evaluation strategies that provide them accurate feedback on children's progress toward targeted goals and objectives. Devising nonintrusive evaluation strategies that yield reliable findings at low cost is a challenge. However, the appropriate use of activity-based intervention is not complete without attention to evaluation of child and family outcomes. A variety of low-cost monitoring strategies is discussed in Chapter 7.

When training team members to use activity-based intervention, we have found it helpful to do so within the context of an actual program with a specific child rather than employing artificial situations. Superimposing training on intervention activities permits addressing real concerns and challenges that team members must confront and solve if the application of the approach is to be successful. Training in the home and classroom should also maximize generalizability of what team members learn.

Our experience suggests that some team members can learn to follow children's leads and subtly direct activities with ease. Following children's initiations appears to come "naturally." These individuals generally require more assistance in learning how to increase the number of training opportunities and in monitoring child progress. Team members who have a long history of directing children and orchestrating their activities may find the use of child initiations difficult. In these cases, considerable effort may be required for team members to change their intervention style in order to recognize and use the subtle cues that children give as springboards for engagement and maintenance of intervention in routine and child-initiated activities.

SUMMARY

It is unfortunate that many local and state agencies have multi-disciplinary diagnostic and evaluation teams that are composed primarily of specialists. In many states or regions, these teams are assigned the responsibility of determining eligibility, writing the IEP/individualized family service plan (IFSP), and often specifying an intervention plan. Because parent participation is often minimal and too frequently no direct service delivery personnel are represented on these teams, the assessment outcomes, the IEP/IFSPs, and intervention plans are of little use or relevance to caregivers and interventionists. To be functional, we believe teams must include as genuine partners family members and the direct service delivery personnel who will be primarily responsible for offering day-to-day services to the child and family. The successful implementation of activity-based intervention requires the collaboration of teams composed of direct service delivery personnel, consultants, and family members.

Clearly, skills and knowledge about child development and recommended practices are essential to the successful application of activity-based intervention by a team; however, as indicated previously, the team members' attitudes are also critical to the successful use of the approach. To summarize, we review three perspectives that we believe provide the necessary foundation for teams to effectively employ activity-based intervention.

First, team members need to have a transactional perspective; that is, they need to recognize that learning occurs as a function of the child's interactions with, and feedback from, the environment (Sameroff & Fiese, 1990). Fundamental to change and growth are the daily interactions that occur between children and their social and physical environments. These exchanges or transactions should serve as the focus of team efforts. Team members should recognize that it is not the behavior of the child or adult in isolation but the cumulative effect of their exchanges that creates change.

A second perspective necessary for the successful implementation of activity-based intervention is a developmental view of how change occurs in children. There is evidence to support the contention that children's growth follows relatively set patterns; however, the patterns and the speed of change can be influenced by the environment (Piper, Darrah, Byrne, & Watt, 1990). For most children, interventions should be formulated based on this developmental knowledge. The establishment of fragmented behavioral targets and the use of training regimens that develop behaviors apart from their placement in the larger developmental context will not produce integrated and useful repertoires for children. Instead, goals and objectives should reflect our best knowledge of development. Children's targets should be selected in reference to their current developmental repertoire and what the most likely ensuing stages will be.

A final perspective has been termed *responsiveness* by Peck (1989). To be effective, team members should react to children in ways that promote learning and growth in desired directions. Included in the concept of responsiveness is the idea that the nature of the response is crucial. It is not adequate that the team provide any type of feedback following a child's questions; the feedback should assist the child in moving forward in the acquisition of a goal. The feedback—responsiveness—should promote a subsequent and preferably more developmentally advanced response from the child. Although feedback cannot always do this, a primary goal should be to work in this direction.

As indicated previously, one of the more important underlying skills for individuals wishing to use activity-based intervention is the ability to be a keen observer of human behavior. To be appropriately responsive, one must be able to critically observe the child's behavior, the larger environmental context, and the effect of transactions on the child's and other's behaviors. In the final analysis, we may find that the most effective team is one who is comfortable in first being able to observe and then being able to respond.

REFERENCES

Bricker, D. (1976). Educational synthesizer. In M.A. Thomas (Ed.), *Hey, don't forget about me! Education's investment in the severely, profoundly, and multiply handicapped* (pp. 84–97). Reston, VA: Council for Exceptional Children.

Bricker, D., & LaCroix, B. (1996). Training practices. In D. Bricker & A. Widerstrom (Eds.), *Preparing personnel to work with infants and young children and their families* (pp. 43–64). Baltimore: Paul H. Brookes Publishing Co.

Bricker, D., & Slentz, K. (1988). Personnel preparation: Handicapped infants. In M. Wang, M. Reynolds, & H. Walberg (Eds.), *Handbook of special education* (Vol. 3, pp. 319–345). Elmsford, NY: Pergamon.

Bricker, D., & Veltman, M. (1990). Early intervention programs: Child-focused approaches. In S. Meisels & J. Shonkoff (Eds.), *Handbook of early childhood intervention* (pp. 373–399). New York: Cambridge University Press.

Bricker, D., & Widerstrom, A. (Eds.). (1996). *Preparing personnel to work with infants and young children and their families.* Baltimore: Paul H. Brookes Publishing Co.

Brown, J., Collins, A., & Duguid, P. (1989). Situated cognition and the culture of learning. *Educational Researcher, 17*(1), 32–42.

Cole, K., Dale, P., & Mills, P. (1991). Individual differences in language delayed children's responses to direct and interactive preschool instruction. *Topics in Early Childhood Special Education, 11,* 99–124.

Dewey, J. (1976). *Experience and education.* New York: Colliers Books.

Education of the Handicapped Act Amendments of 1986, PL 99-457, 20 U.S.C. §§ 1400 *et seq.*

Geik, I., Gilkerson, L., & Sponseller, D. (1982). An early intervention training model. *Journal for the Division of Early Childhood, 5,* 42–52.

Guralnick, M.J. (Ed.). (1997). Second-generation research in the field of early intervention. In M.J. Guralnick (Ed.), *The effectiveness of early intervention* (pp. 3–20). Baltimore: Paul H. Brookes Publishing Co.

Johnson, B., McGonigel, M., & Kaufmann, R. (1989). *Guidelines and recommended practices for the individualized family service plan.* Chapel Hill, NC: National Early Childhood Technical Assistance System.

Jones, H., & Warren, S. (1991). Enhancing engagement in early language teaching. *Teaching Exceptional Children, 23*(4), 48–50.

Klein, N., & Campbell, P. (1990). Preparing personnel to serve at-risk and disabled infants, toddlers, and preschoolers. In S. Meisels & J. Shonkoff (Eds.), *Handbook of early childhood intervention* (pp. 679–699). New York: Cambridge University Press.

McCollum, J., & Catlett, C. (1997). Designing effective personnel preparation for early intervention: Theoretical frameworks. In P.J. Winton, J.A. McCollum, & C. Catlett (Eds.), *Reforming personnel preparation in early intervention: Issues, mod-*

els, and practical strategies (pp. 105–125). Baltimore: Paul H. Brookes Publishing Co.

McCollum, J., & Hughes, M. (1988). Staffing patterns and team models in infancy programs. In J. Jordan, J. Gallagher, P. Hutinger, & M. Karnes (Eds.), *Early childhood special education: Birth to three* (pp. 129–146). Reston, VA: Council for Exceptional Children.

Peck, C. (1989). Assessment of social communicative competence: Evaluating environments. *Seminars in Speech and Language, 10*(1), 1–15.

Piper, M., Darrah, J., Byrne, P., & Watt, M. (1990). Effect of early environmental experience on the motor development of the preterm infant. *Infants and Young Children, 3*(1), 9–21.

Sameroff, A., & Fiese, B. (1990). Transactional regulation and early intervention. In S. Meisels & J. Shonkoff (Eds.), *Handbook of early childhood intervention* (pp. 119–149). New York: Cambridge University Press.

Warren, S. (1991). Enhancing communication and language development with milieu teaching procedures. In E. Cipani (Ed.), *A guide for developing language competence in preschool children with severe and moderate handicaps* (pp. 68–93). Springfield, IL: Charles C Thomas.

Woodruff, G., & McGonigel, M. (1988). Early intervention team approaches: The transdisciplinary model. In J. Jordan, J. Gallagher, P. Hutinger, & M. Karnes (Eds.), *Early childhood special education: Birth to three* (pp. 163–181). Reston, VA: Council for Exceptional Children.

Chapter 5

The Application of Activity-Based Intervention to Individual Children

The previous chapters present detailed descriptions of activity-based intervention, its elements, and the rationale for its underlying structure. This chapter and Chapter 6 describe procedures for the application of activity-based intervention to individual children and to groups of children, respectively. The content contained in these two chapters should permit the reader to use the approach with a wide range of children in home- and center-based settings.

Central to the use of activity-based intervention is the embedding of children's educational and therapeutic goals in a variety of planned, child-initiated, and routine activities. This range of daily activities is the major vehicle through which intervention occurs when using an activity-based approach. Selecting, balancing, and sequencing activities must be carefully done if activity-based intervention is to be successful.

To ensure desired child progress, intervention activities must meet two criteria: 1) children's goals and objectives need to be addressed within activities, and 2) multiple opportunities to practice targeted skills need to be provided during activities. Consistently meeting these two criteria requires a structure that will guide and direct the team's responses to child initiations and the selection of routine and planned activities. The structure that guides the development and use of activities includes program plans, activity schedules, and activity plans. This chapter describes the structure that underlies the use of activities for individual children, whereas Chapter 6 describes the application of the structure for groups of children.

As indicated in Chapters 1 and 4, the term *team* is used to refer to the professionals, paraprofessionals, and parents/caregivers who compose a child's individualized education program (IEP)/individualized family service plan (IFSP) team. The composition of a child's team may vary across children and programs; however, any given team may include parents and other caregivers, interventionists, teachers, consultants, physical therapists, occupational therapists, speech-language pathologists, psychologists, nurses, paraprofessionals, and volunteers. Vital to the implementation of activity-based intervention are teams composed of individuals who have information and knowledge about the child from multiple perspectives. These individuals then are able to share information with each other to gain a complete picture of a child's performance repertoire. Effective and efficient implementation of activity-based intervention is not possible if individuals working with children and families do not share information, expertise, and resources.

Chapter 3 describes a linked systems framework and its relationship to the intervention process. Activity-based intervention is dependent on linking the four program components: assessment, goal development, intervention, and evaluation. To begin, a comprehensive assessment of a child's interests, motivations, and abilities is needed. Once the assessment is complete, the team needs to summarize the results. These results should be used directly to develop an IEP/IFSP that contains goals and objectives to prepare and support a child's independent functioning across environments. We stress in Chapter 3 the importance of using curriculum-based assessments that allow teams to develop goals and objectives that are functional and can be generalized across settings. Intervention planning with the family and program staff follows the development of the IEP/IFSP and should use the strengths and resources of all individuals who care for the child. Once intervention is under way, evaluation procedures are necessary to continually inform the team about child and family progress toward IEP/IFSP goals and outcomes.

The name *activity-based intervention* refers both to "activity" and to "being active." The word *activity* describes the format used by teams to embed opportunities for children to practice their IEP/IFSP goals and objectives. For most children, a combination of child-initiated, routine, and planned activities should be incorporated into their intervention plans. Although some teams continue to recognize or to prefer only one type of activity for intervention, including a variety of activities (e.g., child initiated, planned, routine) is characteristic of activity-based intervention. Providing an array of activities throughout which multiple opportunities for children to practice their individual goals and objectives are woven allows teams to respond to children's varying abilities and needs. For example, some children learn more rapidly using child-initiated activities, whereas others may benefit from the structure of planned activities. It is also possible that initially some children may need the support of a planned activity for the development of certain skills followed by the use of child-initiated or play activities for continued skill refinement and generalization.

Being active describes the expected type of participation by children in their physical and social environments. Active environmental engagement is considered by early childhood educators and early childhood special educators to be a cornerstone of effective learning for children (Carta, 1995). Creating dynamic learning environments for children that inspire their active involvement requires observations of children's actions, initiations, interests, motivations, and abilities across a variety of settings. Comprehensive assessment information assists teams in planning, designing, and organizing the environment in ways that optimally support a child's "active" learning. To the extent possible, children's participation in events and activities should be based on self-determined choice and curiosity rather than on adult direction. Assisting a child to learn and practice new skills using activity-based intervention generally requires using an activity as the vehicle for intervention to gain active child involvement.

As indicated previously, embedding children's goals and objectives in a variety of activities is essential to the implementation of activity-based intervention. *Embedding* refers to a procedure in which opportunities to practice individual goals and objectives are included within an activity or event in a manner that expands, modifies, or adapts the activity/event while remaining meaningful and interesting to children.

The embedding of children's goals and objectives in a variety of daily activities and child initiations is pivotal to offering children a myriad of different opportunities for the meaningful practice of targeted skills. Without consistent practice, progress is likely to be nonexistent or slow. In addition, the embedding of goals or objectives that are developmentally inappropriate, too general, or too narrow may not result in adequate child progress. Given functional and meaningful goals and objectives, most children engage in a range of activities that can be used to embed practice opportunities.

EMBEDDING GOALS: AN EXAMPLE

Tina is an active 2-year-old girl who has been diagnosed with a genetic disorder associated with developmental delays. Tina's team has conducted a careful assessment of her repertoire and selected three IFSP goals and associated objectives. For the Social-Communication Domain, Tina's goal is *to use a variety of object and event labels.* The team first should identify appropriate activities in which to embed this functional goal. Then, the team needs to explore available opportunities for embedding goals while Tina is with her grandparents each weekday morning, with her mother in the afternoons, and at a playgroup at the family's church on Wednesday evenings.

Several routine events at her grandparents' home offer a variety of opportunities for Tina to practice using object and event labels. For example, at breakfast, Tina's grandparents can embed several opportunities to use object labels by asking Tina to indicate her food preferences. Tina can also be offered a variety of toppings for her cereal or pancakes and can be asked to indicate her juice preference, both of which provide additional opportunities to use object labels. When Tina wants more food and juice, her grandparents can use this as yet another opportunity to practice using object labels. The kitchen table sits next to a large window that provides other opportunities for Tina to use object and event labels. For example, a hummingbird feeder hangs from the porch roof, and roses that attract birds, bees, and butterflies line the walkway. Tina's attention is frequently captured by these flying creatures as well as any other surprise visitors who pass in front of the window. Grandma and Grandpa can use Tina's interests as opportunities to encourage her to name objects or events.

At home, Tina practices her social-communication goal when her mom or dad reads a book to her before afternoon naptime and at evening bedtime. Tina uses labels to select the books she wants to have read. Further opportunities to embed this goal can occur while reading books. Her parents can alternate among pauses, questions, and comments, such as "What's he doing?" "Which one do you like?" and "Look at that!" to prompt Tina to name objects/events while looking at the books. Embedding Tina's social-communication goals across daily activities ensures opportunities for repeated practice.

Tina's playgroup at the church can also provide opportunities for Tina to practice using object and event labels. Children in the playgroup range in age from 2 to 6 years, so language skills vary from one-word utterances to complete sentences. One of Tina's favorite activities is playing the game Duck, Duck, Goose. Tina has opportunities to hear her peers model the use of these words as well as use them herself when she is "it." Teachers can vary the game from time to time to maintain the children's interest and expand opportunities for Tina to use new and different object and event labels. The variations can include changing the actions and the name of the game.

As Tina's caregivers practice embedding her social-communication goal into routine morning, afternoon, and evening activities, they will likely become aware of a variety of other opportunities that can also be used to embed training. The embedding of children's goals into daily routines and events is a hallmark of activity-based intervention.

UNDERLYING STRUCTURE: INDIVIDUAL PROGRAM PLANS AND ACTIVITY SCHEDULES

Activities, in and of themselves, do not ensure that children will make desired progress toward their individual goals and objectives even when the activities are attractive to them. Rather, a structure must be present that directs teams to develop activities that provide ample opportunities for practicing and learning targeted skills. It is also critical that systematic monitoring of child progress occur. The structure that underlies activity-based intervention permits team members to coordinate relevant information about a child's interests, strengths, and needs into an intervention plan that, in turn, provides meaningful learning experiences related to children's goals and objectives. The structure for individual children includes 1) individual program plans and 2) individual activity schedules.

Individual Program Plans

The individual program plan is a tool that serves as a 1) systematic guide for planning intervention and 2) record of the intervention process. Prior to planning activities or being able to use routine events or child-initiated actions effectively, an individual program plan should be developed by the team. Individual program plans provide guidelines and criteria for teaching each targeted goal and for evaluating child progress.

Each goal and associated objective on a child's IEP/IFSP should have an associated individual program plan that provides the necessary guidance for planning intervention. For children with severe disabilities, teams may need to develop program steps that also require completion of a program plan. Program steps target skills that are prerequisite, more simple, or smaller components of an objective. For example, a program step for grasping might be extending the arm from the body and/or opening the palm. Program plans are the heart of the successful application of activity-based intervention as they provide the structure that assists teams in planning the appropriate support and feedback necessary to encourage a child to practice his or her targeted skills in child-initiated, routine, and planned activities. Figure 5.1 contains a sample individual program plan that contains the following information:

- **Section One: Identifying Information**

    1. Child's name
    2. Date plan initiated
    3. Date target achieved
    4. Team members' names

- **Section Two: IEP/IFSP Goals/Objectives Specification**

    5. Goal/objective/program step—Indicate type of IEP/IFSP target to be addressed on the individual program plan.
    6. Description—Insert the target goal/objective/program step description taken from the IEP/IFSP when possible.
    7. Criteria—Indicate the criteria to be used to determine satisfactory performance of the target by the child.

- **Section Three: Teaching Considerations**

    8. Antecedents—Specify conditions, setting, or level of support, such as cues or models, used to prompt or elicit target responses.
    9. Responses—Describe specific child behaviors addressed in the goal/objective/program step.
    10. Consequences—Specify logical events following child's response.
    11. Curricular modifications—Identify specific educational and treatment supports needed by the child.

Individual Program Plan
SECTION ONE: IDENTIFYING INFORMATION

1. Child's name: _____

2. Date plan initiated: _____ 3. Date target achieved: _____

4. Team members' names: _____
   _____
   _____

SECTION TWO: IEP/IFSP GOALS/OBJECTIVES SPECIFICATION
(check one)

5. Goal: _____   Objective: _____   Program step: _____

6. Description: _____
   _____
   _____

7. Criteria: _____
   _____
   _____

SECTION THREE: TEACHING CONSIDERATIONS

8. Antecedents	9. Responses	10. Consequences

11. Curricular modifications: _____
    _____
    _____

(continued)

Figure 5.1.   An Individual Program Plan form.

Figure 5.1.   *(continued)*

SECTION FOUR: EVALUATION PROCEDURES

12. Who   13. Where   14. When (circle one)

    _____   _____   Daily Weekly Monthly

    _____   _____   Daily Weekly Monthly

    _____   _____   Daily Weekly Monthly

15. How (check one)

Narrative summary ____   Portfolio ____   Behavioral observations ____

16. Decision rule

If adequate progress does not occur in _____ (specify time frame), the team will:

___ modify intervention strategies

___ modify curricular content (i.e., goal, objective, program step)

___ other (describe) _____

_____

- **Section Four: Evaluation Procedures**

    12. Who—Specify person responsible for data collection.
    13. Where—Indicate where data are to be collected (e.g., meals, circle).
    14. When—Indicate whether data are to be collected daily, weekly, or monthly.
    15. How—Indicate method of data collection.
    16. Decision rule—Specify action if adequate progress does not occur.

The individual program plan includes information found in the IEP/IFSP—for example, child's and team members' names, dates when intervention began and the goal was achieved, goals and objectives, and evaluation procedures. The individual program plan, however, differs from the IEP/IFSP in two significant ways. First, the individual program plan is developed after the IEP/IFSP. As a result, teams have a foundation for planning intervention as well as additional time to develop specific intervention plans to assist a child in achieving targeted goals and corresponding objectives. Developing an individual program plan permits enhancement of the IEP/IFSP and allows teams to develop their intervention efforts in a consistent and collaborative manner. Second, the individual program plan differs from the IEP/IFSP because it is not a legal document. Rather, it is a malleable planning tool that can be altered and modified as a child's interests and needs change to more effectively address a child's IEP/IFSP goals and objectives.

An example of a completed individual program plan addressing the social-communication goal for Hakeem, a 4-year-old boy who has spastic quadriplegic cerebral palsy and is not yet walking independently, is shown in Figure 5.2. Hakeem communicates through facial expressions and vocalizations; however, he is beginning to use word approximations. A switch on his wheelchair can be activated to signal for help. Hakeem appears to enjoy music and prefers toys that make noise. He attends a Head Start classroom in the mornings and an extended child care program until 5:30 P.M. each day. Hakeem's mom brings him to the Head Start classroom on her way to work. A classroom assistant takes Hakeem to his child care program when the morning Head Start session ends. His dad picks him up after work at the child care program.

One evening a week, Hakeem's parents take him to the warm water pool at the Easter Seals Center for "family night." A physical therapist and two assistants are present to help families with their children in the pool. Hakeem enjoys the water, and his parents have the opportunity to meet other families with children who have disabilities.

Prior to developing an individual program plan for Hakeem, the team, including the Head Start teacher, physical therapist, speech-language pathologist, child care teacher, and parents, completed the Assessment, Evaluation, and Programming System (AEPS) Test, the AEPS Family Report, and the AEPS Family Interest Survey (Bricker, 1993). These programmatic tools provide information that is used to directly link assessment to goal development as described in Chapter 3. The team met and summarized their findings, prioritized goals, and developed an IEP. Next, the team used the two selected priority IEP goals to guide the intervention planning.

Individual Program Plan
SECTION ONE: IDENTIFYING INFORMATION

1. Child's name: _Hakeem Alahandro_

2. Date plan initiated: _9-12-97_   3. Date target achieved: _in progress_

4. Team members' names: _Mr. & Mrs. Alahandro, Ms. Johnson (Head_
   Start teacher), Ms. Kim (child care teacher), Mr. Acedo (speech-
   language pathologist), and Mrs. Murphy (physical therapist)

SECTION TWO: IEP/IFSP GOALS/OBJECTIVE SPECIFICATION
(check one)

5. Goal: _X_   Objective: _____   Program step: _____

6. Description: _AEPS Social-Communication Goal 2.0_
   Hakeem will use 10 consistent word approximations to refer to
   objects, people, and/or events.

7. Criteria: _10 times per day for 2 weeks_

_____

_____

_____

SECTION THREE: TEACHING CONSIDERATIONS

8. Antecedents	9. Responses	10. Consequences
• Show object • Model word/phrase • Stop action, give expectant look • Ask questions • Point to person	H produces word approximation appropriate for object, person, event (+) H does not produce word approximation (–) H produces inappropriate word approximation (–)	• Give H object (+) • Express pleasure (+) • Begin action (+) • Imitate H's response (+) • Give H attention (+) • Withhold object, person, action (–) • Model word (–)

(+=correct response; –=incorrect or no response; +=feedback for correct response; –=feedback for incorrect response)

11. Curricular modifications: _Ensure H is positioned correctly in his wheel-_
    chair so he can produce word approximations.

_____

Figure 5.2. A completed individual program plan for Hakeem.

Figure 5.2.   *(continued)*

SECTION FOUR: EVALUATION PROCEDURES

12. Who   13. Where   14. When

    Mr. Acedo   *Snack/Circle*   Daily (Weekly) Monthly

    _____   _____   Daily Weekly Monthly

    _____   _____   Daily Weekly Monthly

15. How (check one)

Narrative summary ____   Portfolio ____   Behavioral observations __X__

                                        (count number of word approximations)

16. Decision rule

If adequate progress does not occur in __*1 month*__ (specify time frame),
the team will:

__X__ modify intervention strategies

____ modify curricular content (i.e., goal, objective, program step)

____ other (describe) _____

_____

The first step in intervention planning was to develop individual program plans for each of Hakeem's two priority IEP goals: 1) Hakeem will use 10 consistent word approximations to refer to objects, people, and/or events; and 2) Hakeem will grasp hand-size objects.

The completed individual program plan for Hakeem shown in Figure 5.2 contains his social-communication goal that was taken directly from the AEPS Test. The team selected this goal by examining Hakeem's performance in the Social-Communication Domain and selecting the next item in the developmental sequence that he was unable to perform (i.e., scored "1" or "0").

Once the goals and objectives were developed, the team was able to complete the section on teaching considerations of the individual program plan. To complete this section, the team referred to the *AEPS Curriculum for Birth to Three Years* (Cripe,

Slentz, & Bricker, 1993). The use of the AEPS Curriculum or similar curricular tools provides information and guidance for selecting antecedents (e.g., environmental arrangements, strategies) and curricular modifications.

The fourth section of the individual program plan is on evaluation procedures. For Hakeem's social-communication goal, the team identified who, where, when, and how to monitor his progress. Finally, the team selected a decision rule to modify the intervention strategy if Hakeem was not making adequate progress within 1 month.

Once an individual program plan is completed for each priority IEP/IFSP goal and associated objectives and, if necessary, program steps, the team is ready to begin intervention. To undertake intervention in an organized fashion, an activity schedule is developed.

Individual Activity Schedules

Individual activity schedules are the second part of the structure underlying activity-based intervention and are essential to the overall planning of intervention efforts for an individual child. Individual activity schedules encourage teams to use a child's routine daily activities as the context for integrating multiple and varied opportunities to embed targeted program steps, objectives, or goals. When working with individual children in the home, classroom, and community, knowledge of the child's daily schedule ensures that the team will consider and plan adequate opportunities for intervention to occur throughout the child's day. This approach to intervention is generally more effective with young children than imposing a set of specific training activities different from a child's daily routines and environments. Furthermore, families find the use of children's daily activities highly compatible with their resources and needs. Families and other team members should work together to make use of activities and materials that are usual parts of the home schedule.

There are two types of activity schedules: individual and group. Individual activity schedules are developed for a single child, whereas group activity schedules are designed to accommodate scheduling for several children. (See Chapter 6 for a discussion of group activity schedules.) Individual activity schedules emphasize the use of routine activities that occur throughout a child's day, and they differ from group activity schedules used in center-based child care and preschool programs. Gathering information through an informal interview with the primary caregiver(s) is often a prerequisite to developing a useful individual activity schedule. Home visits with families can be ideal for obtaining the information necessary to create an activity schedule. Figure 5.3 contains a completed activity schedule information form for Hakeem. The interview outline provides a guide that prompts the interventionist to collect information on the 1) daily family routines, 2) time and frequency of routines, 3) sequence of events occurring in routines, 4) description of child's participation in routines, and 5) whether the routine can be used to embed a child's IEP/IFSP goals.

A discussion with Hakeem's family regarding the use of family routines may indicate, for example, that meals are not a good time to introduce intervention activities because mealtimes are hectic and noisy and, thus, are not conducive to intervention. Without asking questions about family activities, the team might have inappropriately suggested the use of meals for Hakeem to practice his social-communication goals. Intervention will be most successful when team members collaborate with families to determine the match between a child's IEP/IFSP goals and objectives and the family's ability and desire to use a routine activity to provide learning opportunities.

The activity schedule information form provides the necessary information to complete an individual activity schedule such as the one shown in Figure 5.4. Individual activity schedules are designed to describe and reflect the many opportunities that may arise for families and other team members to use daily routines to embed IEP/IFSP goals and objectives. The individual activity schedule is developed for routine activities that occur on a predictable or regular basis, such as meals, diapering, dressing, snacks, clean-up, caring for pets, and traveling to and from designated locations (e.g., school, grocery store). Often, with thought, routine activities can be used or refocused to provide children opportunities to learn new skills or practice emerging skills.

The individual activity schedule provides space to indicate routine activity, routine's time and frequency, and strategies for embedding the child's goals and objectives in each routine activity. Figure 5.4 contains an example of a completed individual activity schedule for Hakeem that addresses his priority social-communication and fine motor goals. Completing an individual activity schedule gives team members concrete ideas of how to use routine activities to embed targeted goals and objectives.

Activity Schedule Information Form

Daily family routines	Routine's time and frequency	Sequence of events occurring in routines	Description of child's participation in routines	Useful to embed IEP/IFSP goals/objectives (yes/no)
Dressing	6:30 A.M. (1x per day)	Remove sleepwear. Retrieve clothes and shoes to wear. Put on clothes and shoes. Wash face.	H moves his head, arms, and legs while Mom dresses him sometimes to indicate he does not want to change clothes and other times to play a game of Catch Me if You Can. H can brush his hair and teeth with hand-over-hand assistance.	Yes
Breakfast	7:00 A.M. (1x per day)	Mom makes breakfast for family. Mom assists H with washing hands and getting into chair. Dad sets table. Family eats breakfast. Mom cleans up (e.g., washes hands, assists H from chair to living room floor, clears table, washes dishes).	H stirs juice in pitcher with sister's help. H needs hand-over-hand guidance to bring food to his mouth on utensil. H's sister often helps H eat breakfast.	No—Parents are not interested in using this routine activity to embed H's goals.
Car travel	8:00 A.M. (1x per day)	Mom puts H in car seat. Mom drops off H's sister at school. Mom removes H from car seat. Mom places H in wheelchair. Mom pushes H to his classroom.	H grasps/releases seat belt. H's sister gives him toys and books. H waves good-bye to his sister. H tries to help mom manipulate wheelchair.	Yes
Bath time	Evening (1x per day)	Run water in bath to fill tub. Remove H's clothes. Place toys in bath. Wash hair and body with soap, and rinse clean. Dry H with towel, and get H dressed.	H grasps toys handed to him in bath.	Yes

Figure 5.3. A completed activity schedule information form for Hakeem. (Based on materials developed by Project Facets in Parsons, KS.)

Individual Activity Schedule

Child's name:_____ Date:_____

Routine activity	Routine's time and frequency	Strategies for embedding goals or objectives	
		Uses consistent word approximations	Grasps hand-size objects
Dressing	6:30 A.M. (1x per day)	• Model a word to indicate preferred clothing. • Point to family members. • Imitate H's approximation.	• Offer H objects (e.g., toothbrush, hairbrush, cup, clothing).
Car travel	8:00 A.M. (1x per day)	• Play radio/cassette in car. • Model a word to indicate familiar location	• Offer H seatbelt, books, or toys from car pocket.
Bath time	Evening (1x per day)	• Look at a book, and model words to refer to common objects.	• Hide objects including soap, shampoo, bottle, washcloth, toys, towel, and robe.

Figure 5.4. A completed individual activity schedule for Hakeem.

In addition to targeting training opportunities during daily routines, it is essential to use child-initiated and play activities for the same purpose. Following is a discussion designed to sensitize team members to the many possibilities for embedding goals and objectives that occur when children initiate actions or are involved in play.

Child-Initiated Activities and Play

Child-initiated activities and play are recognized by many as important opportunities for learning (Linder, 1993; Noonan & McCormick 1993; Widerstrom, 1995). An ensuing question is, "How does a team utilize child-initiated activities and play in ways that encourage and maintain a child's participation in the interaction or event as well as provide varied and frequent opportunities for the child to practice targeted goals and objectives?" Attaining this balance is a challenge. Over the years, we have observed resourceful and skillful team members who successfully use child initiations and children's play to respond to children in a manner that matches and extends their initiations and play and provides many opportunities for children to practice targeted goals and objectives. Three key elements are helpful for shaping children's initiations and play into valuable learning experiences. First, knowledge of children's IEP/IFSP goals and objectives is essential. Second, information about children's interests and abilities is required. Third, a creative and dynamic approach to interacting with children is necessary. Figure 5.5 provides an example of how to transform a child's initiation of mud-puddle play into an opportunity for the child to practice a variety of skills.

Transforming child initiations and play into learning opportunities can be enhanced by following the steps outlined here:

- *List* the child's goals or objectives as shown in Figure 5.5.
- *Observe* the child's interests in his or her environment (e.g., mud puddle).
- *Identify* parts of the activity that encourage and reinforce a child's participation (e.g., splashing of water with feet, squishing of mud through fingers, stirring of water with stick, tossing pebbles into water, watching and commenting on size of splashes created by pebbles).
- *Shape* a child's interactions with his or her environment into opportunities for practicing goals and objectives. For example, if the child is tossing large rocks into the puddle and one of the child's goals is to use a pincer grasp, then hand small pebbles to the child to throw in the puddle.
- *Arrange* the physical and social environments to encourage the child to practice goals and objectives. For example, if a child has a goal of walking independently, then wagons, wheelbarrows, and push carts might be included in the activity. A child could be encouraged to find a mound of dirt and fill her wheelbarrow to cover the mud puddle when she is finished playing. Trips to and from the dirt mound provide many opportunities to walk without adult support. Similarly, arranging the social environment by pairing or grouping particular children can produce opportunities for practicing goals and objectives based on cooperation.

In Section II of this volume, there is a lengthy discussion on the importance of child initiation and play in Chapter 8. The need to capture children's attention and interests to ensure effective and efficient intervention efforts is emphasized. The reader is urged to read Chapter 8 to gain an appreciation for why and how to focus on child initiation.

Developmental domain	Child's goal or objective	Opportunity
Fine motor	Reaches, grasps, and releases a variety of objects from pea size to hand size	Encourage or simply reinforce tossing pebbles, sticks, and other available objects into puddle.
Gross motor	Skips 5 feet Runs 15 feet Hops 3 hops	Introduce or follow a child's lead of playing a game of jumping, running, hopping, or skipping between puddles.
Adaptive	Washes and dries face and hands Removes coat, pants, shirt, socks, and shoes	Follow up with children's comments about their wet clothes by suggesting washing and drying hands/face at bathroom sink. Child practices removing wet and muddy clothing after investigating puddles.
Cognitive	Recognizes and/or demonstrates understanding of a variety of concepts, including • shape • size • spatial relationships	Ask child to find the round, oval, heart-shaped, long, small, and large puddles. Also discuss length of sticks for stirring water in puddle. Participate in tossing pebble or rocks into puddles and asking child, "Can you throw your rock next to mine?" Describe where rock landed (e.g., in front of, next to, behind, on top of).
Social-communication	Uses descriptive words	Prompt child with a variety of questions that encourage the description of the puddles, sticks, and pebbles. Model use of words such as cold, brown, big, small, deep, shallow, long, short, light, heavy, cloudy, and dark.
Social	Resolves conflicts with peers	If water splashes on peers, ask child to think of way he or she can continue playing without getting others wet. If space of puddle is limited, prompt child to think of ways all children can play, such as taking turns or deciding how many children could be at one puddle at the same time.

Figure 5.5. Transforming a child's mud-puddle play activity into opportunities to practice targeted goals and objectives.

SUMMARY

The success of approaches such as activity-based intervention is dependent on a cohesive structure that provides the necessary foundation for selecting and using a variety of activities as the training vehicle. The structure proposed in this chapter for applying activity-based intervention with individual children includes individual program plans and individual activity schedules. This two-part structure provides guidance for using routines, child initiations, and play activities as opportunities for children to address their IEP/IFSP goals and objectives.

We have also sought to emphasize the use of activities that are interesting and meaningful to children. The use of fun and meaningful activities often provides the strongest motivation and reinforcement for encouraging children to practice a variety of skills repeatedly throughout the day.

REFERENCES

Carta, J.J. (1995). Developmentally appropriate practice: A critical analysis as applied to young children with disabilities. *Focus on Exceptional Children, 27*(8), 2–14.

Bricker, D. (Ed.). (1993). *Assessment, evaluation, and programming system for infants and children: Vol. 1. AEPS measurement for birth to three years.* Baltimore: Paul H. Brookes Publishing Co.

Cripe, J., Slentz, K., & Bricker, D. (Eds.). (1993). *Assessment, evaluation, and programming system for infants and children: Vol. 2. AEPS curriculum for birth to three years.* Baltimore: Paul H. Brookes Publishing Co.

Linder, T. (1993). *Transdisciplinary play-based assessment: A functional approach to working with young children* (Rev. ed.). Baltimore: Paul H. Brookes Publishing Co.

Noonan, M.J., & McCormick, L. (1993). *Early intervention in natural environments.* Pacific Grove, CA: Brooks/Cole Publishing.

Widerstrom, A. (1995). *Achieving learning goals through play.* Tucson, AZ: Communication Skill Builders.

Chapter 6

The Application of Activity-Based Intervention to Groups of Children

Chapter 5 discusses the application of activity-based intervention to individual children. This chapter addresses the application of the approach to groups of children using a three-part structure of individual program plans, group activity schedules, and group activity plans. In addition, intervention strategies that are compatible with the use of activity-based intervention are presented. The use of these strategies will likely increase opportunities for children to meaningfully address their individual goals and objectives across activities.

As with individual children, the successful application of the activity-based approach with groups of children is dependent on linking assessment, goal development, intervention, and evaluation. Of particular importance is the need for quality goals and objectives that drive and guide the intervention efforts. As we have suggested previously, the use of curriculum-based assessment/evaluation tools such as the Assessment, Evaluation, and Programming System (AEPS) (Bricker, 1993) is critical to the development of meaningful, functional, and generalizable goals and objectives. Groups are, of course, composed of individual children, and an accurate, reliable measurement of each child's strengths, needs, and interests is necessary for successful intervention.

Teams faced with assessing groups of children may need to devise efficient methods for collecting performance data and other information. The AEPS Tests (Bricker, 1993; Bricker &

Pretti-Frontczak, 1996) offer strategies for the observation and recording of responses for several children simultaneously. Programs that include typically developing children and/or those children who are at risk can assess these children by using the AEPS Family Reports (Bricker, 1993; Bricker & Pretti-Frontczak, 1996). Using the easy-to-administer AEPS Family Reports is an efficient and reliable method for assessing children whose development generally appears typical.

Assessing children and writing quality individualized education program (IEP)/individualized family service plan (IFSP) goals and objectives is no less important for children served in center-based settings than for individual children receiving services at home. Teams need to collect information about children in group settings as the basis for intervention planning and implementation.

PRIORITIZING GOALS FOR GROUPS OF CHILDREN

Critical to planning intervention for groups of children is prioritizing children's IEP/IFSP goals. Prioritization of goals is necessary because children generally have more targeted goals than interventionists and families can comfortably address. Counter to what we believe is good practice, children may have as many as 10–20 goals listed on their IEP/IFSPs. Developing intervention plans that address every child's individual goals becomes a difficult task when several children with disabilities are served in a center-based program. Thus, it is essential to identify the high-priority goals for each child that can be reasonably addressed (McLean, Bailey, & Wolery, 1996).

Once the high-priority goals have been identified for each child, a strategy to help organize the goals and objectives is needed. We recommend the use of a two-way matrix that lists the children's names on the left side and the developmental domains across the top. This type of matrix allows teams to see the variety and developmental range of skills across domains that should be addressed in the group setting. Figure 6.1 provides an illustration of a goal/objective matrix in which a child's goal or objective can be entered at each intersection point. The matrix should be constructed to accommodate changes in children's goals and objectives (e.g., a chalk- or whiteboard that permits erasing or a poster board with Post-it notes). Figure 6.2 provides a blank goal/objective matrix that can be used by the team.

Developmental domains						
Child	**Fine motor**	**Gross motor**	**Adaptive**	**Social-communi-cation**	**Cognitive**	**Social**
Kate	Copies simple shapes		Gets tissue when nose is runny		Follows two-step directions	
Mitch		Pedals riding toys	Uses fork and spoon to eat meals	Uses short sentences to inform (i.e., three to five words in length)		
Trevor	Manipu-lates two small objects	Walks up and down stairs			Uses a variety of problem-solving strategies	
Kylie		Sits balanced without support	Uses toilet			Plays near other peers
Conner	Prints first name			Uses words to label own or others' affect/ emotions	Recalls events immedi-ately after they occur	

Figure 6.1.   A completed goal/objective matrix.

THREE-PART STRUCTURE: INDIVIDUAL PROGRAM PLANS, GROUP ACTIVITY SCHEDULES, AND GROUP ACTIVITY PLANS

Once a goal/objective matrix has been created, teams are ready to develop the three-part structure that underlies the use of activity-based intervention with groups of children. In this chapter, individual program plans, group activity schedules, and group activity plans are discussed in terms of their application to groups of children.

Part One: Individual Program Plans

The process of developing an individual program plan remains the same whether working with a single child or groups of children. Recording the content for the four sections of an individ-

Developmental domains						
Child	Fine motor	Gross motor	Adaptive	Social-communi-cation	Cognitive	Social

Figure 6.2.   A blank goal/objective matrix.

ual program plan, including identifying information, IEP/IFSP goals/objectives specification, teaching considerations, and evaluation procedures, is necessary to provide individualized intervention for children.

Teams may find that completing individual program plans for several children demands both time and resources. Without an individual program plan or a similar written document to guide the intervention, however, the team's efforts are likely to be fragmented and ambiguous. Furthermore, without planning for individual children, group activities may become developmentally inappropriate and meaningless. Developing individual program plans for groups of children accomplishes four important objectives. First, it ties assessment findings to the proposed intervention. Second, it creates a tool for fostering consistency of intervention efforts across team members. Third, it ensures the targeting of developmentally appropriate activities and expectations. Fourth, it sets forth a plan for documenting child progress.

When faced with the responsibility of developing individual program plans for many children, teams need to develop strategies for making the process efficient. Although individualization is essential, some children may have the same or similar goals. In such cases, a single individual program plan can be developed for a specific goal for multiple children. Even if minor to moderate variations are required for children, the team may be able to use the "essence" of an individual program plan for several children. For example, the goal may remain the same for two children, but the consequences each child requires may be different. In another instance, the evaluation procedures may need to be varied for children with the same goal. When individual program plans need to be developed separately for children, teams may find that responsibilities need to be divided to enhance efficiency. Chapter 5 contains an example of an individual program plan.

Part Two: Group Activity Schedules

Once individual program plans have been completed for children's priority goals and objectives, a group activity schedule is generated. The development of a group activity schedule will assist team members in identifying activities that are appropriate for embedding children's goals and objectives. Child care, educational, and treatment programs that serve young children who have or who are at risk for disabilities generally provide a set of activities that follow a predictable sequence (e.g., opening circle, free play, art projects, outdoor play, snacktime, storytime, closing circle). A group activity schedule can highlight activities that can be used to embed children's priority IEP/IFSP goals and objectives. Figure 6.3 presents a completed group activity schedule using a typical preschool classroom schedule that has been individualized for five children. This schedule was developed to offer a balance of routine and planned activities that can provide opportunities to embed children's IEP/IFSP goals and objectives. Each child's name is listed in the left column of the group activity schedule. Prioritized goals and objectives are also listed on the left side of the schedule beside the child's name. The daily program activities are listed across the top of the schedule. Finally, teaching considerations such as antecedents, conse-

Group Activity Schedule

Daily Program Activities

Child	Goals and objectives	Arrival	Center choices	Breakfast	Stories/books	Music and movement
K A T E	Copies simple shapes		• Uses pen or pencil at writing table • Uses marker, chalk, or crayon during art • Makes shopping list in house area • Copies shapes on paper		Traces shapes in books	
	Gets tissue when nose is runny	As needed	As needed	As needed	As needed	As needed
	Follows two-step directions	• Steps down from bus and holds peer's hand to walk to classroom		• Washes/dries hands • Plays Simon Says • Serves self and passes food to peer		• Gets carpet square and places on floor • Participates in songs with simple directions

MITCH					
Pedals riding toys	Rides tricycle from bus to classroom	• Puts backpack in cubby and removes coat • Hangs coat on hook and selects a play center	• Scrapes food into garbage can and rinses plate		Selects song to sing and tells stories
Uses fork and spoon to eat meals		Pretends to eat at restaurant in dramatic play area	Uses fork/spoon with pancake, French toast, applesauce, yogurt, and cereal		
Uses short sentences to inform	Responds to question, "what did you do last night at home?"	Chooses role in dramatic play area and tells peer	• Selects book from choice of two • Tells story about pictures in book		

(continued)

Figure 6.3. A completed group activity schedule for five children. (*Notes*: Goals and objectives taken from the AEPS Test; Snickers & Hoots game is from Krull & Don, 1986.)

95

Figure 6.3. (continued)

Daily Program Activities

Child	Goals and objectives	Arrival	Center choices	Breakfast	Stories/books	Music and movement
T R E V O R	Manipulates two small objects	Unbuttons coat	Puts caps on markers	Takes off and puts lids on plastic food containers		
	Walks up and down stairs	• Walks down bus steps • Walks up classroom steps	Walks up and down indoor climbing structure	Walks up and down steps at sink to wash hands		
	Uses problem-solving strategies		Identifies solution to peer's problem(s)		Responds to adult's questions about problems in stories	• Participates in Snickers & Hoots game • Plays musical chairs
K Y L I E	Sits balanced without support	Sits in seat on bus		Sits in chair at table	Sits on beanbag in book corner	Sits on carpet square during circle
	Uses toilet	Goes to bathroom with adult			Goes to bathroom with adult	

CORNER			
Plays near other peers	Prints first name	Uses words to label own or others' affect/emotions	Recalls events immediately after they occur
Sits next to peer on bus	Prints name on attendance board	Responds to adult's question, "How do you feel this morning?"	Recalls objects/events observed on bus ride
Selects center with other peers	• Prints name on completed projects • Uses alphabet stencils at writing center		
Sits near peer at table			Recalls participation in center(s)
		Names affect/emotions of characters in book	Recalls particular events of a story
• Sits near peers at circle • Participates in musical games (e.g., London Bridge)		Participates in "If You're Happy ..." song	

quences, or curricular modifications can be listed at each intersection of a child's goal/objective and a daily activity. In developing group activity schedules, teams are reminded first to prioritize targeted IEP/IFSP goals and objectives, second to review the "typical" sequence of activities and events of their classroom, and third to identify those activities that can be used to embed children's goals and objectives.

The creation of group activity schedules should not preclude variations and spontaneity in the type and sequence of program activities. If, for example, children introduce a change or an unplanned event occurs that can be used to foster the development of targeted goals and objectives, then team members should not be reluctant to deviate from the group activity schedule. When developing and using activity schedules, it is critical that all team members have a "working" knowledge of children's targeted goals and objectives. A working knowledge of targeted skills allows interventionists to follow children's leads and interests even when they deviate from planned events and ensures multiple opportunities for practice on targeted skills. Teams implementing activity-based intervention should feel free to modify the activity schedule format presented in this chapter.

Figure 6.4 presents another example of a completed group activity schedule developed for a Head Start classroom in which all children have educational goals, many of which are shared (i.e., children share similar targeted skills). As in the previous example of a group activity schedule, the children's names and prioritized goals are listed in the left columns of the schedule and the daily program activities are listed across the top. In addition, the developmental domains of the targeted skills are shown in Figure 6.4. Generation of a group activity schedule should help teams to provide adequate practice time for children who have diverse skills and who function at different developmental levels.

Completing a group activity schedule and then posting it for team members assists in reminding them which goals/objectives can be addressed during which activities. The group activity schedule serves as a visual prompt for team members to seek out opportunities to embed children's goals and objectives across a variety of daily activities and events. Displaying and discussing a group activity schedule with team members can further assist in ensuring that multiple opportunities are provided and used for children to practice targeted skills. The group activity schedule should be developed at the beginning of the

Group Activity Schedule

Child	Goals and objectives	Daily Program Activities				
		Arrival	Lunch	Outdoor play	Circle time	Discovery time
Fine Motor						
Jamal **Kindra** **Aaron** **Breann** **Mikail**	*Prints first name*	*Writes name on name card and sticks on attendance board*	*Prints name on name cards to use for seating arrangements*	• *Writes name with sidewalk chalk* • *Writes name in sand with sticks* • *Writes name on paintings or drawings*		• *Writes name on all completed projects* • *Writes name with stencils at art/writing table* • *Writes name with finger paints*
Tasha **Jorge** **Alex** **Breann** **Dahlia** **Cody** **Sam**	*Uses scissors to cut straight and curved lines*					• *Cuts rolled playdough with scissors* • *Cuts paper at art table* • *Cuts out stamps at post office*

(continued)

Figure 6.4. A completed group activity schedule for children in a Head Start program. (Goals and objectives taken from the AEPS Test.)

Figure 6.4. (continued)

Daily Program Activities

Child	Goals and objectives	Arrival	Lunch	Outdoor play	Circle time	Discovery time
Shelly **James** **Darin** **Marisa** **Gunter**	Threads, zips, and unzips zipper	Unzips and removes coat		Unzips/zips ball bag to remove balls	Zips/unzips zippered pocket books	Zips/unzips dress-up clothing, suitcases, dolls clothing
Gross Motor						
Cody **Dahlia**	Rides and steers toy with pedals			• Rides tricycle around obstacle course • Rides tricycle to storage shed at clean-up time		
Adaptive						
Marisa **Gunter** **Aaron**	Uses napkin to clean face and hands at meals		Wipes face and hands with napkin/towel before, during, and after eating lunch			Uses cloth napkins at restaurant in dramatic play area

Shelly **Jamal** **Alex** **Tasha**	Eats a variety of food types		Selects and eats one food from each of the food groups served			Pretends to eat variety of foods at restaurant in dramatic play area
Gunter **Kindra**	Ties and unties string type fasteners	Unties/ties strings on coat or hat		• Unties/ties bag with sand-box toys • Ties shoes when they come untied		• Unties and ties shoes to participate in movement activities on mats • Unties/ties own shoes and dress-up shoes
Cognitive						
James	Responds appropriately to directions	• Holds hand with peer and walks from bus to classroom • Puts backpack in cubby and selects activity	• Eats lunch with peers at table • Cleans plate and utensils after eating	Participates in small-group organized games such as Duck, Duck, Goose, parachute ball, freeze tag		Participates in adult-planned activity from start to finish
Kindra **Breann** **Mikail**	Demonstrates understanding of six colors	Responds to question, "What color shoes shirt, pants, dress are you wearing today?"	Responds to question about the color of foods served	• Plays Red Light/Green Light outside • Responds to requests for particular color of toy in sand box	Responds to direction, "If you're wearing [blank] color, choose a friend to go to discovery time"	Identifies color of materials desired for use during discovery time (e.g., paints, dress-up clothes, blocks)

(continued)

Figure 6.4. (continued)

Daily Program Activities

Child	Goals and objectives	Arrival	Lunch	Outdoor play	Circle time	Discovery time
Cognitive						
Jorge Shelly Darin	Demonstrates understanding of five different concepts about time	Responds to question, "what did you do last night with your family?"	Responds to question "when have you eaten [blank] food before?"			
Jamal	Gives possible cause for some event	Identifies cause for peer's or adults' absence	Suggests why a particular item is missing at lunch		Responds to adult's questions about problems in stories read	
Tasha James	Counts 10 objects	Counts pockets/buttons on clothes	• Counts number of food items served on plate • Counts cups, plates, utensils on table	• Counts to 10 while playing Hide and Seek • Counts objects in sandbox, flowers/vegetables in garden, found objects such as rocks or sticks	Counts in songs/fingerplays	Counts number of children playing in area

102

Alex	Asks what and where questions	Smells food cooking for lunch and asks, "What is for lunch?"	Notices absent peer or adult and asks, "Where is [blank]?"	Plays Hide and Seek and asks peer/adult, "Where is [blank]?"	• Asks what and where questions about objects brought for sharing day • Participates in animal charades asking, "Where do you live and what do you eat?"	Asks where are objects when too few objects are present in areas
Jorge Dahlia	Uses adjectives to make comparisons	Describes texture and color of clothing on self and others	Describes textures and colors of food items served		Describes items felt in feely bag	Describes and compares completed projects of peer/self

(continued)

Figure 6.4. (continued)

Daily Program Activities

Child	Goals and objectives	Arrival	Lunch	Outdoor play	Circle time	Discovery time
Social-Communication						
Darin Sam Mikail Aaron	Shares or exchanges objects	Shares umbrella with peer while walking from bus to classroom	Exchanges plates/bowls of food with peers	Shares or trades objects when enough are not available		• Shares watercolor palette • Trades objects in any area selected • Shares large paper to paint/write/draw • Shares big blocks • Trades puppets
Sam	Knows gender of self and others	• Walks in line with boys to classroom from bus • Places attendance card on bulletin board next to a boy's or a girl's card			Responds to song directions specifically for boys	• Plays doctor's office in dramatic area that requires practice in giving identifying information such as name, address, gender
Jamal Marisa Cody	Accurately identifies own affect/emotions	Responds to questions, "How do you feel today?" "How do you think [blank] feels today?"	Identifies likes and dislikes	Identifies affect/emotion of children experiencing conflict or injury	Identifies affect/emotion of people in books	

year and changed as children achieve their goals and objectives and/or as other conditions change (e.g., staff, setting). Figure 6.5 provides a blank group activity schedule that can be used by the interventionist.

Part Three: Group Activity Plans

In shifting the focus from the individual child to groups of children, planned activities become an important method for addressing children's targeted goals and objectives. Planned activities refer to activities that require adult planning, preparation, and guidance. Examples of planned activities can include preparing snacks, taking field trips, having special science or art projects, and preparing circle time events. The process of planning group activities may be as vital as the execution of the activity with the children. Planning group activities benefits teams in at least two ways. First, a team that plans group activities may discover opportunities to embed children's goals and objectives that were not obvious or apparent prior to the planning. Second, teams may enhance their cooperation, collaboration, and use of limited resources through their discussions on planning group activities. A group activity plan is composed of nine components:

1. Activity name
2. Materials—Indicate the materials necessary to conduct the activity.
3. Environmental arrangements—Recommend changes in physical space and/or social organization necessary to make the activity successful.
4. Description of activity
   a. Introduction—Indicate how to obtain the children's attention and set the stage for the ensuing activity.
   b. Sequence of events—Identify an order for the parts of the activity to occur that lead to its completion.
   c. Closing—Indicate how to end and summarize the activity.
5. Opportunities to embed children's goals and objectives—Identify specific planned opportunities the interventionist can provide individual children to practice goals and objectives.
6. Planned variations—Indicate possible variations that could be used in the activity.
7. Vocabulary—List possible words/gestures/signs that could be used/targeted during the activity.

Group Activity Schedule

Child	Goals and Objectives	Daily Program Activities				

Figure 6.5. A blank group activity schedule.

8. Peer interaction strategies—Describe methods for encouraging peer interactions.
9. Parent/caregiver input—List parent suggestions or concerns.

The following sections provide detailed descriptions of Components 2 through 9.

Materials and Environmental Arrangements

Prior to the introduction of a planned group activity, it is useful for the team to consider what materials and types of environmental arrangements are necessary for the activity to be successful. Consideration of environmental arrangements is important for several reasons. First, it may be that some activities require the interventionist to assemble or purchase materials ahead of time (e.g., shaving cream for a shaving cream activity). Second, some activities may require such extensive shifts in the physical environment that they can only be done, for example, at the end of the day (e.g., setting up an obstacle course). Third, appropriate numbers of "things" and sufficient space should be available to accommodate children during specific activities (e.g., for a dress-up activity, enough clothing for each participating child). Fourth, some children may require special equipment (e.g., communication board, orthopedic chair) to participate in the activity. Review of materials and environmental arrangements should not only prepare the interventionist for the activity but should allow for individualization and keep transitions and "dead time" for the children to a minimum.

Description of Activity—
Introduction, Sequence of Events, and Closing

The introduction, sequence of events, and closing sections of a group activity plan provide a description of the activity from its initiation to its ending. Introduction, as well as other components of a group activity plan, are effective when interventionists consider children's interests, motivations, and developmental abilities. The introduction describes how a planned activity is to begin. When possible, the introduction should include opportunities for children to help with the activity. For example, an introduction to a pretend picnic activity might begin with the interventionist asking, "Who would like to come with me on a picnic outside under the big oak tree?" Once the children's interest is aroused, the interventionist might produce a list and ask the children to help gather the items on the list for the picnic, or the children might generate the list themselves. The list could include the names of picnic items such as plates, cups, forks, milk, crackers, apples, and so forth. Each word on the list could have a picture of the item beside it for children who are not yet ready to recognize words by sight. The interventionist could show the children a large basket in which they could place the items that they retrieve from the classroom. After the children and the interventionist have gathered the items on the list and placed them in the basket, everyone is ready to go on the picnic.

The introduction to an activity includes opportunities for children to practice multiple goals and objectives from fine motor, gross motor, social-communication, and cognitive domains. For example, tailoring the picnic list to include names of objects that target children's language goals and objectives provides at least three opportunities for children to practice saying or imitating specific words: 1) when the picnic activity is first introduced, 2) while collecting items for the picnic basket, and 3) when the interventionist reviews the list of items against the contents of the picnic basket. Placement of the picnic basket in a particular area of the classroom offers children opportunities to practice a variety of gross motor skills, such as 1) walking to and from the picnic basket, 2) pulling to stand at the table that holds the picnic basket, and 3) sitting unsupported on the carpet to review items gathered for the picnic with the interventionist. The introduction also encourages practice of cognitive skills that include locating familiar objects such as fruits, vegetables, bread, cheese, and drinks; matching pictures from the list with picnic items; and imitating words and actions associated with picnics, such as eating, spreading the blanket on the ground, and playing games. Slight variations in the introduction could allow for other goals and objectives to be embedded in this part of the planned group activity.

The sequence of events section of the group activity plan encompasses the primary events "expected" to occur during the activity in an outline form. This part of the activity, however, should be shaped by children's interests and may change as the activity proceeds. Team members can adapt to children's directions and use unplanned opportunities for intervention by knowing children's goals and objectives. An essential element of planning the events section of an activity plan is to consider the developmental range of children who are to participate in the activity. Team members should examine expected events to determine if all children in the group will be able to participate and interested in participating in the activity. Asking the following questions may be useful:

1. Do the planned events cover the spectrum of children's interests, abilities, and needs?
2. Can the activity's events be modified to accommodate a particular child or group of children?
3. Do the events include a sufficient variety for providing feedback to children and maintaining their engagement?
4. Do the events create multiple opportunities for embedding children's IEP/IFSP goals and objectives?

Reviewing the goal/objective matrix contained in Figure 6.1 provides a visual picture of each child's goals/objectives to be targeted for intervention and the range of developmental targets present in a group of children. For instance, the matrix may show that a particular group of children's play skills range from parallel play to cooperative play or that their fine motor skills lie on the continuum from beginning to grasp objects to using writing instruments for printing letters. Knowing the range of children's goals/objectives helps prepare team members in planning the sequence of events in an activity so it is both developmentally and individually appropriate for a particular group of children. For example, a sequence of events for a gardening activity might include digging or raking the dirt, scooping and filling containers with topsoil or water, opening seed packets, placing individual seeds in the ground, patting the ground around the seeds, watering the seeds with spray bottles or watering cans, and laying a ground cover over seeds to facilitate germination. In this sequence of events, both children who are at the stage of dumping and pouring materials and children who are capable of following an entire series of steps to complete a final project can be included in the activity. Allowing children to participate in the activity at their developmental level and for the amount of time they choose requires thoughtful arrangement of the environment. If one child wants to only dig and scoop dirt for the duration of the activity whereas several others want to move through the entire sequence of events in the activity, then it is necessary to make one area available for digging and scooping and another area available for children to complete the gardening activity.

Teams can increase the value and meaningfulness of an activity for children when they have a planned closing that offers children the opportunity to participate in the activity from start to finish. Similar to introductions, closings can provide significant learning opportunities to practice many different skills across domains. For example, the following are skills generally used by children during routine clean-up activities: 1) cognitive skills such as problem solving, sorting, classifying, and numbering and comparing objects; 2) social skills such as cooperating with peers, taking turns, following routines, and resolving conflicts; 3) social-communication skills such as naming and locating familiar objects and recognizing letters and names; and 4) gross and fine motor skills such as crawling, standing, walking, stooping, moving around obstacles, and using hands and fingers to grasp objects.

The closing of an activity should include clean up and recalling or summarizing the activity. Learning to clean up not only is a useful skill for children but also may provide many opportunities to practice targeted skills. One team's solution to using mealtime closings more effectively was to develop a plan that created multiple opportunities for children to practice daily their goals and objectives. The original closing required children to place dirty dishes and napkins in a container at the end of the meal. The new closing involved the creation of a designated clean-up area. The team placed a table near the eating area with wash, rinse, and drain tubs on top of the table and a garbage can next to it. Much of the additional clean-up process formerly assigned to an adult was redesigned to include children, allowing for the targeting of multiple IEP/IFSP goals and objectives. For example, children were assisted in following a simple four-step clean-up process: 1) scraping leftover food from plates into the garbage can, 2) washing plates in the wash tub, 3) rinsing plates in the rinse tub, and 4) stacking plates in the drain tub. Children also had access to dustpans, mops, sponges, and child-size brooms to further assist in clean-up.

Recalling or summarizing the activity is also an important aspect of closing and involves a discussion between children and adults about what happened or what was learned during the activity. For example, an interventionist might ask children to review the steps of planting seeds in a garden activity. Or, the interventionist might show the children a picture of a garden and ask them to make comparisons between the picture and the garden they planted at school. Closings like these provide excellent opportunities for children to practice a variety of social-communication and cognitive skills.

Opportunities to Embed Children's Goals and Objectives

This section of the activity plan provides specific information about how parts of an activity may be used or enhanced by an interventionist to offer individual children additional opportunities to practice their goals and/or objectives. Children's initials can be listed and corresponding opportunities can be described regarding how each goal/objective might be embedded in the group activity. Figure 6.6 illustrates how children's goals/objectives listed in the goal/objective matrix in Figure 6.1 can be embedded in a gas station activity. Providing children with multiple opportunities for practicing targeted and emerging skills is particularly important for promoting the growth and development of children with disabilities. Teams should ensure that adequate exposure and practice time are occurring within the context of meaningful routine, planned, and child-initiated activities.

Planned Variations

Group activities for children can be enhanced by variations. Variations seek to build on the basic structure of an activity by introducing one or more changes that can be used if children display little interest in the original planned activity or to expand the activity in a meaningful way. Many variables affect children's interest, and any well-planned or favorite activity may become unappealing on a particular day. Variations also allow for multiple opportunities to embed targeted goals and objectives. For example, if during the gas station activity two children discover a small pile of rocks that they decide to load in their wagons, then the children can be encouraged to repeatedly transport rocks, thus needing to fill up at the gas station. This subtle variation may provide many additional opportunities to embed children's targeted goals and objectives.

Vocabulary

Although it is likely that most teams will use developmentally appropriate language with children, team members may not consider specific vocabulary items to target in an activity or be aware of the vocabulary they routinely use in an activity. Selection of vocabulary items should represent a range of words/signs used to convey thoughts, wants, needs, and descriptions of objects or events. Selection of vocabulary items should also be based on children's assessment information and include familiar and new words/signs to gradually build children's vocabulary. A communication specialist can assist in selecting vocabulary items that target particular sounds that children might need practice producing. Depending on the words/signs selected for the activity, teams may need to review their materials list. It may be that a particular material must be included in an activity

GROUP ACTIVITY PLAN

Gas Station

Materials

Toy gas pump, variety of double-seated riding toys, tricycles, wagons, work shirts with zippers, tire pump, zippered bag for work shirts, empty spray bottle, cloth rags, empty clean quarts of oil, several plastic crates, scratch pad, pencils, happy face stickers, Velcro belt for riding toy

Environmental Arrangements

Gas station is set up near tricycle and riding toy path. Plastic crates and gas pumps define space. One adult is assigned to area to monitor and facilitate children's play.

Description of Activity

Introduction
- Children set up gas station with adults.
- Children remove riding toys from toy shed.
- Children and adults carry all other materials to center of riding area to create a gas station. Plastic crates are used to define space and contain the quarts of oil, rags, and spray bottles.

Sequence of Events

- Children select riding toys and ride around gas station.
- Children identify their roles (e.g., who will be a gas station attendant, what he or she will do).
- Children on riding toys stop at gas station for gas, air for tires, and getting windows washed.
- Children running gas station ask, "Do you want gas? Air for your tires? Windows washed? Oil checked?"
- Children make request for services desired.
- Children pay attendant by slapping his or her hand the number of times equivalent to dollar amount.
- Attendant wishes peer a good day and attends to next peer on riding toy.

Closing

- Interventionist gives 5-minute warning before clean-up bell is rung.
- Interventionist tells children they can take one more turn at the gas station.

_____

(continued)

Figure 6.6.   A completed group activity plan for a gas station activity. (*Note:* Letters in parentheses refer to the initials of a specific child.)

Figure 6.6.   *(continued)*

- Children participate in clean up by riding toys to shed and assisting with carrying other materials to shed.
- Children line up at shed and return to classroom when finished with clean-up.

Opportunities to Embed Goals[a]

Present choice of riding toys with pedals. (MK)
Encourage riding of tricycle to gas station. (TO)
Suggest selecting a double-seated riding toy or riding with a peer. (KA)
Ask, "Which riding toy do you have?" (MK)
Ask, "What would you like to do in the gas station?" (KA)
Give zipper bag with work shirts to pass out to children. (TO)
Encourage B to help peers zip their shirts. (BW)
Identify children's expressions when they arrive at gas station (e.g., happy, excited, tired). (CT)
Give happy face stickers to M to hand out to children once they've paid for their gas. (MK)
Give directions to follow, including fill gas tank and wash windows; say hello and ask, "How much gas do you want?"; check oil and get quart of oil to pour in; put away tricycle and remove work shirt. (KA)
Pedal tricycle to shed. (MK)
Prompt C to assist peers who need assistance carrying objects or moving riding toys to shed. (CT)
Ask M what he did on his riding toy when waiting in line to return to class. (MW)

   [a]This section to be completed by the team for individual children based on their targeted goals and objectives.

Planned Variations

1. Add different props to gas station, such as paper money, wallets, purses, and cash register.
2. Set out road signs on riding toy path.

Vocabulary

- Hello, good-bye
- Please, thank you
- Numbers 1–20
- Tire
- Window
- Oil, gas
- Wash
- Dollar
- Peers' names

(continued)

Figure 6.6.   *(continued)*

Peer Interaction Strategies

1. Two or more children operate the gas station together.
2. Children ride double-seated riding toys or ride/pull wagons.
3. Children push vehicles to gas station that break down or run out of gas.
4. Children request services from peers at gas station.

Parent/Caregiver Input

1. Children visit a gas station where a parent works.
2. Parents donate chamois cloths, spray bottles, and empty clean quart oil containers.
3. Children bring a picture of their family car to classroom.

to ensure that the interventionist targets identified words, signs, or sounds. For example, including a variety of colors, sizes, and textures of blocks in the block area creates opportunities to target many different words and sounds with children who enjoy using blocks.

Peer Interaction Strategies

It is not within the scope of this book to address the topic of inclusion; however, increasing numbers of community-based programs are serving children with disabilities. Consequently, many teams are faced with the challenge of designing and maintaining environments that build and encourage interaction between children with diverse behavioral repertoires. Creating and maintaining successful (i.e., positive and constructive) interactions between children with different developmental levels, skills, and interests requires thoughtful planning and adult guidance (Bricker, 1995; Odom & Brown, 1993; Turnbull & Turbiville, 1995).

Ensuring positive and constructive peer interactions requires that teams have two types of knowledge or information. First, knowledge of children's cognitive, linguistic, and social development is required. Second, children's IEP/IFSP social goals/objectives should be identified. Information on children's development and selection of appropriate social goals requires the administration of a programmatic measure that yields useful and functional assessment information across domains. Once this information is available to the team members, they can design activities that will promote and sustain appropriate interactions with a variety of peers across the day. The group activity plans included in the appendix at the end of this chapter provide examples of peer interaction strategies that can be integrated into group activities.

Parent/Caregiver Input

Suggestions and input from parents/caregivers enable teams to plan activities with an eye toward family priorities and concerns while using families' strengths and resources. Seeking parent input will likely result in planned activities being meaningful to children while providing opportunities for family and professional team members to work together.

Family input related to activities for individual children may be obtained in several ways, including 1) written communication with families through traveling notebooks and daily notes home, 2) formal communication with families during home visits and conferences, or 3) informal communication during children's arrival and departure from the program. An option for gathering family input as a group is through parent meetings. Parent meetings can be organized to generate and discuss the next month's planned activities for the classroom. Teams can structure such discussions by using a "mapping" procedure for incorporating family input (Perrone, 1994). Figure 6.7 illustrates a sample "map" for involving families in group activity planning around children's interests in dinosaurs.

The "map" encourages families to share ideas for activities with the team that are based on knowledge of their child's interests with materials and activities at home or in the community. Likewise, the team is prompted to share knowledge about children's interests in classroom materials and activities. Together, the team generates a range of activities that build on the children's current and individual interests and strengths while providing opportunities to experiment with new and challenging activities and skills. Team members discuss resources, contributions, and concerns they have related to the ideas for activities. The combination of information prepares the team to support children's learning at home and in the classroom.

GUIDELINES FOR SELECTING ACTIVITIES AND MATERIALS

The success of using activity-based intervention depends, in part, on the team's choice of activities and the materials to be used in the selected activities. In the following sections, a set of guidelines for choosing activities and materials is offered to assist teams.

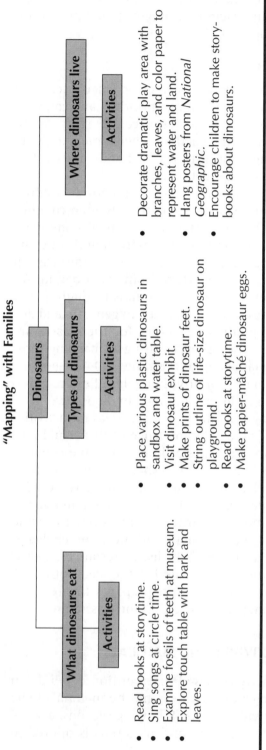

"Mapping" with Families

Dinosaurs

What dinosaurs eat

Activities

- Read books at storytime.
- Sing songs at circle time.
- Examine fossils of teeth at museum.
- Explore touch table with bark and leaves.

Types of dinosaurs

Activities

- Place various plastic dinosaurs in sandbox and water table.
- Visit dinosaur exhibit.
- Make prints of dinosaur feet.
- String outline of life-size dinosaur on playground.
- Read books at storytime.
- Make papier-mâché dinosaur eggs.

Where dinosaurs live

Activities

- Decorate dramatic play area with branches, leaves, and color paper to represent water and land.
- Hang posters from *National Geographic.*
- Encourage children to make story-books about dinosaurs.

Parent ideas

- Visit museums that have fossils.
- Read books about dinosaurs.
- Make papier mâché dinosaur eggs.
- Decorate dramatic play area like landscape where dinosaurs used to live.
- Share dinosaur collection.

Concerns

- Ensure that there is adequate number of adults to supervise children on field trip to museum.

Resources/contributions

- J's father works at museum and could be the tour guide.
- Parents can contribute newspaper for papier-mâché eggs.
- S's mother is a sculptor and could share some of her projects with the children.
- Several families eat at fast-food restaurants that give children dinosaur fact cards.
- K has a cassette tape with dinosaur songs.

Figure 6.7. Sample "mapping" procedures for use with families when planning group activities. (*Source:* Perrone, 1994.)

Activity Guidelines

Because the use of planned activities is a fundamental part of activity-based intervention, it is important that teams give thought to their selection and development. We have found the guidelines discussed here to be helpful in ensuring the selection of appropriate activities for groups of children.

Guideline One: Activities Should Be Meaningful to Children

Activities that are meaningful to children are those that tap into children's interests and motivations and have relevancy for them. As Dewey (1959) argued, education should be a continual restructuring of children's experiences. In addition, children should have the necessary behaviors in their repertoire to participate meaningfully in an activity. Daily experiences (e.g., dressing, eating, problem solving) often meet these criteria and provide children with the opportunity to interact using functional behaviors.

Guideline Two: Activities Should Have an Action Component

Activities provide frequent and useful opportunities for embedding children's goals when they incorporate action components. Motor development is a significant part of children's overall development and should be used to encourage a variety of other skills. Children are often engaged in some form of action, and a team can use these actions to assist children in acquiring desired skills (e.g., by asking children to run to a specific location to find hidden objects).

Guideline Three: Activities Should Foster Independence

Activities that provide few opportunities for children to complete the majority of tasks on their own do little to encourage independence. Teams must continually encourage children's independence in activities rather than "step in" and complete the activity for a child. When children become frustrated in completing a task, it is more helpful to the child if an adult engages the child in problem solving rather than rescue the child from trying to complete the skill.

Guideline Four: Activities Should Be Balanced

Activities selected for intervention should include a balance of child-initiated, routine, and planned activities. Children's days should not be composed entirely of a series of planned activities.

Guideline Five: Activities Should
Be Compatible with Typical Routines

Routine activities that occur during the day can be used to increase the number of opportunities for children to work on targeted skills. Intervention should not interfere with the primary purpose of these activities. For example, snacktime can be used to enhance communication, social, and motor skills as long as the training does not overpower the primary purpose of gaining nourishment.

Guideline Six: Activities Should Be
Adjusted as Children Reach Their Objectives

When children are able to complete a targeted skill, an activity may need to be adjusted to address new skills. This does not mean that when a child can consistently make his or her preferences known at snacktime that the team should abandon the snack; rather, it means that if the child has acquired one-word requests, then multiple-word requests should become the target during snacktime. If, during bath time, a child learns all of the body parts, then a new objective can be targeted for this routine activity (e.g., following simple directions such as "wash your face"). Teams will know when to change objectives only if they monitor child change and attend to the next level of skill acquisition indicated by the child's assessment.

Guideline Seven: Activities Should Include Repetition

Children appear to enjoy as well as learn from various forms of repetition. Planned and spontaneous repetition of activities and/or responses within activities provide an ideal mechanism for enhancing opportunities for practicing goals and objectives. Repetition can be used as a strategy for increasing opportunities to practice targeted behaviors in three ways: 1) by initiating the same activity over time (e.g., a restaurant, circus, or post office activity can continue across several days), 2) by including an action across activities throughout the day (e.g., labeling objects during circle time, a post office activity, or trip to museum), and 3) by repeating elements within an activity (e.g., catching paper fish repeatedly provides multiple opportunities for eye–hand coordination, turn-taking, and counting).

Guideline Eight: Activities Should
Include Imitation and Role Playing

Imitation seems to be a precursor to role playing as children begin imitating a person's behavior and then developing more complex skills to assume the role completely. Role playing permits children opportunities to practice turn taking with peers, initiating and maintaining interactive play, communicating with peers, problem solving, and carrying out sequential actions. A variety of problem-solving skills can also be practiced or learned during role-play activities such as negotiation (e.g., who gets which role), use of symbolic actions and objects, and increasing action sequences to represent complex events. Imitation and role playing consistent with a child's developmental level should be encouraged. Early imitation and role playing should center around experiences familiar to a child. Including brief scripts for a role-play scenario in planned activities may assist children who typically do not engage in role plays. Often, children spontaneously generate a script within an activity, and the interventionist need only observe and listen to know when it is appropriate to join in their play and assist children in making use of their ideas and imaginations to practice their goals and objectives.

Materials Guidelines

Another important consideration when employing activity-based intervention is the selection of intervention materials. As with intervention activities, the most critical aspect of materials selection is that such materials assist children in reaching their goals and objectives. Toys and materials, no matter how charming to adults and children, are of little value if they cannot be used to enhance children's growth and development. In addition, the careful selection of materials may do much to stimulate child initiations and actions. Well-selected materials can reduce the need for direct intervention by caregivers and professionals and afford them opportunities to respond to children's initiations. The following sections discuss the guidelines that should be considered when selecting intervention materials.

Guideline One: Materials
Should Be Relevant to Daily Activities

An essential guideline for selection of materials used in the activity-based approach is that they must be relevant to daily activities and not simply attractively packaged, commercial toys. A common concern in intervention settings is that large investments are made in costly commercial products that may not enhance learning as readily as materials adapted from the child's daily environment. For example, an egg carton and bottle caps or pinto beans can be used as counting devices as easily as commercially purchased plastic egg cartons with plastic eggs. Real crackers and fruit can be used at a tea party instead of plastic fruits and vegetables. The use of materials from the child's environment is another way of ensuring that activities incorporate the cultural values and diversity of children and families. The materials must be interesting, but they need not be costly and "slick."

Guideline Two: Materials
Should Be Multidimensional

Single-dimension materials offer little opportunity for children to initiate new activities, whereas materials with multiple properties may facilitate child-initiated activities. For example, a commonly advertised toy for toddlers is a jack-in-the-box consisting of a toy clown that jumps out of a box after a crank has been turned. The toy may have bright colors or play music, but it is unidimensional in its use of jumping and surprising (or scaring) the child. Balls and blocks, however, can be used in a variety of ways during activities designed by interventionists or initiated by children. Multidimensional materials, such as blocks, provide children with opportunities to discover for themselves the qualitative properties of the materials as well as opportunities to establish relationships between entities and events.

Guideline Three: Materials
Should Be Developmentally Appropriate

Materials should also be developmentally appropriate. Children first learn to stack large plastic blocks, then they advance to smaller uniform shapes, and finally they develop skills and interests in multiple shapes and sizes with arches and openings. Early "cooking" activities involve spreading peanut butter and later progress to making pizzas with several different ingredients. Children progress by exploring the object's physical properties first (e.g., spinning the wheels of the fire truck, ringing the bell) to later experimenting with the material's potential (e.g., hauling blocks as fire buckets to put out the fire).

Guideline Four: Materials Should
Enhance Training Opportunities and Generalizations

Finally, materials should be chosen that increase training opportunities and facilitate generalization. Selecting a variety of common materials that children will likely encounter to enhance acquisition and response fluency may do much to assist children in developing genuinely functional responses that generalize across settings, conditions, and people.

NONDIRECTIVE INTERVENTION STRATEGIES

The activity-based intervention approach was designed for use with nondirective teaching strategies. Although the use of massed trials and drill is not incompatible with activity-based intervention, this approach recommends that interventionists and caregivers use, to the extent possible, intervention strategies that are responsive to a child's initiations and that are compatible with daily routines and meaningful planned activities.

A variety of nondirective intervention strategies have been described in the language intervention literature under the rubric of naturalistic approaches (Duchan & Weitzner-Lin, 1987), joint action routines (Snyder-McLean, Solomonson, McLean, & Sack, 1984), and milieu teaching (Kaiser, Hendrickson, & Alpert, 1991). Fey (1986) referred to these strategies as hybrids and defined them as "naturalistic" procedures designed to facilitate the development of functional skills. These hybrid strategies are compatible with an activity-based approach if woven into ongoing activities that maintain child interest. Several of these nondirective strategies are described in the following sections.

Forgetfulness

The strategy of *forgetting* can be used by interventionists and caregivers to encourage action and problem solving by children. It is an effective strategy for determining what children know and can do. Forgetting can occur when the adult fails to provide the necessary equipment or materials or overlooks a familiar or important component of a routine or activity. Examples include not having food immediately available for snacktime, paintbrushes available for painting, or books available for storytime. When this occurs, the interventionist's or caregiver's goal is that the children recognize the missing element and convey this information by asking questions, searching for materials, or engaging in other appropriate problem-solving actions.

Novelty

Interventionists and caregivers are aware that children are generally enticed by new toys or activities. The careful introduction of *novelty* may stimulate desirable reactions from children. For infants and children with severe disabilities, this strategy may be more effective if the novelty is introduced within the context of a routine or familiar activity; for example, a new action could be added to a familiar song or a familiar nursery game. For older or more capable children, examples might include a new way to enter the building from the playground or the addition of different toys to the water play activity. For most infants and young children, the introduction of novelty is most effective if the change is not dramatically discrepant from their expectations. For example, the appearance of a giant white rabbit at an Easter party introduces novelty, but it can also introduce terror and an almost complete cessation of activity by the children except for crying and escape behaviors.

Visible but Unreachable

A strategy that generally requires only simple environmental manipulation is placing objects so that they are *visible but unreachable*. Placing objects within children's sight but out of their reach can facilitate the development of social, communication, and problem-solving behaviors. When using this strategy, it is important that the child is able to see the object and that a peer or adult is available to retrieve the object unless independent problem solving is being encouraged. Placing objects out of reach is often an effective strategy to use with children who are learning early communication skills. Preferred foods or objects can be placed in sight but out of reach, requiring the child to use some form of communication to obtain the item.

Violation of Expectations

Omitting or changing a familiar step or element in a well-practiced or routine activity is a strategy known as *violation of expectations*. Many violations may appear comical to children. For example, the interventionist may try to draw or write with a pencil while using the eraser; the caregiver may try to comb her hair with a spoon or place a block on the child's plate for a snack. The purpose of these violations is twofold: 1) children's recognition of change provides information about their discrimination and memory abilities, and 2) such violations provide ideal situations for evoking a variety of communicative and problem-solving responses (e.g., the child verbalizes a protest, the child turns the pencil so the pointed end is down). Children with severe disabilities can often recognize violations, such as putting a mitten on a foot, and communicate this recognition. The alert caregiver or interventionist can often shape these communicative responses into functional behaviors.

Piece by Piece

Another often easy to execute intervention strategy can be used when activities require materials that have many pieces. The interventionist can ration giving access to something in particular by separating it into pieces so that the child must request materials *piece by piece*. For example, when working on a puzzle, pieces can be handed out as a child asks for them. Labeling of the piece or action can be encouraged or required. This strategy may be used effectively when children use paint, glue, paper, crayons, blocks, or other small items. Snacktime with foods such as cereal, raisins, or apple pieces also presents opportunities for employing this strategy.

Interventionists should be alert, however, to the introduction of too many disruptions. For example, having a child ask for each puzzle piece may destroy the continuity of the activity and interfere with its meaningfulness for the child. The interventionist should balance providing opportunities to practice skills with the children's needs to become actively and genuinely involved in the activity.

Assistance

Another intervention strategy is the use of materials or engagement in activities that require adult or peer *assistance*. To have access to materials or to complete an activity, the child will need some form of assistance from an adult or peer. This strategy can be effective in the development of a range of skills in the adaptive, fine motor, gross motor, and communication areas. Placing a snack in a container with a lid that the child cannot remove independently may set the stage for the child to seek assistance. Once the request is made and the lid is loosened, the child can then practice his or her pincer grasp and wrist rotation to complete the opening of the container and retrieve the snack. Wind-up toys offer another example of materials that often require assistance from an adult.

Interruption or Delay

Interruption requires that the interventionist or caregiver stop the children from continuing a chain of behaviors. For example, if tooth brushing has become a routine, the caregiver can stop the child from getting the toothpaste and ask, "What do you want?" The child will have to indicate what is needed to complete the behavior chain. This intervention strategy has been effective with individuals with severe disabilities (Goetz, Gee, & Sailor, 1985).

The *delay* strategy introduces a pause, or a small delay, in an activity in order to prompt a response from the child. Delaying fits easily into many activities but should be employed with sensitivity. Time delay as described by Halle, Baer, and Spradlin (1981) has been shown to be effective in increasing the initiations of requests by preschool-age children.

Two points should be emphasized when using the intervention strategies described in this section. First, as discussed previously, the interventionist and caregiver should be guided by children's goals and objectives. The strategies should be used only when they assist in helping children reach their designated goals and objectives. Employing these strategies without careful integration with children's overall intervention plans will likely yield unsatisfactory outcomes.

Second, intervention strategies should be used in a thoughtful and sensitive manner. The overuse of any strategy will likely produce an undesired outcome. For example, if interruptions or delays are overused, then children may experience frustration that leads to the onset of an emotional outburst. Activity-based intervention encourages the use of nondirective intervention strategies, but they should be used with sensitivity and monitored carefully.

SUMMARY

The intent of this chapter has been to describe the three-part structure (i.e., individual program plans, group activity schedules, and group activity plans) that underlies the application of activity-based intervention to heterogeneous groups of children. Besides describing the three-part structure, guidelines for activity and materials selection and nondirective intervention strategies have been discussed.

Without a structure for addressing children's individual goals and objectives in a group setting, several unfortunate outcomes will likely occur. First, interventionists and caregivers may miss many opportunities to target children's goals and objectives. Second, activities that do not match children's developmental levels or that fail to target children's goals/objectives may be used. Third, disorganization may occur in terms of planning and executing program schedules and activities. Finally, teams may have significant difficulty monitoring child change over time.

REFERENCES

Bricker, D. (Ed.). (1993). *Assessment, evaluation, and programming system for infants and children: Vol. 1. AEPS measurement for birth to three years.* Baltimore: Paul H. Brookes Publishing Co.

Bricker, D. (1995). The challenge of inclusion. *Journal of Early Intervention, 19*(3), 179–194.

Bricker, D., & Pretti-Frontczak, K. (Eds.). (1996). *Assessment, evaluation, and programming system for infants and children: Vol. 3. AEPS measurement for three to six years.* Baltimore: Paul H. Brookes Publishing Co.

Dewey, J. (1959). *Dewey on education.* New York: Columbia University, Teachers College, Bureau of Publications.

Duchan, J., & Weitzner-Lin, B. (1987). Nurturant-naturalistic intervention for language-impaired children. *Asha, 29*(7), 45–49.

Fey, M. (1986). *Language intervention with young children.* San Diego: College-Hill Press.

Goetz, L., Gee, K., & Sailor, W. (1985). Using a behavior chain interruption strategy to teach communication skills to students with severe disabilities. *Journal of The Association for Persons with Severe Handicaps, 10,* 21–30.

Halle, J., Baer, D., & Spradlin, J. (1981). Teachers' use of delay as a stimulus control procedure to increase language use in handicapped children. *Journal of Applied Behavior Analysis, 14,* 389–409.

Kaiser, A., Hendrickson, J., & Alpert, K. (1991). Milieu language teaching: A second look. In R. Gable (Ed.), *Advances in mental retardation and developmental disabilities* (Vol. IV, pp. 63–92). London: Jessica Kingsley Publishers.

Krull, S.W., & Don, N. (1986). *Play power games and activities for young children.* Orinda, CA: Play Power Publishing.

McLean, M., Bailey, D., & Wolery, M. (1996). *Assessing infants and preschoolers with special needs* (pp. 491–518). Columbus, OH: Charles E. Merrill.

Odom, S.L., & Brown, W.H. (1993). Social interaction skills interventions for young children with disabilities in integrated settings. In C.A. Peck, S.L Odom, & D. Bricker (Eds.), *Integrating young children with disabilities in community programs: Ecological perspectives on research and implementation* (pp. 39–64). Baltimore: Paul H. Brookes Publishing Co.

Perrone, V. (1994, February). How to engage students in learning. *Educational Leadership,* 11–13.

Snyder-McLean, L., Solomonson, B., McLean, J., & Sack, S. (1984). Structuring joint action routines. *Seminars in Speech and Language, 5,* 213–228.

Turnbull, A., & Turbiville, V. (1995). Why must inclusion be such a challenge? *Journal of Early Intervention, 19*(3), 200–202.

Appendix

GROUP ACTIVITY PLAN

Snack

Materials

Fruits, vegetables, drinks, grain items, cheese or other spread, cups, bowls, child-size pitcher, napkins, vinyl place mats, wash/rinse/drain containers, towels, sponges, dustpans, child-size broom and mop, stickers, two or three kidney-shaped tables, 15–20 child-size chairs, one child-size rectangular table, two large storage containers for snack materials

Environmental Arrangements

During transition to snack tables, one interventionist assists the children with hand washing, while the other interventionist sits at the snack table to welcome the children as they arrive at the table. The children sit at kidney-shaped tables with one interventionist per table. All food and materials are prepared and placed in a large plastic container with a lid prior to the snack. The interventionist brings a container with the snack to the table and sits with the children to serve and eat the snack.

Description of Activity

Introduction

- The interventionist welcomes the children to the snack table and hands the children their place mats.
- The children are given a choice of stickers with which to decorate their mats as they wait for their peers to finish washing their hands.
- Two children who have been identified as the snack helpers pass out cups, utensils, and napkins.

Sequence of Events

- The interventionist shows and names each snack item before serving it family-style (i.e., pass items around table with children serving themselves).
- Once items have moved around the table, the interventionist places items in center of table.
- Children eat their snacks and request more as desired.
- The interventionist and children talk about previous activities or current topics of interest.

Closing

- When children are finished with snack, they scrape the leftover snacks into the garbage and wash/rinse/drain the cups, utensils, and bowls at a specified clean-up table.
- The children select a center activity when finished with clean-up.

Opportunities to Embed Goals[a]

[a]This section to be completed by the team for individual children based on their targeted goals and objectives.

Planned Variations

1. The children help prepare snack prior to eating it.
2. The children eat snack in a different location (e.g., outside/picnic style).
3. The interventionists prepare snacks and place in paper sacks with children's names on them. Sacks are hidden on playground for children to find and then have snack.
4. The children are given paper place mats and crayons.

Vocabulary

- Peers' names
- Interventionists' names
- Colors of foods (e.g., green, brown, yellow, orange)
- Texture of foods (e.g., soft, chewy, crunchy, hard, rough, smooth)
- Numbers 1–10
- Questions (e.g., "Who's missing today?" "How many [blanks] did you eat?" "How many [blanks] are in the bowl?")
- Sentences to inform (e.g., "I'm going to use tongs to pick up the [blank]")

Peer Interaction Strategies

1. Two children choose to be the snack helpers each week.
2. The interventionist encourages the children to help each other with serving themselves.

Parent/Caregiver Input

1. Parent/caregiver joins the children for snack on special days (e.g., birthdays, holidays).
2. Parent/caregiver shares with the class favorite snack foods served at home .
3. Parent/caregiver donates food from work place such as bagels, yogurt, produce, and pizza.

GROUP ACTIVITY PLAN

Dump Trucks and Gravel

Materials

Large plastic crate for dump trucks; variety of small- to large-size dump trucks; large, sturdy box lid or plastic container for holding gravel; 10–20 pounds of gravel; tarp on which roads are drawn; Fisher-Price houses and trucks, and people to place in the toy trucks and homes; books about dump trucks or pictures of dump trucks; child-size broom and dustpan

Environmental Arrangements

Activity begins inside with the interventionist and children seated on the carpet reading a book to introduce activity. The rest of the activity occurs outside. Spread tarp on ground away from flow of traffic. Set Fisher-Price houses on tarp. Fill box lid with gravel, and set it next to the tarp.

Description of Activity

Introduction

- The interventionist announces to the children, "I have a book of big trucks, and the father of someone in our classroom drives a big truck at work."
- The interventionist reads the book and engages the children in conversation about big trucks.
- The interventionist asks the children, "Who would like to play with dump trucks and gravel today?"
- The interventionist shows the children the container with the dump trucks and asks the children to select one dump truck to take to the activity.

Sequence of Events

- The children examine trucks and push them on floor.
- The children carry trucks outside to the prepared activity with the tarp and houses.
- The children put gravel in their trucks and dump it out.
- The children push trucks on roads drawn on tarp.
- The children engage in imaginary play with toy trucks, houses, and little people.

Closing

- The interventionist gives a child a bell to ring to signal clean-up time.
- The children scoop gravel into trucks from the tarp and return the gravel to the container. The children place trucks in crate. The children sweep off of the sidewalk the gravel that is too small to pick up.

Opportunities to Embed Goals[a]

[a]This section to be completed by the team for individual children based on their targeted goals and objectives.

Planned Variations

1. Use sand with dump trucks.
2. Add trailers that the children can attach to their dump trucks.
3. Allow children to make a gravel pathway on the playground.
4. Provide semi-trucks or trains and a variety of materials for children to fill and transport.
5. Add wood toy roads and bridges children can put together.

Vocabulary

*   Sizes (e.g., small, large)
*   Quantities (e.g., full, empty, half-full)
*   Location (e.g., in, under, behind, first)
*   Quality (e.g., heavy, light, rough)

Peer Interaction Strategies

1. The interventionist uses only very large trucks and provides one for every two children.
2. The interventionist encourages the children to assume roles (e.g., some children drive trucks, some children fill trucks, some children spread gravel to make roads).
3. The interventionist prompts the children to trade trucks with each other.
4. The interventionist prompts the children to observe and imitate one another's actions.

Parent/Caregiver Input

1. Parent/caregiver arranges to bring dump truck to program one day and tell children about his or her job. Children get to sit in dump truck and honk air horn.
2. Parent/caregiver shares snack recipe for creating vehicles with fruit, vegetables, and toothpicks.
3. Children add pictures of their families' trucks and cut ones from magazines to create a children's bulletin board for a week.

GROUP ACTIVITY PLAN

Brushing Teeth

Materials

Toothbrush holders, masking tape on which the children's names are written and placed in front of hole on toothbrush holder, toothpaste, one plastic cup for each child with his or her name on it, poster near sink outlining steps for brushing teeth, mirror above sink, step stool, towel dispenser, waste basket, liquid soap and dispenser, paper towels

Environmental Arrangements

All required materials are stored at the sink area. Step stool is placed in front of sink. Children brush teeth in pairs.

Description of Activity

Introduction

The interventionist asks the children two at a time to come to the sink and brush their teeth during morning choice-time activities, which follows breakfast.

Sequence of Events

- The children find their toothbrushes by identifying their names written on the masking tape in front of each toothbrush.
- The interventionist gives a cue if necessary to assist the children in locating their toothbrushes.
- The interventionist squirts toothpaste onto bottom of plastic cup. Children scrape toothpaste from bottom of cup onto toothbrush with their toothbrushes.
- The children brush their teeth for 10–20 seconds.
- The children turn over cup and fill with water at sink.
- The children rinse out their mouths with water.
- The children rinse their toothbrushes with water from the faucet. Each child returns his or her toothbrush to the holder.

Closing

- The interventionist asks the children to show their smiles. The interventionist comments on the brightness of children's smiles as a result of brushing their teeth.
- Children return to the activity in the classroom.

Opportunities to Embed Goals[a]

[a]This section to be completed by the team for individual children based on their targeted goals and objectives.

Planned Variations

1. The interventionist changes the posters around the sink throughout the year to renew interest in messages about brushing teeth.
2. The interventionist gives children new toothbrushes every 3 months, which offers children an opportunity to select new colors.

Vocabulary

- Brush, rinse, smile, scrape
- Cup, toothpaste, teeth
- Names of different types of teeth
- Beginning sounds of children's names
- Colors of toothbrushes

Peer Interaction Strategies

1. The children go to the sink in pairs.
2. The interventionist encourages a peer to observe and comment on child's clean teeth.
3. A peer assists child with locating toothbrush in holder.

Parent/Caregiver Input

1. The children can take a field trip to visit a dentist's office, or a dentist or hygienist can be invited to the classroom to describe proper care of teeth and his or her job.
2. The interventionist can read books about the care of teeth during story-time.
3. The interventionist can send home recipes for healthy snacks.

GROUP ACTIVITY PLAN

Washing Bicycles and Other Riding Toys

Materials

Tricycles, ride-on cars, wagons, bicycles with training wheels, double-seated riding toys, buckets, spray bottles filled with soapy water, sponges, towels, hose, plastic crates, poster with order of events for washing bicycles, mops, brooms, dustpan

Environmental Arrangements

Activity is set up near a water faucet and away from main traffic flow. Children are asked to choose roles (e.g., one is in charge of rinsing the bicycle with the hose, one is in charge of washing the bicycle with the sponge, one is responsible for drying the toys with a towel). Organize materials in plastic crates. The children can turn over crates and sit on them to wash toys once materials are removed from them. One interventionist facilitates activity with children.

Description of Activity

Introduction

- The interventionist announces to the children that a special area is going to be set up outside that day for washing bicycles and riding toys.
- The interventionist shows the children a poster board with a picture description of the process for washing bicycles.
- The interventionist shows the children materials they can use to wash the bicycles (e.g., hose, sponges, buckets, spray bottles, towels).
- The interventionist asks the children which role they would like to have in washing the bicycles and riding toys.

Sequence of Events

- The children select a role and receive the materials they need. The children then carry the materials outside to the designated area.
- The children ride the bicycles or other riding toys from the shed to the washing area.
- The children rinse, wash, scrub, and dry the bicycles and riding toys.
- The interventionist names parts of a car (e.g., wheels, seat, horn, tires) as children are cleaning them.
- The children ride the bicycles and other riding toys.

Closing

- The interventionist gives one child a bell to ring to signal clean-up time.
- The children finish washing/drying bicycles and then return bicycles and materials to their designated areas (i.e., bicycles to shed and cleaning materials to labeled crates).
- The children line up at the gate to return to classroom. While in line, the interventionist reviews the activity with children by asking several questions, such as, "Who washed the bicycles?" "How many bicycles did you wash?" "What did you like best about washing bicycles?"

Opportunities to Embed Goals[a]

[a]This section to be completed by the team for individual children based on their targeted goals and objectives.

Planned Variations

1. The children wash the interventionists' cars or program vans.
2. The children wash other outside toys such as sandbox toys and balls.
3. The children wash toys (e.g., dolls, doll clothes, manipulatives) inside if the weather is not good.
4. The children pretend to clean the housekeeping area with mops, brooms, dustpan, vacuum cleaner, spray bottles, and cloths.

Vocabulary

- Parts of a bicycle (e.g., wheel, spoke, handle bar, seat, horn, pedals)
- Descriptive words (e.g., fast, slow, stop, go)
- Action words (e.g., squeeze, dip, spray, rinse, wash, dry)
- Peers' names
- Types of transportation (e.g., wagon, bicycle, tricycle)

Peer Interaction Strategies

1. The children work in pairs to fulfill different activities of washing bicycles.
2. The children switch activities and share materials.
3. The children ride double-seated riding toys together.

Parent/Caregiver Input

1. Parents/caregivers can contribute materials for washing bicycles, such as clean, empty spray bottles; chamois cloths; buckets; and sponges.
2. Families plan a car-washing fund-raiser for the program followed by a potluck lunch/dinner to celebrate efforts.

GROUP ACTIVITY PLAN

Potato Head Pals Game

Materials

Two Potato Head Pals game sets; blanket; large dice; plastic, rectangular container for storing game pieces

Environmental Arrangement

Spread blanket on carpeted area of room for children to sit on. The blanket defines space for children.

Description of Activity

Introduction

- The interventionist asks, "Who would like to play the Potato Head Pals game?"
- The interventionist asks the children to help spread out the blanket on the floor and then shows the children game materials (i.e., potato heads, body parts, spinner board).
- The interventionist explains the rules of the game.

Sequence of Events

- The children shake and roll the dice to see who starts the game.
- The children take turns spinning the spinner board to create a potato head pal based on where the spinner lands.
- The children spin the spinner until all of the potato head pals are complete.
- Children play the game again.

Closing

- The interventionist gives one child a bell to ring when it is clean-up time.
- The children put game materials in marked containers with lids.
- The interventionist asks children to recall what their potato head pals looked like when they had all of their body parts.

Opportunities to Embed Goals[a]

[a]This section to be completed by the team for individual children based on their targeted goals and objectives.

Planned Variations

1. The interventionist adds a picnic basket of plastic food. The children can pretend to have a picnic with the potato head pals once the pals are assembled.
2. The interventionist provides soft potato head pals and/or large plastic potato head pals with the small potato head pals.
3. The interventionist adds Fisher-Price houses and lets the children play with the pals and houses.
4. The interventionist makes clothes for the potato head pals and lets the children dress the potato head pals.

Vocabulary

• Prepositions (e.g., on, in)
• Body parts (e.g., arms, legs, eyes, nose, mouth, ears)
• Clothing (e.g., hat, shoes, tie, bow)
• Sequence (e.g., first, second, third, fourth, fifth, last)
• Taking turns (e.g., my, your, his, or her turn)

Peer Interaction Strategies

1. The number of potato head pals are limited so that the children must create the pals together.
2. The interventionist asks the children to hand their peers body parts of the potato head pal.
3. The interventionist asks the children to show their completed pals to each other.
4. The interventionist prompts the children to introduce their pals to each other by having children give their pals a name.

Parent/Caregiver Input

1. A game lending library is created whereby families can check out games for use at their homes.
2. The interventionist provides families with names of games that are developmentally appropriate for children.

GROUP ACTIVITY PLAN

Mealtime (Breakfast/Lunch)

Materials

Place mats; bowls; cups; napkins; utensils; food and drinks; sponges; garbage basket; wash and rinse tub; dish drainer; two kidney-shaped tables; 12–15 child-size sturdy chairs; one rectangular-shaped table on which there is a place to wash, rinse, and drain containers for clean-up

Environmental Arrangements

The interventionist sits at the U-shaped part of the table in order for him or her to have access to all of the children. The rectangular table is placed approximately 6 feet from the kidney-shaped tables. It is away from the wall with enough room for the children to stand on both sides of it to clean up their plates.

Description of Activity

Introduction

- One child per table passes out the place mats, bowls, cups, napkins, and utensils. The children should be given the opportunity to assume this role on a daily or weekly basis.
- The interventionist asks the children which song/fingerplay they would like to sing before eating.

Sequence of Events

- The interventionist removes covers of dishes and names each food. Children are asked to which food group each food belongs.
- The interventionist begins passing food around the table for children to serve themselves.
- The children are asked to take a specified amount of food, such as five grapes.
- The children pour milk/juice/water from the pitcher into cups.
- The children eat and request more food.
- The interventionist responds to children's conversations or initiates a conversation related to previous events of the day.

Closing

- The children carry dishes, utensils, and napkins to the designated clean-up area (i.e., rectangular table).
- The children place the appropriate materials in the garbage.
- The children wash and rinse the dishes and then stack them in drainer.
- The children move to the next activity.

Opportunities to Embed Goals[a]

[a]This section to be completed by the team for individual children based on their targeted goals and objectives.

Planned Variations

1. The interventionist introduces breathing exercises before children eat.
2. The children cook the meal.

Vocabulary

- Names of food served (e.g., pancakes, strawberries, syrup, milk, juice)
- Numbers 1–10
- Peers' names
- Descriptive words related to food (e.g., texture, temperature, colors, size)
- Names of food groups (e.g., dairy, grains, meat, fruits, vegetables)

Peer Interaction Strategies

1. The children assist each other in serving and pouring the food. For example, peer holds the cup for the child while child pours milk.
2. The interventionist suggests group problem solving when conflict occurs.
3. The interventionist assigns preselected seating arrangements to encourage social communication at table.
4. Pairs of children set the table.

Parent/Caregiver Input

1. The children eat foods of their ethnic origin.
2. Parents/caregivers are occasionally invited to eat lunch or snack with children.
3. Parents/caregivers share recipes of children's favorite meals with interventionist.

GROUP ACTIVITY PLAN

Playdough (Birthday Time)

Materials

Playdough of different colors; birthday candles; small plastic plates; butter knives; birthday crown; large, round cookie cutters; container for utensils; vinyl place mats for each child; puppet; long, rectangular table; rolling pins; bucket with several damp sponges; broom and dustpan

Environmental Arrangements

Each child is given a place mat to define their area for using playdough at the table. Name cards are placed at the table for seating arrangement. One interventionist should be seated at the table with the children. This activity should take place away from other activities as children will be singing and talking throughout. Select a puppet of high interest to children or one that fits in with the theme of the week/month.

Description of Activity

Introduction

- The interventionist announces, "I have a puppet friend who is 4 years old today. Who would like to help give my friend a birthday party? What do children like to eat on their birthdays?"
- The interventionist then asks the children which kind of cake they like.
- The interventionist tells children that the art table has playdough and utensils for making a pretend cake for the puppet.

Sequence of Events

- The children select the color of the playdough that they want to use for making the cake.
- The children use utensils as desired by requesting them from peers/interventionist.
- The children place candles on the cake.
- The children sing "Happy Birthday" to the puppet.
- The children repeat the above steps.

Closing

- The interventionist gives a 5-minute warning to signal the closing of the activity.
- The interventionist suggests that the children do one last thing to their cakes before they return the playdough to its container.
- The children return playdough utensils to basket.

- The children take a sponge from the bucket and wipe the table where they were using playdough.
- The children move to next activity.

Opportunities to Embed Goals[a]

[a]This section to be completed by the team for individual children based on their targeted goals and objectives.

Planned Variations

1. The children make playdough cookies for a cookie monster puppet. The children should be given cookie sheets instead of place mats to make the cookies.
2. The children make playdough to take home.
3. Different textures can be added to the playdough such as cornmeal, coarse salt, and party confetti.

Vocabulary

- Colors (e.g., yellow, pink, green, orange, brown)
- Name of puppet
- Words of "Happy Birthday" song
- Prepositions (e.g., beside, next to, on)
- Utensils and materials (e.g., knife, rolling pin, sponge, plate, place mat, cookie cutter)
- Numbers 1–4
- Directions (e.g., cut, blow out, share)
- Peers' names
- Flavors (e.g., strawberry, chocolate, lemon, orange, vanilla)

Peer Interaction Strategies

1. The interventionist places name cards at the activity table prior to children's arrival to ensure that particular children sit near one another to increase social communication between children.
2. The interventionist encourages children to cut their cakes and to serve them to their peers.

Parent/Caregiver Input

1. Children celebrate their birthdays in the classroom with peers. Parents/caregivers provide a special treat for snack.
2. Children visit a bakery and observe the baker decorating a cake.

GROUP ACTIVITY PLAN

Sand Table with Dinosaurs

Materials

Water table; wet sand; plastic eggs; bucket; small dinosaurs; variety of large dinosaurs; plastic plants, trees, and leaves; bark; moss; dinosaur mobile; tarp

Environmental Arrangements

Tarp is spread on the floor under the water table. The corners of tarp are taped to the floor with duct tape. Fill table with wet sand and hide eggs with small dinosaurs in them before activity. Hang mobile above sand table.

Description of Activity

Introduction

- The interventionist shows the children the bucket of dinosaurs to play with in the sand table. One child passes out dinosaurs, and children discuss names of dinosaurs.
- The interventionist asks children to help remove cover on texture table.

Sequence of Events

- The children engage in imaginary play with dinosaurs.
- The children make dinosaur sounds to communicate between dinosaurs.
- The children find eggs, inside of which are baby dinosaurs, in the sand.
- The children arrange plastic trees, bark, leaves, and moss in the sand to create dinosaur habitat.

Closing

- The interventionist gives 5-minute warning that activity will end.
- The children return the dinosaurs to the bucket and place cover on table.
- The interventionist reviews with the children how they played with the dinosaurs in the sand.

Opportunities to Embed Goals[a]

[a]This section to be completed by the team for individual children based on their targeted goals and objectives.

Planned Variations

1. The interventionist includes wind-up dinosaurs.
2. The interventionist makes the sand table a "Dinosaur Dig" table. Small bones and rocks are buried in the sand that have fossilized plants embedded in them. The interventionist provides a small shovel, paint brushes, and magnifying glasses. The interventionist hangs a poster near the table with different types of bones buried for the children to make comparisons.

Vocabulary

- Dinosaur sounds (e.g., grrr, rrrr)
- Natural materials (e.g., leaves, bark, moss, tree, sand)
- Dinosaur names (e.g., Tyrannosaurus Rex, Duckbill, Brontosaurus, Triceratops, Brachiosaurus)

Peer Interaction Strategies

1. The interventionist gives one child the bucket of dinosaurs to pass out to his or her peers at beginning of the activity and collect at end of activity.
2. The interventionist allows only four children at one time to play at the table with two on each side of it.
3. The interventionist encourages children to imitate their peers' actions with dinosaurs.

Parent/Caregiver Input

1. Children can take a field trip to a natural history museum.
2. The interventionist can contact a professor of a geology class and ask if a student might be willing to make a presentation to the interventionist's classroom to show children paleontological tools and pictures of digs where dinosaur fossils are found.
3. The interventionist can check out books from the library about dinosaurs and read them during storytime.

GROUP ACTIVITY PLAN

Blocks, Ramps, and Small Vehicles

Materials

Variety of small vehicles (e.g., cars, trucks, buses, vans, motorcycles); variety of sizes and shapes of wood blocks; two to four long, sanded wood boards for ramps; one long, rectangular, child-size table; buckets with picture labels of small vehicles; variety of road sign displays

Environmental Arrangements

The interventionist places rectangular, child-size table on carpet in block area. The children build roads/garages with wood blocks on top of table. The children prop long, sanded boards against table to create ramps.

Description of Activity

Introduction

- The interventionist introduces the activity by showing children baskets that contain a variety of vehicles.
- The children name a vehicle that they would like and reach into basket to obtain the vehicle.
- The interventionist shows the children blocks and road signs and asks children how they could use these materials to make roads and garages for the cars.

Sequence of Events

- The children use blocks and boards on the table in the block area.
- The children create roads, ramps, and garages.
- The children place vehicles on roads and move vehicles on them.
- The children place road signs at various locations on the roads.

Closing

- The interventionist gives 5-minute warning to signal clean-up and end of activity.
- The children return vehicles to basket with matching picture label.
- The children place blocks on shelves.
- The children carry long boards to storage room with interventionist.
- The children convene on carpet.
- The interventionist asks the children to recall one thing they did during the activity.
- The interventionist records the children's statements.

Opportunities to Embed Goals[a]

[a]This section to be completed by the team for individual children based on their targeted goals and objectives.

Planned Variations

1. The interventionist adds large vehicles.
2. The interventionist adds props such as a Fisher-Price gas station with people.
3. The interventionist tapes a large sheet of paper on the table and lets the children draw roads.
4. The interventionist places materials in the sandbox outside.
5. The interventionist provides hats for the children to wear, which correspond with vehicles (e.g., firefighter hat, police officer hat, chauffeur hat).

Vocabulary

- Colors (e.g., blue, yellow, red, black, green, orange)
- Sizes (e.g., big, small, long, short, wide, narrow)
- Names of vehicles
- Speed (e.g., fast, slow)
- Location (e.g., up, down, around, in, out, beside, next to, on, under)
- Names of signs (e.g., stop, yield, curve, railroad crossing)

Peer Interaction Strategies

1. Long boards require two children to pick up and move them.
2. The interventionist directs children's attention to peers' actions in activity.
3. The interventionist prompts children to imitate a particular action of peer.
4. The children plan together roads they will lay out on the floor with boards and blocks.

Parent/Caregiver Input

1. Parents can provide different types of blocks.
2. Visit worksites of parents who use particular vehicles for their jobs (e.g., mail trucks, fire trucks, police cars, dump trucks, school bus).

GROUP ACTIVITY PLAN

Name

Materials

Environmental Arrangements

Description of Activity
Introduction
Sequence of Events
Closing

Opportunities to Embed Goals[a]

[a]This section to be completed by the team for individual children based on their targeted goals and objectives.

Planned Variations

Vocabulary

Peer Interaction Strategies

Parent/Caregiver Input

Chapter 7

Monitoring and Evaluating Child Progress

At workshops on activity-based intervention, we have asked participants how they monitor and evaluate child progress. Most people indicated that they do *not* use any strategy to determine the effects of intervention. A small number answered that they administer standardized tests at the beginning and end of the year. An even smaller number answered that they systematically monitor child change (i.e., collect daily/weekly child progress data). To date, few workshop participants have indicated that they collect both overall program impact and systematic child progress data.

Findings from these informal surveys are worrisome because monitoring and evaluating the effects of intervention efforts is an essential feature of quality early intervention/early childhood special education programs. Without systematic documentation of child change, or lack of it, direct service providers, consultants, and caregivers cannot evaluate the effects of intervention. Furthermore, without the establishment and use of reliable data collection procedures, interventionists and caregivers will have an inadequate basis on which to judge whether the child's participation in a variety of activities is producing the desired effect or outcome. Finally, without the collection of systematic and objective child change data, interventionists and caregivers are not employing activity-based intervention as it is described in this volume.

PURPOSE OF MONITORING AND EVALUATING INTERVENTION

Monitoring, as used in this volume, refers to the systematic collection of information that provides ongoing feedback on children's performance over time. Monitoring allows teams to track the effects of intervention efforts in relation to children's individualized education program/individualized family service plan (IEP/IFSP) goals and objectives, global curriculum goals, and overall development. *Evaluation,* as used in this volume, refers to the systematic collection of comparative data to determine the significance or impact of intervention on individual children or groups of children. Evaluation allows teams to make decisions and to judge the worth of intervention efforts.

Both monitoring and evaluation are seen as integral parts of the linked systems framework described in Chapter 3 and are essential to the successful application of activity-based intervention. Formal and informal monitoring and evaluation activities are necessary to 1) identify children's needs for services, 2) target important IEP/IFSP goals and objectives, 3) individualize intervention procedures and activities, and 4) assess child progress. In addition to these general purposes, monitoring and evaluation data have significant utility. Some of the potential uses of monitoring and evaluation data include the following:

- Determining individual children's developmental status at a given time and their progress and change over time
- Gaining valuable information about children's strengths, interests, and needs
- Ensuring that teaching strategies are effective
- Discovering trends in children's learning
- Making sound decisions regarding curriculum implementation and individualization
- Identifying family priorities and concerns
- Collaborating and communicating
- Appraising the effects of staff behaviors on children
- Obtaining information about needed staff development
- Determining program effectiveness
- Meeting federal guidelines

Despite the number of potential uses for monitoring and evaluation data, most team members concentrate their data collection efforts on appraisals of children's initial functioning and year-end evaluations. This narrow use of data may occur because of the challenges and barriers teams face in systematically monitoring and evaluating child progress. Attempting to measure the effects of child progress when intervention is embedded in a variety of activities can present additional barriers and challenges. Unlike traditional teacher-directed, massed-trial data collection approaches, collecting data with an activity-based approach requires making multiple decisions about which measurement strategies are appropriate given children's targeted goals and objectives.

Although clearly challenging, the successful user of activity-based intervention is required at the very least to systematically monitor and evaluate child progress toward IEP/IFSP goals and objectives. Thus, the purpose of this chapter is to assist team members in developing and using child progress monitoring and evaluation systems that are compatible with activity-based intervention. Teams should also be concerned with evaluating other program components (e.g., parent outcomes, staff training), but describing these efforts is beyond the scope of this volume. Assistance in evaluating other program components can be found in Bricker (1989, 1996a, 1996b), Dunst and Trivette (1990), Krauss and Jacobs (1990), and Snyder and Wolfe (1997).

This chapter is divided into five major sections. The first section describes an overall measurement framework and guidelines for monitoring and evaluating child progress and discusses guidelines for monitoring and evaluating child progress. The second section reviews a decision-based model for monitoring and evaluating child progress. The third section presents examples of three data collection systems that are compatible with an activity-based approach. The fourth section offers assistance in data summarization. The fifth section guides the team in data interpretation and application.

OVERALL MEASUREMENT FRAMEWORK

An overall framework for monitoring and evaluating child progress is important because it provides a structure for understanding and implementing a variety of measurement strategies. The framework presented here is composed of three interrelated levels and is shown in Figure 7.1. Although this framework presents a strategy for designing and managing data collection for

---

Level One Activities—Weekly Child Progress

Purpose: Monitor and evaluate child progress toward prioritized IEP/IFSP goals and objectives.

Procedure: Collect weekly data.

Level Two Activities—Quarterly Child Progress

Purpose: Monitor and evaluate child progress toward prioritized IEP/IFSP goals and objectives, global curricular goals, and overall development.

Procedure: Administer quarterly program-relevant, criterion-referenced test.

Level Three Activities—Annual Child Progress

Purpose: Evaluate general program effect.

Procedure: Administer pre- and poststandardized or criterion-referenced test.

Figure 7.1.   Three-level measurement framework for monitoring weekly, quarterly, and annual child progress. (Adapted from Bricker, 1989, and Bricker & Gumerlock, 1985.)

child change, it should be noted that it does not address the need to evaluate other programmatic components such as family outcomes and staff functioning.

The arrows connecting the three levels of this framework indicate the need for an ongoing relationship between the information obtained and the procedures used at each level. In a well-designed system, the data collected at Level One can be used to complement and support data collected at Level Two, and Level Two data can likewise be used to complement data collected at Level Three.

Level One activities monitor and evaluate children's weekly progress toward selected IEP/IFSP targets or more specific program steps. For many infants and children, a goal or an objective may require responses that are too advanced for them to perform. In these cases, the skill needs to be divided into simpler components (i.e., program steps) to be targeted. The type of data collection procedures used at Level One should permit 1) monitoring of a child's IEP/IFSP goals and objectives;

2) meeting family, interventionist, and program needs; and 3) gauging the effects of weekly intervention efforts. Weekly monitoring and evaluation activities may enhance the prospects of demonstrating individual improvement and program efficacy at quarterly and annual evaluations by providing ongoing feedback that will allow interventionists to detect and remedy ineffective program targets and strategies that impede child progress.

Level Two activities provide systematic and comparative feedback on children's growth and development through the repeated administration (e.g., every 3–4 months) of a program-relevant, criterion-referenced instrument (e.g., the *Assessment, Evaluation, and Programming System (AEPS)* [Bricker, 1993]; *The Carolina Curriculum for Infants and Toddlers with Special Needs, Second Edition* [Johnson-Martin, Jens, Attermeier, & Hacker, 1991]; *ABACUS* [McCarthy, Lund, & Bos, 1986]). The outcomes from such instruments are useful for gauging the effects of intervention on individual children as well as groups of children. For example, if a child does not reach his or her established objectives in the Gross Motor Domain or is having difficulty with skills in the Social Domain of the AEPS Test, then interventionists or caregivers may not be providing adequate practice in these areas or the teaching strategies being used may be ineffective. In either case, results from the quarterly evaluation may suggest that modification of the program is in order. Thus, information from quarterly evaluations provides feedback about the child's developmental progress and helps clarify where intervention modifications or revisions may be necessary.

Level Three activities require the administration of standardized norm-referenced (e.g., Bayley Scales of Infant Development—II [Bayley, 1993]) or criterion-referenced (e.g., HELP [VORT Corp., 1995]) tests that are usually administered at the beginning and end of the school year. The outcomes from such testing are useful to evaluate general program effects for groups of children; however, these outcomes may not be useful for measuring the progress of individual children or monitoring progress toward targeted IEP/IFSP goals and objectives.

In addition to the three-level measurement framework, teams that are interested in implementing activity-based intervention are encouraged to follow a set of guidelines for systematically monitoring and evaluating child progress. The set of guidelines is designed to increase the likelihood that teams will monitor and evaluate child progress and to clarify the purpose for collecting data. Table 7.1 summarizes these guidelines.

Table 7.1.   Guidelines for monitoring and evaluating child progress

Guideline	Description
1	Data collection systems should be designed to address team's purposes.
2	Children's IEP/IFSPs should guide data collection efforts.
3	Data collection systems should be flexible (i.e., adjust to age, developmental level, and targets) and applicable across settings, events, and people.
4	Data collection systems should yield valid and reliable data.
5	Data collection responsibilities should be shared by team members (i.e., interventionists, consultants, and caregivers).
6	Data collections should be compatible with available resources (e.g., time, skills, materials).

A DECISION-BASED MODEL
FOR MONITORING AND EVALUATING CHILD PROGRESS

A variety of data collection systems are available to systematically monitor and evaluate child progress. No universal data collection system exists that is appropriate for use with all children and across all goals or programs nor will one system necessarily remain appropriate as children's goals change. However, teams will likely function more effectively if they adopt a decision-based model that guides their activities. A decision-based model, such as the one proposed by McAfee and Leong (1997), can offer a useful framework that addresses important questions associated with data collection systems. These types of models 1) emphasize the cyclic nature of the monitoring and evaluation process and 2) begin and end with the purpose or reason for monitoring child progress. Decision-based models allow interventionists to collect both ongoing feedback data (i.e., weekly and quarterly child progress data) and impact data (i.e., annual child progress data).

Why to Monitor and Evaluate Child Progress

Why child progress should be monitored and evaluated is the first issue that a team should address. Systematic monitoring and evaluation data can be collected for several reasons including, but not limited to, 1) modifying or changing intervention strategies and activities (e.g., increase the number of practice opportunities), 2) providing additional support for child learning, 3) communicating with other team members, 4) determining whether the child is ready to move to the next goal or objective, 5) planning for the next environment (e.g., making the transition to preschool), 6) determining when and where a child demonstrates a behavior, and 7) examining a particular aspect of the behavior (e.g., frequency, quality, duration). Determining *why* data are being collected should guide subsequent decisions and should increase the validity and utility of the data.

What to Monitor and Evaluate

Typically, *what* to monitor and evaluate at Levels One and Two of the measurement framework is decided by the goals and objectives that are selected, prioritized, and written on children's IEP/IFSPs. An appropriate and useful IEP/IFSP specifies both targeted behaviors and the manner in which the success of the intervention will be evaluated (i.e., specific criteria should be included). *What* to evaluate at Level Three is determined by classroom or program goals (e.g., important global developmental skills such as improving play skills and promoting compliance).

Who Will Monitor and Evaluate Child Progress

A third decision that should be made is *who* will collect the data. Assigning team members responsibility for specific data collection activities is essential. Without specific assignments, it is likely that systematic monitoring and evaluating of child progress will not occur. Data collection assignments should match time and other resources available to team members. Responsibility should be shared across team members for at least three reasons. First, sharing permits the collection of information across perspectives and settings. Second, sharing distributes the responsibility more or less in an equal manner, potentially allowing for more opportunities to collect data. Third, sharing helps involve each team member (in particular, family members) in the important activity of monitoring and evaluating child progress.

Where to Monitor and Evaluate Child Progress

Deciding *where* to monitor and evaluate child progress should be based on the situation in which children need to use the targeted response. For example, if the target skill is *use of phrases for requesting an object,* then data should be collected in those situations in which the child actually needs to make a verbal request. For example, snacktime, when the child wants more juice or a cracker, may be an ideal time to determine his or her progress toward verbal requesting. Interventionists and caregivers cannot always collect data during ongoing activities such as snack-time, but with planning it may be possible. If, for example, a data recording form were taped to the table, then the interventionist might be able to quickly mark the number of requests produced by the child during the snack period.

Although it may be simpler to collect child progress data by taking the child to a quiet, individual setting, the outcomes produced under these conditions may not accurately reflect the child's usual performance. For example, we have found that children may not reliably label pictures in isolated test settings but that they will use targeted words when they desire a particular object for play. An example illustrates this point. An interventionist was surprised by a child's ability to print his name without a model. Initially, the interventionist assessed the child's writing skills by asking him to trace or copy his name from a model. Under these conditions, the child had difficulty tracing or copying the letters of his name. One day, during an integral part of a library activity, the interventionist asked the child to sign his name on a blank sheet of paper when he checked out a book. To the interventionist's surprise, during this meaningful activity the child was able to write his name independently.

When to Monitor and Evaluate Child Progress

Deciding *when* to monitor and evaluate child progress depends on the program, staff, children, and targeted skills. In general, data on children's progress toward targeted IEP/IFSP goals and objectives should be collected systematically on specified days. Finding time to collect systematic data is not easy, but it is integral to effective intervention. Team members should select days and times for data collection that offer appropriate opportunities for monitoring and evaluating child progress, and data should be collected when children are comfortable and motivated.

How Often to Monitor and Evaluate Child Progress

In deciding *how often* to monitor and evaluate child progress, teams should consider which aspect of prioritized goals/objectives is of interest (e.g., frequency, duration, latency), their resources (e.g., training, time, staff availability), and which level of child progress they are going to monitor and evaluate (i.e., Level One, Two, or Three). In general, teams need to monitor and evaluate child progress frequently enough to provide them with an accurate picture of the child's functioning across important environments (e.g., home, school). Data should also be collected based on specified criteria for targeted IEP/IFSP goals and objectives, preferably on a weekly basis (i.e., Level One). We have found that most interventionists are able to collect information on targeted goals and objectives only once or twice per week. Data on global curricular skills or developmental skills can be collected less frequently than data for targeted IEP/IFSP goals and objectives but should still be collected at regular intervals (i.e., every 3–4 months [Level Two]). Comparative data used to evaluate child change can be collected once at the beginning of the year and again at the end of the year (i.e., Level Three).

How to Monitor and Evaluate Child Progress

Deciding *how* to monitor and evaluate child progress presents a challenge because a universally applicable system/tool/procedure does not exist. Depending on previous decisions made by the team (e.g., the purpose for monitoring and evaluating child progress, when child progress will be monitored and evaluated), *how* child progress is actually monitored and evaluated may differ. For example, if the team members are interested in monitoring how often a child shares materials with a peer during free play, then they may choose a simple probe system composed of a series of tally marks versus the creation of a portfolio or the administration of a lengthy assessment/evaluation tool.

Teams interested in collecting child progress data can use any of the following types of measurement systems:

- **Narrative Summaries:** Anecdotal records, running records, specimen descriptions
- **Portfolios:** Indicator systems, work samples, permanent records
- **Behavioral Observations:** Sampling (e.g., category, event, time), rating scales, probe recording systems, levels of assistance, task analytic ratings

Alberto and Troutman (1995) and McLean, Bailey, and Wolery (1996) provided detailed examples of each of these types of data collection systems and corresponding data collection forms.

Key variables of the decision-based model described previously appear on the individual program plan described in Chapter 5. The evaluation procedures section of the individual program plan was designed to prompt team members to consider why they are collecting data; what they will monitor and evaluate; who will collect the information; where, when, and how often they will collect data; and how the data will be collected.

Team members interested in monitoring and evaluating child progress at quarterly intervals can use a range of assessment/evaluation tools. Readers are encouraged to review Chapter 3 for a discussion of selecting appropriate assessment/evaluation tools. Teams interested in evaluating child progress to determine program effect can use norm-referenced or criterion-referenced assessment/evaluation tools pre- and posttest for comparative purposes.

In general, teams should adopt data collection systems and procedures that are reliable, are valid, match program resources, and produce the type of data needed for making sound decisions. McComas and Olson (1996) urged teams to keep evaluation of child progress simple by 1) *M*aking the system accessible and usable, 2) *A*voiding the placement of too much information on the data collection form and the use of too many papers for data recording, 3) *K*eeping writing to a minimum, and 4) *E*xplaining recording terms and symbols.

Monitoring and Evaluating Child Progress: An Example

Stacy is a 32-month-old child with Down syndrome. Stacy attends a playgroup five mornings a week and goes to a child care center each afternoon. The teachers at the playgroup are interested in monitoring and evaluating 1) Stacy's progress on targeted IFSP goals and objectives, 2) Stacy's growth across developmental areas and global skills, and 3) the effect of the playgroup on Stacy's development. Recently, the teachers in Stacy's playgroup have begun to implement intervention strategies they learned from the occupational therapist. The strategies were designed to promote Stacy's learning and development on two of her targeted IFSP goals. Using a decision-based model, Stacy's team decided it needed to monitor and evaluate her progress to ensure that its efforts were effective and to modify the new intervention strategies if necessary (i.e., the team members first determined *why* they were evaluating Stacy's progress).

Deciding *what* to evaluate was straightforward because the team members used Stacy's IFSP goals to guide their efforts. The two goals targeted were 1) participating in group activities and 2) drinking from a cup without assistance. The team also decided to assess Stacy's overall growth by looking at key developmental milestones across developmental areas. Finally, the team was interested in evaluating the effect of the playgroup on Stacy.

The team then decided *who* would collect the data. The team wanted to share data collection responsibilities across team members in order to maximize use of its limited resources and to gain information from across settings. It was determined that the teachers would monitor Stacy's progress at the playgroup, the occupational therapist would monitor and evaluate Stacy's progress during monthly visits to the home or to the playgroup, and Stacy's mother and father would monitor her progress on targeted goals each week at home.

The team then examined *where* Stacy would need to use the targeted goals (e.g., participates in group activities). Three activities (circle time, outdoor time, and snacktime) were selected by the team as ones that would provide frequent opportunities for Stacy to practice her targeted goals and objectives and provide the team multiple opportunities to observe her performance (i.e., during activities *where* Stacy would need to demonstrate the targeted skills).

Next, the team members determined *when* they would be able to monitor and evaluate Stacy's progress on the two targeted goals. They decided that several adults were present during circle time and outdoor time, which would give them the necessary resources to collect data on Stacy's group participation. They also decided that, despite the lack of resources during snacktime, the team would try to collect data during this activity because this was when Stacy would need to use the targeted skill of drinking from a cup.

The team members then decided *how often* they would evaluate Stacy's progress by reviewing each goal's criteria found on the IFSP and their resources for monitoring and evaluating progress. It was decided that Stacy's participation during group activities would be evaluated at least twice a week for a period of 3 weeks. Stacy's progress on drinking from a cup would be evaluated at least once a day during snacktime, for a 2-week period.

Finally, the team members decided *how* they would collect the data. They explored several options including narrative summaries, portfolios, behavioral observations, and administration of assessment/evaluation tools. For Stacy's targeted goal of group participation, team members decided to collect anecdotal records that would describe how Stacy participated during different group activities (e.g., Did Stacy tend to watch, listen, or share materials during group activities?). For Stacy's goal of drinking from a cup without assistance, the team decided to create a simple data collection form that would indicate the number of times Stacy was able to drink from a cup without spilling. These two systems would allow the team to monitor and evaluate Stacy's progress on a weekly basis. Because the team members were interested in looking at Stacy's overall development and the effect of the playgroup, they decided to administer the AEPS Test at quarterly intervals and the Bayley Scales of Infant Development at the beginning and end of the year.

By using a decision-based model, the members of Stacy's team will likely be successful in collecting valuable child progress data.

That is, they considered *why* they were collecting data, *what* skills they were interested in monitoring and evaluating, *who* would be responsible for collecting the data, *where* and *when* they would collect the data, *how often* they would need to collect data, and *how* they would collect data to meet their needs. If team members do not take the time to discuss these issues, they will face many challenges and will not have an adequate base from which to make decisions.

DATA COLLECTION SYSTEMS AND ACTIVITY-BASED INTERVENTION

Three types of data collection systems are particularly applicable for evaluating child progress within an activity-based approach: 1) anecdotal records, 2) portfolios, and 3) probe recording systems.

Anecdotal Records

Anecdotal records are a type of narrative description that provide accounts of a single child, groups of children, or a particular activity or event (McLean et al., 1996). These types of accounts are often less objective and more interpretative than data collection systems that focus on describing more discrete behaviors. For example, an interventionist may describe a child's behavior when he or she arrives each morning, or the interventionist may describe where and with whom the child chooses to play. Anecdotal records can be useful in monitoring and evaluating child progress; however, we recommend that they be used as supplements to other, more objective data collection procedures.

Anecdotal records are compatible with an activity-based approach because the observations can be conducted 1) across a variety of daily activities, 2) by any of the team members including the family, and 3) through brief exchanges and interactions. Five primary recommendations exist for collecting anecdotal records: 1) writing the anecdote while it occurs or as soon afterward as possible; 2) describing the key behaviors and people present during the situation; 3) recording the time, location, and basic sequence of events; 4) keeping inferences and opinions of the observer to a minimum; and 5) describing responses and reactions of others to the activity or event (McLean et al., 1996).

Portfolios

"A portfolio is an organized, purposeful compilation of evidence documenting a child's development and learning over time"

(McAfee & Leong, 1997, p. 111). Portfolios provide ongoing information regarding a child's development and include representative samples of performance. Portfolios can contain a variety of documents including notes, test results, artwork, and checklists. Two basic approaches exist for organizing information into a portfolio: indicator systems and work sample systems. An example of a portfolio planning sheet created by McComas and Olson (1996) is provided in Figure 7.2.

Portfolios are compatible with an activity-based approach because they contain information from multiple sources and across time, give access to a range of subjective and objective documentation, allow for flexibility in type and amount of data collected given program resources, assist in monitoring child

---

Portfolio plan for _____ (child's name) _____

Prioritized goal/objective(s): _____

_____

_____

Documents to be collected (e.g., artwork, videotape): _____

_____

_____

Opportunities to collect documents: _____

_____

_____

When and _how_ documents will be collected: _____

_____

_____

Additional notes and comments: _____

_____

_____

_____

Figure 7.2. A portfolio planning sheet. (Adapted from McComas & Olson, 1996.)

change, and emphasize the process of development/change rather than test scores.

Probe Recording Systems

Given adequate staff or caregiver time, we recommend a probe recording system for use with an activity-based approach for two reasons. First, the probe system can be designed to collect objective information in terms of the different types of responses (e.g., frequency, duration). Second, data can be collected while children are engaged in their daily environmental interactions and, therefore, should reveal whether the child uses a response in functional ways.

Probe recording systems can be defined as mini-tests or as quick snapshots of children's behavior. Probes can be conducted prior to, during, or at the end of an activity. The interventionist or caregiver simply introduces one or two "test trials" (i.e., probes) and then records the outcomes (i.e., child's performance). In the case of Stacy (see the previous vignette), her targeted goal of drinking from a cup without assistance could be monitored using a probe recording system. For example, during a snack activity, interventionists can observe Stacy drink from a cup or prompt Stacy to take a drink. Interventionists then record whether Stacy was able to drink from the cup independently or whether she needed assistance. Figure 7.3 contains an example of a probe recording system data collection form completed for Stacy and another child.

Probe recording system data collection forms may vary but should include 1) situation information (i.e., setting, who was the observer, goals or objectives being measured, when the observation occurred [e.g., week, day]) and 2) performance information (i.e., actual record of child's response to probes [e.g., correct or incorrect]). Figure 7.4 provides a copy of a blank probe recording system data collection form.

Probe recording systems can also be employed in home-based settings. For example, caregivers and interventionists can modify the individual activity schedule described in Chapter 5 to track child progress toward targeted goals and objectives. Figure 7.5 provides an example of a modified individual activity schedule that can be used for monitoring and evaluating child progress.

Probe recording systems have several advantages over anecdotal records and portfolios because they 1) require minimal training for use, 2) take little time to administer, 3) provide

Probe Recording System Data Collection Form

Setting: _Playgroup_

Observer: _Ms. Hill_

Week: _October 7–11_

ACTIVITIES

Outside / Opening circle / Free play / Snacktime / Choice time / Closing circle

Child's name	Goal or objective	Outside M T W Th F	Opening circle M T W Th F	Free play M T W Th F	Snacktime M T W Th F	Choice time M T W Th F	Closing circle M T W Th F
Stacy	1. Drinks from a cup				I W W		
	2. Participates in group activities	N W W	W	W			
Steve	1. Makes verbal requests	C	C			C	C
	2. Walks unassisted	W	W			C	

Figure 7.3. An example of a completed probe recording system data collection form. (I = incorrect, C = correct, W = with assistance, N = no attempt.)

Probe Recording System Data Collection Form

Setting:_____

Observer:_____

Week:_____

Child's name	Goal or objective	ACTIVITIES
		M T W Th F M T W Th F M T W Th F M T W Th F M T W Th F M T W Th F

Figure 7.4. A blank probe recording system data collection form.

Individual Activity Schedule

Child's name: _Hakeem_   Date: _9-97_

Child's goals or objectives

Routine activity	Routine's time and frequency	Uses consistent word approximations	Grasps hand-size objects
Dressing	6:30 A.M. (1x per day)	• Approximates a word to indicate preferred clothing and responds to questions [C][C][N][C][C] • Approximates a word to indicate family members [C][C][C][ ][ ] • Approximates a word used by family members [C][N][N][ ][ ] Comments: _____ _____ _____	• Grasps objects (e.g., toothbrush, hairbrush, cup, clothing) [W][W][W][ ][ ] • Grasps clothing [W][W][W][C][ ] Comments: _____ _____ _____
Car travel	8:00 A.M. (1x per day)	• Approximates a word heard from radio/cassette in car [C][C][ ][ ][ ] • Approximates a word to indicate familiar location [ ][ ][ ][ ][ ] Comments: _Used_ _verbal prompt_ _____ _____	• Grasps seat belt [W][W][ ][ ][ ] • Grasps books or toys from car pocket [C][ ][ ][ ][ ] Comments: _____ _____ _____
Bath time	Evening (1x per day)	• Approximates a word to refer to common objects [C][C][C][ ][ ] Comments: _____ _____ _____	• Grasps objects including soap, shampoo, bottle, washcloth, toys, towel, and robe [W][W][W][C][ ] Comments: _____ _____ _____

Figure 7.5. Individual activity schedule modified for collecting child progress data. (*Note:* A checkmark can be placed in each box when the child performs the skill, or a simple coding system can be used [e.g., C = correct, W = with assistance, N = no attempt].)

useful information about the functional use of targeted responses, 4) allow children to remain engaged in the ongoing activity, and 5) can indicate the presence or absence of a behavior
as well as the assistance a child needs to perform a behavior.

DATA SUMMARIZATION

Monitoring and evaluation data can be summarized by using
numbers (e.g., frequencies, percentages) or verbal descriptions.
Summaries of data provide teams with important information
about children's progress across developmental areas, settings,
and time. When numerical summaries are used, teams can
transpose weekly data into percentages and plot results on
graphs. For example, the percentage of time a child spends in
playing with peers each week, the percentage of correct responses, or the percentage of intelligible words used can all be
plotted on a graph to summarize the child's progress. In the case
of Stacy (see the previous vignette), the data collected on the
weekly probe recording system data collection form can be
transposed into the percentage of correct cup-drinking responses, and then the percentage correct over time plotted on a
graph and used to monitor her progress toward independent
cup drinking. For example, at the end of the first week of intervention (as shown in Figure 7.3), the team summarized Stacy's
performance across three snack activities. Stacy drank from a
cup with some spilling on Monday (incorrect) and drank from a
cup with assistance on Wednesday and Friday. These observations can be summarized and plotted on a graph each week. A
summarized example of cup drinking data for Stacy is plotted
for 4 weeks in Figure 7.6.

Narrative summaries can also be used to describe a child's
level of functioning on an IEP/IFSP and to communicate with
other team members about a child's performance at school or at
home. The following are several guidelines for creating narrative summaries:

- Collect and summarize data by developmental areas or tar-
  geted skills.
- Write positively, objectively, and without jargon.
- Use examples of children's behaviors whenever possible.
- Include evaluation data from across people and settings.

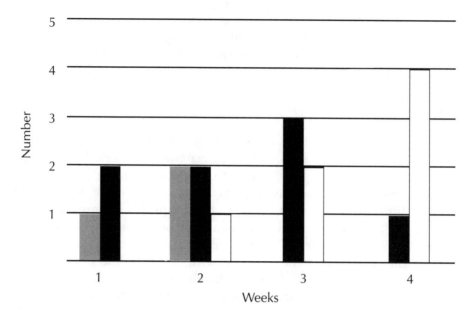

Figure 7.6. A summarization of Stacy's cup-drinking performance across 4 weeks of intervention. (▨ = incorrect, ■ = with assistance, □ = correct.)

DATA INTERPRETATION AND USE

There is no point in collecting data if the team is not going to use it to make sound decisions, particularly about intervention content. An interventionist may ask whether children are making progress when goals and objectives are embedded into daily activities, but this question can be answered only by evaluating child progress.

There are at least six steps teams can follow to adequately interpret and use data (McAfee & Leong, 1997). Step One requires team members to summarize data whenever possible to avoid making decisions based on isolated or random bits of information. Step Two requires team members to use their knowledge of typical sequences and timetables of development when interpreting a particular child's performance (Greenspan & Meisels, 1995). In Step Three, team members should consider how the data collected match or relate to other aspects of a child's development and learning. Step Four requires team members to collect data across settings, measures, perspectives, and time (i.e., to obtain a picture of the "whole" child). In Step Five, a child's unique pattern or learning style should be factored into how data are interpreted as well as environmental factors that may have influenced a child's performance. In Step Six, team members should determine whether a child's performance across critical areas of development is improving as expected.

SUMMARY

The use of an intervention model that capitalizes on child-initiated, routine, and planned activities requires that attention be given to the development of objective child evaluation systems that can provide staff and caregivers with the necessary information to make timely and appropriate programmatic changes. Without the establishment and use of sound evaluation procedures, interventionists and caregivers will have an inadequate basis on which to judge whether the child's participation in a variety of activities is producing the desired effect (i.e., improvement in IEP/IFSP goals and objectives). By using a decision-based model such as the one described in this chapter, teams should be able to overcome many of the challenges of monitoring and evaluating child progress, particularly within an activity-based approach to intervention.

REFERENCES

Alberto, P., & Troutman, A. (1995). *Applied behavior analysis for teachers* (4th ed.). Upper Saddle River, NJ: Prentice-Hall.

Bayley, N. (1993). *Bayley Scales of Infant Development—Second Edition manual.* San Antonio, TX: The Psychological Corporation.

Bricker, D. (1989). *Early intervention for at-risk and handicapped infants, toddlers, and preschool children.* Palo Alto, CA: VORT Corp.

Bricker, D. (Ed.). (1993). *Assessment, evaluation, and programming system for infants and children: Vol. 1. AEPS measurement for birth to three years.* Baltimore: Paul H. Brookes Publishing Co.

Bricker, D. (1996a). Assessment for IFSP development and intervention planning. In S. Meisels & E. Fenichel (Eds.), *New visions for the developmental assessment of infants and toddlers* (pp. 169–192). Washington, DC: National Center for Clinical Infant Programs.

Bricker, D. (1996b). Using assessment outcomes for intervention planning: A necessary relationship. In M. Brambring, H. Rauh, & A. Beelmann (Eds.), *Early childhood intervention theory, evaluation, and practice* (pp. 305–328). Berlin/New York: Aldine de Gruyter.

Bricker, D., & Gumerlock, S. (1985). A three level strategy. In J. Danaher (Ed.), *Assessment of child progress* (pp. 7–17). Chapel Hill, NC: Technical Assistance Development System.

Dunst, C., & Trivette, C. (1990). Assessment of social support in early intervention programs. In S. Meisels & J. Shonkoff (Eds.), *Handbook of early childhood intervention* (pp. 326–349). New York: Cambridge University Press.

Greenspan, S., & Meisels, S. (1995). A new vision for the assessment of young children. *Exceptional Parent, 25*(2), 23–25.

Johnson-Martin, N.M., Jens, K.G., Attermeier, S.M., & Hacker, B.J. (1991). *The Carolina curriculum for infants and toddlers with special needs* (2nd ed.). Baltimore: Paul H. Brookes Publishing Co.

Krauss, M., & Jacobs, F. (1990). Family assessment: Purpose and techniques. In S. Meisels & J. Shonkoff (Eds.), *Handbook of early childhood intervention* (pp. 303–325). New York: Cambridge University Press.

McAfee, R., & Leong, D. (1997). *Assessing and guiding young children's development and learning.* Needham Heights, MA: Allyn & Bacon.

McCarthy, J., Lund, K., & Bos, C. (1986). *Arizona basic assessment and curriculum utilization system (ABACUS).* Denver: Love Publishing Co.

McComas, N., & Olson, J. (1996). *Building effective successful teams series: Module 2—Activity-based approach to learning.* [Supported by U.S. Department of Education Grant #H024P50019; unpublished.] University of Idaho, Moscow.

McLean, M., Bailey, D., & Wolery, M. (1996). *Assessing infants and preschoolers with special needs.* Columbus, OH: Charles E. Merrill.

Snyder, P., & Wolfe, B.L. (1997). Needs assessment and evaluation in early intervention personnel preparation: Opportunities and challenges. In P.J. Winton, J.A. McCollum, & C. Catlett (Eds.), *Reforming personnel preparation in early intervention: Issues, models, and practical strategies* (pp. 127–171). Baltimore: Paul H. Brookes Publishing Co.

VORT Corp. (1995). *Hawaii Early Learning Profile (HELP): HELP for preschoolers* (pp. 3–6). Palo Alto, CA: Author.

Why to Use
Activity-Based Intervention

Chapter 8

Naturalistic
Teaching Approaches

Our work has centered on activity-based intervention that both
we and others have placed in the larger context of "naturalistic"
teaching approaches. If the literature is a measure, then the discussion and use of naturalistic teaching approaches with young
children with disabilities is on the upswing, particularly in the
areas of language and communication. The growth of naturalistic teaching approaches has at least four potential explana-
tions. First, as the inclusion of children with disabilities into
community-based programs increases, there is an associated
need for approaches that better fit the values and strategies used
in these programs (Atwater, Carta, Schwartz, & McConnell,
1994). Second, many parents appear to understand and appreciate the use of strategies that can be easily integrated into their
family's daily routines. Third, the use of adult-directed, highly
structured training regimes has not produced the desired response generalization we seek for children with learning and
developmental disabilities (Warren & Horn, 1996). Fourth, the
growing popularity of developmentally appropriate practice
(DAP) for children with disabilities has encouraged the adoption of approaches that can be usefully blended with DAP
guidelines (Novick, 1993; Wolery & Bredekamp, 1994).

Given the growth and popularity of naturalistic teaching
approaches, it is of interest to us and others (Hepting & Goldstein, 1996) that the descriptions, definitions, and conceptual
parameters of approaches classified as *naturalistic* are brief (e.g.,
Noonan & McCormick, 1993), general (e.g., Cole, Dale, & Mills,
1991), confusing (e.g., Barnett, Carey, & Hall, 1993), or focused

173

on a particular area such as language (e.g., Kaiser, Yoder, & Keetz, 1992). The remainder of this chapter examines the definitional problems surrounding naturalistic teaching approaches, compares features associated with these approaches, and proposes a reformulation that includes the elements found in activity-based intervention.

NATURALISTIC TEACHING

As Hepting and Goldstein (1996) observed, the term *naturalistic* as a descriptor for language intervention appears with increasing frequency in the literature. That increase is not limited to the area of language but rather can be seen across the entire spectrum of early intervention literature (e.g., Noonan & McCormick, 1993). An analysis of how the term *naturalistic* is used in language training and the broader context of early intervention approaches suggests two major definition problems: the parameters of the term and the definitions themselves. To us, much of the writing focused on naturalistic teaching approaches does not make clear distinctions between the setting (i.e., where training occurs) and the teaching strategies used (e.g., following the child's lead, using daily routines). Although some authors make the distinction between natural environments and naturalistic teaching approaches (Noonan & McCormick, 1993), many authors muddy this distinction to the extent that it is not clear whether the writer is referring to a naturalistic setting or a naturalistic training strategy. A discussion of this issue and other issues surrounding the definition of naturalistic teaching follows.

Definitions

Since the 1950s and 1960s, the lack of generalization from training environments to nontraining environments has plagued investigators, particularly those using operant training techniques. The need for an individual to generalize behavior learned under specific training conditions to his or her natural environment was recognized (Guess, Sailor, & Baer, 1974). Also recognized was that "many aspects of a child's 'natural' environment can be used to shape his or her behavior toward the desired target response" (Bricker & Carlson, 1981, p. 507). Two of the early investigators to address this problem were Hart and Risley (1968), who designed and evaluated a strategy that they called "in vivo" or "incidental" teaching to promote the use of trained language structures in children's daily preschool environments.

Hart and Risley suggested that incidental teaching can occur in natural environments when children initiate an interaction and the teaching includes the following features:

> First, incidental teaching is conducted within the very setting conditions that naturally maintain language use. . . . Second, incidental teaching is conducted casually throughout the child's day, at various times and in various contexts. . . . Third, incidental teaching is by its nature loose training (Stokes & Baer, 1977). . . . Also, fourth, the conditions of incidental teaching are such that the actual contingencies of reinforcement are likely to be much less discriminable than those in a one-to-one training session. . . . Perhaps most importantly, incidental teaching establishes a class of behavior, language use, which is likely to be generalized by stimulus similarity across settings and occasions. (1980, pp. 409–410)

In 1985, Hart wrote a chapter entitled "Naturalistic Language Training Techniques" that focused on a discussion of environmental interventions. Although she did not define naturalistic, she identified three naturalistic processes (incidental teaching, mand-model, and delay) that could be used to promote language usage. In that chapter, Hart arrived at an interesting and important conclusion: "What makes training programs effective is not the occurrence, or even the frequency of aspects such as imitation, prompting, or modeling, but the process of which they are a part" (1985, p. 68).

Moving forward with the notion of embedding training in daily activities, several investigators proposed an approach termed *milieu language training,* which incorporates a variety of naturalistic language training strategies (Kaczmarek, Hepting, & Dzubak, 1996; Kaiser et al., 1992; Warren, 1991; Warren & Kaiser, 1988). Definitions of milieu teaching have been relatively consistent. For example, Warren and Kaiser suggested the following:

> Milieu teaching approaches are characterized by the use of dispersed training trials, attempts to follow the child's attentional lead while teaching in the context of normal conversational interchanges, and an orientation toward teaching the form and content of language in the context of normal use. (1988, p. 93)

Warren (1991) went on to suggest that two important elements of milieu language teaching are the targeting of specific responses and the use of increasingly specific prompts.

For Kaiser et al., "milieu teaching is a naturalistic strategy for teaching functional language skills" (1992, p. 9). According to these authors, milieu teaching shares several common features with a variety of naturalistic language teaching procedures: 1) teaching follows the child's lead or interest; 2) multiple, natural occurring examples are used; 3) the child's language productions are prompted; 4) consequences that are natural to the teaching context are used; and 5) teaching episodes are embedded in ongoing interactions. Other investigators have adopted these features as the defining parameters of naturalistic teaching approaches (Fox & Hanline, 1993). Hancock and Kaiser offered a variation of the above definitions: "Milieu teaching involves naturalistic, conversation-based strategies to elicit child communication responses" (1996, p. 169).

Although not referred to as milieu teaching, Halle and his colleagues have championed the use of functional language training strategies (Drasgow, Halle, Ostrosky, & Harbers, 1996). In 1982, Oliver and Halle observed that "language training in the natural environment offers an exciting alternative to traditional, structured training sessions for obtaining the goal of functional use" (p. 61). Halle, Alpert, and Anderson classified a variety of strategies as natural environment language training procedures that share the following characteristics:

a) brief and positive
b) carried out in the natural environment where opportunities for teaching functional language naturally occur, and
c) occasioned by child interest in the topic to which training will relate. (1984, p. 44)

Although much of the work on naturalistic approaches has focused on language, a number of writers have broadened naturalistic approaches to include other domains of behavior or to describe a general intervention approach. For example, Noonan and McCormick offered the following definition: "Naturalistic teaching approaches are structured approaches that use natural routines and activities in natural environments as the teaching context" (1993, p. 22). An interesting point is that these authors listed the defining characteristics for naturalistic teaching approaches as those offered by Warren and Kaiser (1988) for milieu teaching. In their discussion, Noonan and McCormick (1993) also defined the natural environment, which is important because of the apparent conceptual confusion by some writers between a strategy and a setting. According to Noonan and McCormick, "At the broadest level, the term natural environments refers to all integrated community settings . . . where the majority of participants are nondisabled persons" (1993, p. 238).

A further excursion into the literature reveals many slightly different definitions surrounding the concept of naturalistic. A listing of the features associated with naturalistic approaches reveals both differences and similarities. Table 8.1 contains a list of definitions, whereas Table 8.2 contains a list of the features that authors have associated with a variety of naturalistic training approaches. These lists of definitions and features are not exhaustive, but they do provide the reader with a sense about which features appear frequently and which do not; these lists should also further point to some of the important conceptual discrepancies that surround the terms *natural* and *naturalistic*. An analysis of the conceptual agreements and disagreements contained in the definitions and associated features may lead to a useful conclusion about the salvageability of these terms and may serve as a useful platform for a reformulation.

FEATURES OF NATURALISTIC APPROACHES

One feature that consistently appears in the literature on naturalistic approaches is the need to follow the child's lead and interest. The need to capitalize on the child's motivation is consistently emphasized across definitions and features (see Tables 8.1 and 8.2). There appears to be little disagreement that intervention will be effective when it is tied directly to actions and activities initiated by children and for which children show clear evidence of interest. There is disagreement, however, about the adult's role in the process. Some of the definitions imply that an approach is naturalistic only when the adult follows the child's initiations, which suggests that the adult's role is primarily as a responder. Other approaches, such as the activity-based approach, make it clear that the adult is not passive but must be both an initiator and responder. Some definitions appear to suggest that any structure provided by the adult would obviate a naturalistic approach. An interesting point is that observations of mother–infant interactions (thought to be natural) do not reveal mothers who relinquish total control to their young child in terms of conversational topics or actions. Mothers can be

Table 8.1. Selected definitions of naturalistic intervention

Definition	Source
Naturalistic intervention includes those that may be incorporated into the routine of caregivers or those that unobtrusively extend or modify experience that occurs within the settings important to children.	Barnett, Carey, & Hall (1993)
"Naturalistic intervention design stresses understanding of, and capitalization on, the natural interactions between the referred child and persons in closest contact with him or her" (p. 473).	Barnett et al. (1997)
"The term natural means that the unit for analysis is found in nature and is not based on a contrived assessment or measurement construct" (p. 474).	
Naturalistic teaching approaches are structured approaches that use natural routines and activities in natural environments as the teaching context.	Noonan & McCormick (1993)
The main goal of the naturalistic curriculum model is to increase the infant/young child's control, participation, and interaction in natural, social, and physical environments.	
"A prominent feature [of the program] is the firm belief that 'play is the child's genetically determined and inherent means of learning.' . . . Through this self-initiated, intrinsically rewarding activity, the child integrates the internal and external worlds" (p. vii).	Sheridan, Foley, & Radlinkski (1995)
"Incidental language teaching refers to interactions between an adult and a child that arise naturally in an unstructured situation and are used systematically by the adult to transmit new information or give the child practice in developing a communication skill" (p. 291).	Warren & Kaiser (1986)
"Naturalistic teaching strategies involve brief interactions between children and adults, provide children with opportunities to learn new skills or practice existing ones, and result in access to natural reinforcers" (p. 13).	Wolery (1994)

Table 8.2. Selected list of features associated with naturalistic intervention approaches

Title of approach	Features	Source
Incidental teaching	1. Contingent delivery of materials	Hart & Risley (1974)
	2. Hierarchical contingent instruction (teacher prompts)	
	3. Occurs within typical childhood activities with toys and other children	
	4. "Working" speech	
In vivo, incidental teaching	1. Conducted within the very setting conditions that naturally maintain language use	Hart & Risley (1980)
	2. Conducted casually throughout the child's day at various times and contexts	
	3. Loose training	
	4. Contingencies of reinforcement are less discriminable	
	5. Establishes a class of language behavior likely to generalize	
Natural environmental language training	1. Brief and positive	Halle, Alpert, & Anderson (1984)
	2. Conducted in the "natural" environment where opportunities for teaching functional language occur	
	3. Tied to child interest in a topic	
Naturalistic approaches	1. Occurs in the child's natural environment	Warren & Kaiser (1986)
	2. Uses conversational contexts	
	3. Uses a dispersed trials training approach	
	4. Emphasizes following the child's attentional lead	
	5. Uses functional reinforcers indicated by child requests and attention	

(continued)

Table 8.2. *(continued)*

Title of approach	Features	Source
Incidental teaching	1. Brief and positive interactions	Warren & Kaiser (1988)
	2. Designed to communicate	
	3. Resembles mother–child interaction	
	4. Focuses on specific targets	
	5. Uses increasingly specific prompts	
Milieu teaching	1. Disperses training trials	Warren & Kaiser (1988)
	2. Follows child's attentional lead	
	3. Teaches language form/content during daily activities	
Milieu teaching	1. Follows child's lead/interest	Kaiser, Yoder, & Keetz (1992)
	2. Uses multiple, naturally occurring examples to teach language	
	3. Prompts child production of language	
	4. Uses natural consequences including those associated with specific linguistic forms and those natural to the teaching context	
	5. Embeds teaching episodes in ongoing interactions	
Naturalistic approaches (parent training)	1. Primary focus is interaction between parent and child	Tannock & Girolametto (1992)
	2. Orientation is toward communication rather than language	
	3. Uses spontaneously occurring events that arise in play or daily routines	

Term	Characteristics	Citation
Naturalistic teaching	1. Occurs in the natural environment 2. Brief and spaced over period of hours/days 3. Child initiated 4. Uses natural consequences	Fox & Hanline (1993) (cited in Kaiser, Yoder, & Keetz [1992])
Naturalistic teaching approaches	"1. Teaching occurs in the natural environment. 2. Individual teaching interactions are typically very brief and distributed or spaced over a period of hours and days. 3. Instructional interactions are typically child-initiated. 4. Instruction uses natural consequences (objects and events are highly salient and desired by the child)." (p. 238–239)	Noonan & McCormick (1993), (cited in Warren & Kaiser [1988])
Naturalistic (milieu) strategies	1. Uses ongoing activities and interactions 2. Uses repeated brief interactions between children and adults 3. Responds to children's behavior 4. Provides feedback and naturally occurring consequences to children 5. Requires purposeful planning by adult	Wolery (1994)
Naturalistic approaches (e.g., milieu teaching)	1. Uses naturally occurring patterns of mother–child interactions 2. Targets skills that are immediately functional 3. Promotes skills that are useful in acquiring language	Kaiser, Hester, Alpert, & Whiteman (1995)
Milieu and responsive interaction, naturalistic teaching	1. Occurs in informal settings with activities not designed for language intervention 2. Addresses topics of interest to child 3. Linguistic input is appropriate to child's level of language functioning 4. Provides consequences that are part of communication episodes 5. Uses a range of specific language facilitation techniques	Yoder et al. (1995)

(continued)

Table 8.2. *(continued)*

Title of approach	Features	Source
Developmental approach	1. Uses natural environment 2. Follows child's interest 3. Promotes generalization of skills 4. Distributes practice 5. Focuses conversation on communication intent	Cole, Mills, Dale, & Jenkins (1996)
Natural language paradigm	1. Child-selected activities 2. Uses multiple examples in natural environment 3. Explicitly prompts language 4. Uses direct, natural consequences 5. Reinforces child's attempts 6. Promotes natural interaction	Koegel (1996)
Integrated therapy	1. Embeds training in ongoing routines, activities 2. Follows child's attentional lead 3. Chooses functional and immediately useful goals	Warren & Horn (1996)
Natural literacy	1. Children construct knowledge with help of adults/peers 2. Passive and active learning 3. Examples and concepts presented in meaningful contexts, presented on multiple occasions, and reflect child's interest 4. Various levels of participation are possible within activities 5. Focus of activity is on child's capabilities and extending knowledge 6. Heterogeneous groupings permit modeling and diversity	Watkins & Bunce (1996)

seen to focus their infants' attention and even be relatively directive if necessary. The important notion here is that the mother varies her natural interaction to meet the contextual demands. So, too, the effective interventionist does not always defer to the child's actions but uses a variety of techniques appropriate to the contextual demands. Clearly, it is important that children frequently initiate actions and activities; however, there will be times when it is entirely appropriate for the adult to initiate and to direct the child's actions. The goal is the adult's skillful blending of initiations and responses that capitalizes on the child's motivation and also keeps actions focused on acquiring and generalizing skills that enhance the child's behavioral repertoire.

A second feature that is contained in the definitions of naturalistic teaching approaches is the use of routines, daily activities, and play as a context for training. Although each venue may be valid, it seems appropriate to point out that play differs considerably from routines and daily activities. Perhaps the commonality they share is that each presents repeated opportunities for learning and practicing skills throughout the child's day.

Routines and daily activities are those in which each of us must participate, more or less, to maintain some semblance of order and substance to our lives (e.g., personal care, food preparation, cleaning). Such activities often occur by necessity, and, therefore, they tend to be meaningful in the sense that one cannot get along well without engaging in them. It seems capricious to ignore routines and daily activities as frequent and meaningful training opportunities for children. Or, said another way, because we have to do these routines and daily activities anyway, why not capitalize on their occurrence for enhancing children's skills, particularly because many of the skills to be learned during these routines are essential for becoming independent?

Although different, play also presents children with opportunities to acquire and generalize skills. Because most children play frequently and because play activities are often self-selected, there exist multiple opportunities to work on targeted goals. There are important conceptual differences, however, in how to think about play, routines, and daily activities. In particular, Hart (1985) referred to such activities as nontraining environments, whereas others use play and daily activities as primary training vehicles (e.g., activity-based intervention). Hart and others appear to be suggesting that preliminary or acquisition training can be conducted apart from children's daily activities and then the generalization of skills can be practiced in nontraining environments (e.g., play or incidental opportunities that present themselves throughout the day). In activity-based intervention, play, routines, and daily activities serve as primary training environments and are not to be thought of as nontraining settings or merely incidental.

A third widely espoused feature is that naturalistic approaches incorporate consequences (or reinforcements) as part of the action or activity. The consequence of asking for a drink of juice should be that the child receives the juice not that he or she is congratulated with "Good talking." Of course, life is more complicated in the sense that we learn about secondary reinforcements and that we learn (at least some of us do) to accept delayed reinforcement. For most young children, however, learning appears to be promoted when there are relatively direct ties between their actions and the consequences that occur. Therefore, it is recommended practice, when possible, to integrate consequences that occur as a direct result of these activities or actions into children's activities and actions. For example, pulling a chair to the counter gets the child the desired toy; requesting food or drink gets the child the desired item; responding to mom's question gets the child attention and a reciprocal response; asking a question may get the child the wanted information; using a new word improves the child's ability to communicate; using a pincer grasp permits the child to eat small pieces of food; learning color names gets the child the desired crayon; sitting upright permits the child to play next to a peer; saying "hi" and "bye" may get the child attention and a smile; saying "stop" may result in the child keeping a toy another child is trying to take; and putting one foot in front of another and maintaining his or her balance may permit the child to move to a desired location. Children's worlds are full of repeated opportunities to learn a variety of essential human skills. Effective intervention takes advantage of these multiple opportunities as primary teaching vehicles that not only are meaningful to children but also have inherently positive consequences that are directly linked to the children's actions.

A fourth feature frequently identified in definitions and features of naturalistic approaches is the need for training to occur across a range of conditions (e.g., events, people, settings, times of day). Training embedded across a range of conditions offers children multiple opportunities to learn targeted skills and also to ensure generalization of the skills across relevant conditions. Take, for example, a toddler with a moderate motor disability who was unable to walk independently. The intervention staff worked diligently to provide supports to encourage his independent stepping in the classroom. As good teachers will do, they carefully faded the external supports until this small boy was able to toddle across the classroom floor with relatively few falls. The approach of spring and a warm, sunny day sent the staff and children outside. To the dismay of the staff, when the toddler's feet made contact with grass, his walking skills failed him. He sat down and refused to stand up or take a step. During the remainder of that spring, the teachers recycled through the toddler's walking program with appropriate modifications, and by summer he was able to negotiate walking through grass. Although he learned to generalize his walking skills, this toddler was resistant to transferring his "new" walking skills to other settings. Had this toddler's initial training been more varied, he would probably have learned to negotiate variations in terrain more efficiently, and his resistance to change would have likely been significantly diminished. Variations in life's conditions (conditions are rarely identical) require that children develop repertoires to effectively manage change.

To a few writers, brief episodes that occur across the day are a defining feature of naturalistic approaches. Although it may be that some naturalistic teaching occurs in brief interactions, this is not a requirement. Why would an extended, meaningful interaction for a child be necessarily "unnatural?" For example, a child who has a target of expanding her vocabulary finds a small insect and points to the insect, the adult may respond, "Bug. It is a bug." The child may spend the next several minutes watching the bug, moving the bug, and talking about the bug, which all provide the adult many opportunities to introduce new words and to practice previously learned words. The adult might suggest that the child try to paint a picture of the bug or place the bug in a box and look for other bugs outdoors. As long as the child's interest is maintained and opportunities for learning targeted skills occur, it would be completely appropriate to continue with an activity or a child's focus of interest. Likewise, the requirement that brief episodes occur throughout the day could be troublesome. It may be better that children have the opportunity to practice and generalize skills across the day, but is it "unnatural" if opportunities to practice some skills only occur intermittently? For example, taking one's coat off and putting it on meaningfully may happen only once or twice a day or may not happen at all. Does this make it an unnatural activity?

A review of the definitions contained in Table 8.1 and the features in Table 8.2 reveal what we believe is a serious disagreement about the need for structure to underlie naturalistic approaches. Many definitions and descriptions suggest an informal approach that is permitted to happen as it will. This position suggests that there is no formal planning involved; rather, opportunities that occur by happenstance should be used to generalize targeted skills. Other approaches, such as activity-based intervention, have an underlying structure that guides the interventionist and ensures that routines, play, and daily activities are systematically targeted as teaching opportunities.

Providing structure does not mean that child initiations and motivation are ignored or compromised. The appropriate structure offers a framework to ensure systematic attention to child initiation as well as the development and use of other available opportunities for teaching. A few distinctions may be instructive. There are at least three types of actions/activities that are typically classified as *natural*. First are those child-initiated activities in which the interventionist's role is to follow the child's lead with the intent of enhancing the child's skill. As important, but less often addressed, is that the skillful interventionist can often guide off-target child initiations to become vehicles for learning or generalizing a targeted skill. In either case, it seems essential that an underlying structure be present to assist the interventionist in the effective use of child initiations. The second and third types of natural activities are routines and play. The importance of and reasons for using such activities are discussed previously. Again, the issue is whether the use of such activities should be left to happenstance or whether there should be an underlying structure that helps direct the interventionist and caregiver to the successful use of these activities. Observations across numerous classrooms and homes suggest that most interventionists and parents miss literally hundreds of "teachable" moments during play and routine activities. A structure that directs the adult's attention to daily routines and play activities and how to effectively introduce targeted skills during them should lead to a more efficient and effective use of daily activities and play than if these activities are used in an informal manner. Structure does not mean totally adult-directed, orchestrated training activities, but rather it means providing an underlying framework that orients the adult to the multiple opportunities for promoting children's learning throughout the day.

The dominant theme that underlies definitions of naturalistic approaches is that the acquisition and use of meaningful skills across the range of conditions experienced in day-to-day living environments can be enhanced in young children by using the daily environmental activities for teaching. Unfortunately, none of the definitions in Table 8.1 make particularly clear the parameters of naturalistic approaches, nor do they necessarily agree on essential features that supposedly define the approach. Is the term *naturalistic* salvageable? Perhaps yes but only as a general rubric for classifying an array of intervention strategies. The more important issue becomes the presentation of a framework that permits displaying potentially useful intervention strategies that can be operationalized. We need to make it clear that effective intervention is composed of a variety of strategies that need to be constantly tailored, adjusted, and modified to fit the particular child, setting, and goals. Whether these strategies are termed *naturalistic* is far less important than interventionists' understanding of the need to focus on functional goals that should be addressed frequently in meaningful contexts throughout the child's day-to-day activities.

REFORMULATION

We propose that a general goal for early intervention/early childhood special education (EI/ECSE) is to orchestrate environmental input, both physical and social, to maximize children's motivation to acquire and generalize targeted information and skills that will enhance their independence, problem-solving skills, and adjustment across a range of changing conditions and settings. Underlying this goal are three important assumptions that provide a conceptual base for recommended practice in early intervention.

Children's Motivation Is Critical
to Effective Learning and Generalization

The first assumption is that the child's motivation is pivotal to acquisition and generalization of targeted responses. If information and skills are to be acquired and generalized, then children need to be motivated (i.e., see a reason) to learn the targeted information and skills. Rather than relying on external and artificial consequences (i.e., a consequence not associated with an action or activity), the hope is that the child's responses are acquired and used because of the consequences inherent in the action or activity or because of the functionality of the response (i.e., leading to the desired outcomes). The goal is to have children act on the environment to produce outcomes they desire. Consequently, the focus of the entire intervention enterprise is turned from adults directing activities to adults observing child initiations and daily activities and using them as primary, but not exclusive, training strategies.

It is important to note that the use of child initiations or daily routines are not the only training options. On the contrary, it is essential that the adult not relinquish control entirely to the child. Following children's leads and appreciating their motivations does not negate the use of adult-directed strategies nor does it preclude the interventionist's redirecting or modifying a child initiation. The effective interventionist is able to use a variety of strategies calibrated to the child's response, setting, and goals.

Intervention Should Focus on Targeted Skills and Information

The second underlying assumption is the need to focus on targeted information and skills. Effective intervention is not a laissez-faire arrangement in which children are permitted to engage in any action or activity without direction; rather, the adult role is to capitalize on children's behaviors and environmental events by using them as opportunities to help children learn targeted goals and objectives. To use child initiations, daily routines, and play as training vehicles requires two caveats: first, the adult must be familiar with and knowledgeable about children's goals and objectives; and, second, the goals must be appropriate, functional, and timely for the child. This second caveat requires the use of assessment/evaluation tools that produce information that permits the targeting of appropriate and functional goals (Bernheimer & Keogh, 1995; Bricker, 1993).

Learning Requires Multiple Opportunities to Practice Across Changing Conditions

The third assumption underlying the goal for EI/ECSE is that children have multiple opportunities to practice and use new skills and information across a range of conditions and settings. Preferably, these conditions and events closely parallel those in which the skill and information can be meaningfully and legitimately used. One of the strongest recommendations for using child initiations, daily activities, and play is that use of these events significantly expands the potential number of times children will have to practice targeted skills. Data on the amount of time teachers engage in instructional activities are troubling in that their engagement is often found to be minimal (Bricker & Pretti-Frontczak, 1997; Fleming, Wolery, Weinzierl, Venn, & Schroeder, 1991; Pretti-Frontczak, 1996; Schwartz, Carta, & Grant, 1996). It appears, therefore, that for many children with developmental, learning, or adjustment disabilities, the time spent or opportunities presented to learn or to practice a new skill are limited. This reality may help explain the lack of child progress often seen on developmental measures. In addition to opportunities for practicing targeted skills is the need for children to be able to practice across a range of conditions and settings. As we have stated previously in this chapter, events do not replicate exactly, and, therefore, children must learn how to adapt or modify either a little or a lot to changing conditions (Stokes & Baer, 1977). One must be able to open doors that are small, that are large, that stick, that are heavy, or that are light; when it is raining or the wind is blowing; and while talking or carrying something in one's arm. Such commonplace realities mitigate strongly against teaching children highly predictable routines conducted under static conditions if, indeed, the goal is to help children acquire generalized repertoires that assist them in adapting to changing environmental conditions.

WHAT'S IN A NAME?

We began this chapter with an analysis of naturalistic teaching approaches and found that although there is some basic agreement about what constitutes such approaches, important differences exist. This has led to the following conclusion: Except for the need for general classification rubrics (Hobbs, 1975), the use of vague and poorly operationalized terms such as *naturalistic* may serve as a hindrance. An alternative is to define and operationalize the critical features that contribute to recommended practices in EI/ECSE. Interventionists can then use a particular approach that will have benchmarks or parameters for determining the fidelity of treatment (i.e., how closely the practice meets the stated criteria).

We recommend that EI/ECSE teams give serious consideration to including the following five recommended practice features in their intervention efforts:

- Providing multiple practice opportunities
- Encouraging child initiations
- Varying training conditions
- Targeting functional responses
- Using logical consequences

Under most circumstances, it will not be if these features are present or absent but rather how fully and how frequently the recommended practice features are employed. Although the fidelity should be apparent, the frequency of use of the features needs to be adjusted to each child, goal, setting, and other relevant conditions. For example, there may be times when it is important to observe children and follow their leads, but there are also times when the interventionist should exert control or redirect children when their responses appear to be nonproductive.

Providing multiple practice opportunities is the first recommended practice feature and emphasizes the need to provide children multiple opportunities to practice targeted goals and objectives. The importance of providing children many opportunities throughout their day to practice (i.e., acquire and generalize) verbal, problem-solving, and motor skills that will expand their behavioral repertoires is discussed previously. However, it appears neither sensible nor advisable to attempt to specify a general rule for the frequency of practice. This recommended practice feature is dependent on the child and his or her goals and settings as well as on an appreciation for other recommended practice features. For example, multiple opportunities to practice may be of little use if they all are teacher directed, occur under the same conditions, involve nonfunctional responses, or involve the use of artificial consequences. Practice of inappropriate targets may do little to enhance and expand children's repertoires in desired directions. This reality highlights the interactive nature of the five recommended practice features.

The second feature, *encouraging child initiations,* captures the importance of children's motivation for fueling and directing their learning. An interventionist's success in responding to and subtly redirecting child initiations is likely critical to the efficiency with which children acquire targeted goals and objectives. Child initiations refer to those responses that appear to emanate from the child without any direct request or prompting—although environmental events may serve to trigger these initiations. Through observation of children's behaviors, adults may find numerous child initiations that should be encouraged or that can be shaped into desired directions. For example, if a child initiates play with toy vehicles that he pushes on the floor, then the adult can encourage labeling of targeted objects (e.g., car, floor, road) and practicing targeted words (e.g., stop, go) and/or sounds or motor skills (e.g., eye–hand coordination by placing a box in front of the vehicle as a garage). Child initiations that produce unwanted outcomes (e.g., hurting other children) or that appear unproductive (e.g., sitting for extended periods of time, picking at one's fingers) should not be encouraged, nor is it desirable for children to constantly be the initiators. Learning to respond appropriately is as important as the initiation of behavior. As with the recommended practice feature of providing multiple practice opportunities, the frequency of encouraging and responding to child initiations is dependent on the child, goal, setting, and other recommended practice features.

The third feature, *varying training conditions,* provides an important qualifier to the recommended practices of encouraging child initiations and providing multiple practice opportunities when teaching both acquisition of new responses and generalization of responses. Multiple opportunities provided under conditions that are relatively constant likely will not produce a response that children can use in a flexible and functional way. If practice is tied to a specific set of eliciting conditions, then children may not be able to generalize the response to other appropriate settings and events. In fact, as indicated previously, this lack of generalization led in large part to developing "loose" intervention techniques (Stokes & Baer, 1977). Recommended practice dictates that, whenever possible, training should occur under a variety of conditions as long as it is appropriate and functional for the targeted response.

The dichotomy between training and nontraining environments suggested by some writers (Hart, 1985) is not a useful distinction; rather, we see the child's day-to-day environment as isomorphic with his or her training environment as useful and appropriate events and circumstances arise or are planned. Use of routines, child initiations, and planned activities provides a variety of training conditions that assist children in acquiring responses that are functional across a range of changing conditions. It is also important to note that circumstances will arise for some children and some goals for which training across a variety of conditions is not effective. For example, children with severe behavior problems may need from time to time training that is conducted under relatively stable conditions, and children with significant developmental delays may need repeated practice of a skill under unchanging conditions. Training introduced across daily living activities is not at odds with repeated practice under set conditions; rather, dispersed and repeated training opportunities represent anchoring points on a continuum. In general, the choice should be to intervene using varied conditions because generalization is enhanced; however, times occur when the better choice is repeated practice under relatively unchanging conditions. As with other recommended practice features, the adult's appropriate use of varied conditions is dependent on the child, the goal, and other relevant conditions associated with the training environment.

Pivotal to the recommended practice features described previously is *targeting functional responses* for children. The previous recommended practice features yield little benefit if the targets of choice are nonfunctional for children because they require learning skills too advanced; they target responses that the child consistently uses appropriately; or the response does not enhance the child's communication, problem solving, and adjustment to environmental demands. Observations of many infant and preschool intervention programs indicate that children spend considerable time working on learning nonfunctional skills (e.g., putting pegs in boards, stacking "donuts" on rings, pasting objects on paper). Although many of these activities may be fun for children, those who have or who are at risk for disabilities must acquire skills that keep their developmental levels as close as possible to that of typically developing children. Interventionists and caregivers should be committed to targeting goals and objectives that are fun for children but that also ensure the development of skills that allow children who have or who are at risk for disabilities to be included in programs with typically developing children. This need raises the topic of planned activities.

Experience suggests that using daily routines, play, and child initiations often does not provide an adequate number of training opportunities for children with disabilities to acquire and use their targeted goals and objectives. It is often necessary and desirable to introduce and use a variety of planned activities. As long as planned activities capture the attention of children and maintain their interest, we see nothing "unnatural" about them. Planned activities do not have to be completely adult directed but often only have to be adult introduced and guided. For example, an interventionist may plan a walk that takes a route that will challenge many children's motor skills and social interaction skills. During the walk, children may initiate a variety of unplanned activities as well as be able to practice targeted motor and social skills. Planned activities should be specifically designed to offer and promote multiple opportunities for children to engage in targeted skills, and adults should always be alert to variations introduced by children or nonplanned events as useful modification of the planned activity. A critical feature of activity-based intervention is its systematic use of planned activities.

The critical need to select goals and objectives that are functional emphasizes the importance of assessment and evaluation. The selection of IEP/IFSP goals and objectives that are developmentally accurate (i.e., not too advanced or not too simple), that are chronologically age appropriate, and that target skills or information that improve the child's ability to meet environmental demands (i.e., functional) is essential. The development of IEP/IFSP goals that meet these criteria is dependent on conducting an evaluation of the child's repertoire with a measurement tool that is comprehensive, provides developmental hierarchies that permit the selection of developmentally appropriate goals, and yields outcomes that can be directly used to select targets that are educationally/therapeutically relevant. Without the use of curriculum-based assessment tools, IEP/IFSP goals and objectives for children are likely to be ambiguous, nonfunctional, and fragmented (Bricker & Pretti-Frontczak, 1997; Cripe, 1990; Notari & Bricker, 1990; Notari & Drinkwater, 1991). Targeting functional responses is critical to recommended practices in EI/ECSE. Critical to the selection of functional responses is the use of measurement tools that produce such information.

The fifth recommended practice feature is *using logical consequences*. Using logical consequences means that the consequence, or what follows a child's response, is a part of the action or activity or has some direct connection to the action or activity. This recommended practice feature underlies the importance of targeting functional responses and activities for children. To move from a room with a closed door, the functional response is to open the door. The logical consequence is letting oneself out of the room. The logical consequence of calling mom is that she pays attention to the child. The logical consequence of asking for a toy is that the child receives it. The response for which most people look for when asking a question is that an answer is provided. It is important to note in these examples that the consequences are directly linked to the action, which likely makes them meaningful (i.e., make sense to the child). Providing a child with a star when he or she labels an object or a picture may not be meaningful and may even result in confusion (Mahoney & Weller, 1980).

The use of artificial or nonassociated contingencies or consequences may be the result of asking children to engage repeatedly in actions or activities that do not interest or motivate them. Maintaining their participation requires the use of consequences apart from the activity because the activity is not associated with a functional, meaningful, or desirable outcome. Although we recommend keeping these activities to a minimum, especially for young children, Sulzer-Azaroff (1992) correctly pointed out that for some children acquiring educational goals is not naturally reinforcing, regardless of teacher effort. She commented that "if their natural consequences are insufficient or punishing, we have to supplement those consequences with more powerful, positive stimuli" (Sulzer-Azaroff, 1992, p. 82). If logically occurring contingencies fail to produce desired outcomes, it may be necessary to use artificial contingencies; however, artificial contingencies should be faded quickly and used sparingly (Sulzer-Azaroff, 1992). Clearly, the goal is a quick return to the use of logical consequences.

SUMMARY

The purpose of this chapter is to provide an examination of the terms *natural* and *naturalistic* as applied to intervention approaches. Except as a means for loosely grouping approaches under a general rubric, the varying definitions and features associated with these terms create confusion and lead to imprecise and differing notions about what constitutes these approaches. As a solution, we recommend that attention be directed to the identification and operationalization of teaching strategies that reflect state-of-the-art practice.

We offer a set of basic assumptions that we believe underlie recommended practices and have recommended five practice features that emanate from these assumptions. Both the assumptions and recommended practice features described in this chapter are integral to activity-based intervention.

REFERENCES

Atwater, J., Carta, J., Schwartz, I., & McConnell, S. (1994). Blending developmentally appropriate practice and early childhood special education: Redefining best practice to meet the needs of all children. In B. Mallory & R. New (Eds.), *Diversity and developmentally appropriate practices* (pp. 185–201). New York: Teachers College Press.

Barnett, D., Carey, K., & Hall, J. (1993). Naturalistic intervention design for young children: Foundations, rationales, and strategies. *Topics in Early Childhood Special Education, 13*(4), 430–444.

Barnett, D., Lentz, F., Bauer, A., MacMann, G., Stollar, S., & Ehrhardt, K. (1997). Ecological foundations of early intervention: Planned activities and strategic sampling. *Journal of Special Education, 30*(4), 471–490.

Bernheimer, L., & Keogh, B. (1995). An approach to family assessment. *Topics in Early Childhood Special Education, 15*(4), 415–433.

Bricker, D. (Ed.). (1993). *Assessment, evaluation, and programming system for infants and children: Vol. 1. AEPS measurement for birth to three years.* Baltimore: Paul H. Brookes Publishing Co.

Bricker, D., & Carlson, L. (1981). Issues in early language intervention. In R. Schiefelbusch & D. Bricker (Eds.), *Early language: Acquisition and intervention* (pp. 477–515). Baltimore: University Park Press.

Bricker, D., & Pretti-Frontczak, K. (1997, November 21). *Examining treatment validity: A critical and often overlooked construct in evaluating assessment instruments.* Paper presented at the International Conference for the Division of Early Childhood, New Orleans.

Cole, K., Dale, P., & Mills, P. (1991). Individual differences in language delayed children's responses to direct and interactive preschool instruction. *Topics in Early Childhood Special Education, 11*(1), 99–124.

Cole, K., Mills, P., Dale, P., & Jenkins, J. (1996). Preschool language facilitation methods and child characteristics. *Journal of Early Intervention, 20*(2), 113–131.

Cripe, J. (1990). *Evaluating the effectiveness of training procedures in a linked system approach to individual family service plan development.* Unpublished doctoral dissertation, University of Oregon, Eugene.

Drasgow, E., Halle, J., Ostrosky, M., & Harbers, H. (1996). Using behavioral indication and functional communication training to establish an initial sign repertoire with a young child with severe disabilities. *Topics in Early Childhood Special Education, 16*(4), 500–521.

Fleming, L., Wolery, M., Weinzierl, C., Venn, M., & Schroeder, C. (1991). Model for assessing and adapting teachers' roles in mainstreamed preschool settings. *Topics in Early Childhood Special Education, 11*(1), 85–98.

Fox, L., & Hanline, M. (1993). A preliminary evaluation of learning within developmentally appropriate early childhood settings. *Topics in Early Childhood Special Education, 13*(3), 308–327.

Guess, D., Sailor, W., & Baer, D. (1974). To teach language to retarded children. In R. Schiefelbusch & L. Lloyd (Eds.), *Language perspectives: Acquisition, retardation, and intervention* (pp. 529–563). Baltimore: University Park Press.

Halle, J., Alpert, C., & Anderson, S. (1984). Natural environment language assessment and intervention with severely impaired preschoolers. *Topics in Early Childhood Special Education, 4*(2), 36–56.

Hancock, T., & Kaiser, A. (1996). Siblings' use of milieu teaching at home. *Topics in Early Childhood Special Education, 16*(2), 168–190.

Hart, B. (1985). Naturalistic language training techniques. In S. Warren & A. Rogers-Warren (Eds.), *Teaching functional language* (pp. 63–88). Baltimore: University Park Press.

Hart, B., & Risley, T. (1968). Establishing use of descriptive adjectives in the spontaneous speech of disadvantaged preschool children. *Journal of Applied Behavior Analysis, 1,* 109–120.

Hart, B., & Risley, T. (1974). Using preschool materials to modify the language of disadvantaged children. *Journal of Applied Behavior Analysis, 7*(2), 243–256.

Hart, B., & Risley, T. (1980). In vivo language intervention: Unanticipated general effects. *Journal of Applied Behavior Analysis, 13*(3), 407–432.

Hepting, N., & Goldstein, H. (1996). What's "natural" about naturalistic language intervention? *Journal of Early Intervention, 20*(3), 250–264.

Hobbs, N. (1975). *The future of children.* San Francisco: Jossey-Bass.

Kaczmarek, L., Hepting, N., & Dzubak, M. (1996). Examining the generalization of milieu language objectives in situations requiring listener preparatory behaviors. *Topics in Early Childhood Special Education, 16*(2), 139–167.

Kaiser, A., Hester, P., Alpert, C., & Whiteman, C. (1995). Preparing parent trainers: An experimental analysis of effects on trainers, parents, and children. *Topics in Early Childhood Special Education, 15*(4), 385–414.

Kaiser, A.P., Yoder, P.J., & Keetz, A. (1992). Evaluating milieu teaching. In S.F. Warren & J. Reichle (Eds.), *Communication and language intervention series: Vol. 1. Causes and effects in communication and language intervention* (pp. 9–47). Baltimore: Paul H. Brookes Publishing Co.

Koegel, L.K. (1996). Communication and language intervention. In R.L. Koegel & L.K. Koegel (Eds.), *Teaching children with autism: Strategies for initiating positive interactions and im-*

proving learning opportunities (pp. 17–32). Baltimore: Paul H. Brookes Publishing Co.

Mahoney, G., & Weller, E. (1980). An ecological approach to language intervention. In D. Bricker (Ed.), *Language intervention with children* (pp. 17–32). San Francisco: Jossey-Bass.

Noonan, M., & McCormick, L. (1993). *Early intervention in natural environments.* Pacific Grove, CA: Brooks/Cole.

Notari, A., & Bricker, D. (1990). The utility of a curriculum-based assessment instrument in the development of individualized education plans for infants and young children. *Journal of Early Intervention, 14*(2), 117–132.

Notari, A., & Drinkwater, S. (1991). Best practices for writing child outcomes: An evaluation of two methods. *Topics in Early Childhood Special Education, 11*(3), 92–106.

Novick, R. (1993). Activity-based intervention and developmentally appropriate practice: Points of convergence. *Topics in Early Childhood Special Education, 13*(4), 403–417.

Oliver, C., & Halle, J. (1982). Language training in the everyday environment: Teaching functional sign use to a retarded child. *Journal of The Association for the Severely Handicapped, 8,* 50–62.

Pretti-Frontczak, K. (1996). *Examining the efficacy of embedding young children's goals and objectives into daily activities.* Unpublished doctoral dissertation, University of Oregon, Eugene.

Schwartz, I., Carta, J., & Grant, S. (1996). Examining the use of recommended language intervention practices in early childhood special education classrooms. *Topics in Early Childhood Special Education, 16*(2), 251–272.

Sheridan, M., Foley, G., & Radlinkski, S. (1995). *Using the supportive play model: Individualized intervention in early childhood practice.* New York: Teachers College Press.

Stokes, T., & Baer, D. (1977). An implicit technology of generalization. *Journal of Applied Behavioral Analysis, 10,* 349–367.

Sulzer-Azaroff, B. (1992). Is back to nature always best? *Journal of Applied Behavioral Analysis, 25,* 81–82.

Tannock, R., & Girolametto, L. (1992). Reassessing parent-focused language intervention programs. In S.F. Warren & J. Reichle (Eds.), *Communication and language intervention series: Vol. 1. Causes and effects in communication and language intervention* (pp. 49–79). Baltimore: Paul H. Brookes Publishing Co.

Warren, S. (1991). Enhancing communication and language development with milieu teaching procedures. In E. Cipani (Ed.), *A guide for developing language competence in preschool children with severe and moderate handicaps* (pp. 68–93). Springfield, IL: Charles C Thomas.

Warren, S.F., & Horn, E.M. (1996). Generalization issues in providing integrated services. In R.A. McWilliam (Ed.), *Rethinking pull-out services in early intervention: A professional resource* (pp. 121–143). Baltimore: Paul H. Brookes Publishing Co.

Warren, S., & Kaiser, A. (1986). Incidental language teaching: A critical review. *Journal of Speech and Hearing Disorders, 51*(4), 291–299.

Warren, S.F., & Kaiser, A.P. (1988). Research in early language intervention. In S.L. Odom & M.B. Karnes (Eds.), *Early intervention for infants and children with handicaps: An empirical base* (pp. 89–108). Baltimore: Paul H. Brookes Publishing Co.

Watkins, R., & Bunce, B. (1996). Preschool intervention programs. *Topics in Early Childhood Special Education, 16*(22), 191–212.

Wolery, M. (1994). Instructional strategies for teaching young children with special needs. In M. Wolery & J. Wilbers (Eds.), *Including children with special needs in early childhood programs* (pp. 119–140). Washington, DC: National Association for the Education of Young Children.

Wolery, M., & Bredekamp, S. (1994). Developmentally appropriate practice and young children with disabilities: Contextual issues in the discussion. *Journal of Early Intervention, 18*(4), 331–341.

Yoder, P., Kaiser, A., Goldstein, H., Alpert, C., Mousetis, L., Kaczmarek, L., & Fischer, R. (1995). An exploratory comparison of milieu teaching and responsive interaction in classroom applications. *Journal of Early Intervention, 19*(3), 218–242.

Chapter 9

The Historical Basis
of Activity-Based Intervention

Since the initiation of early intervention programs in the late 1960s and early 1970s, significant progress has been made in providing quality services to young children with disabilities. Federal- and state-supported education, mental health, and social services programs have been expanded to include services for infants and young children who have or who are at risk for disabilities (Bricker, 1989; Odom, 1988). In the brief history of early intervention, program approaches, preparation of personnel, approaches to assessment and evaluation, curricular focus, and instructional strategies have changed considerably as a result of clinical experience, consumer feedback, and empirical study. The passage of federal and state legislation during the 1980s has made early intervention a legitimate enterprise that provides services to thousands of families and their infants and young children who have or who are at risk for disabilities (Cutler, 1993; Shonkoff & Meisels, 1990).

Early intervention programs assist in offsetting the potentially negative impact of medical, biological, and environmental conditions associated with developmental disabilities (Brooks-Gunn et al., 1994; Guralnick, 1997; Ramey & Ramey, 1991). Although educational, medical, and social services personnel associated with early intervention programs have reason to be proud of the services delivered to participating children and families, challenges still remain, and further improvement of intervention services is clearly an important goal.

We believe two changes are fundamental to the improvement of services offered in early intervention programs. First, the development of systematic approaches to early intervention that link assessment, intervention, and evaluation processes will improve the effectiveness and efficiency of current intervention services (Bagnato, Neisworth, & Munson, 1997; Bricker, 1989; Hutinger, 1988). Using a linked systems approach enables personnel to accomplish four essential goals:

- To accurately identify appropriate individualized education program/individualized family service plan (IEP/IFSP) goals and objectives for children and families
- To formulate appropriate educational/therapeutic plans of action
- To establish intervention content to reach selected goals and objectives
- To monitor children's/families' progress using timely and appropriate strategies

A second change necessary is the shift away from intervention approaches that direct children through a series of fragmented, nonmeaningful training routines or from approaches that do not provide adequate structure or direction for children. Intervention approaches are being developed that capitalize on the use of children's daily interactions with their social and physical environments as training opportunities. In these approaches, functional goals are selected to enhance children's independence, problem-solving abilities, and adaptability. These approaches respect and incorporate children's motivations and initiations to ensure individualization of instruction and identification of meaningful instructional activities.

EARLY INTERVENTION APPROACHES: A HISTORICAL PERSPECTIVE

Early intervention programs for young children who have or who are at risk for disabilities have emerged as a synthesis of philosophies, curricular approaches, and instructional methodologies of special education, general early childhood education, applied behavior analysis, developmental psychology, and speech-language pathology (Odom, 1988; Warren & Kaiser, 1988). Although this convergence of disciplines has not occurred without debate (Atwater, Carta, Schwartz, & McConnell, 1994; Carta, 1995; Carta, Schwartz, Atwater, & McConnell, 1991; Novick, 1993), there is a clear move toward the development of unified, transdisciplinary intervention approaches, such as activity-based intervention.

Visiting an early intervention classroom in the early 1970s would have been a very different experience from visiting one in the late 1990s. In these initial programs, skills were generally taught in a "didactic" fashion that employed one-to-one, highly structured, adult-directed, massed-trial training approaches. These initial intervention approaches were primarily downward extensions of procedures used with adults in institutional settings and with school-age children in special education classrooms (Bricker & Bricker, 1974a, 1974b). These clinical and educational procedures relied on behavior analysis principles that carefully structure antecedents, specify precise responses, and deliver tangible consequences not associated with the response or activity.

These behavioral techniques were used with young children for at least two reasons. First, many of the investigators who originally worked with older individuals in institutions shifted their attention to children and used techniques previously found to be effective. Second, impressive data were available on the effectiveness of the behavior analytic techniques for changing behavior. Consequently, many of the early intervention programs initiated during the 1970s relied on careful structuring of antecedent events, learning of specific responses, and delivering tangible consequences (Bricker, Bricker, Iacino, & Dennison, 1976; Shearer & Shearer, 1976).

The field of early intervention emerged from clinical work with young children who demonstrated some form of deviant behavior (e.g., Risley & Wolf, 1967) and a few pioneer programs employing behavioral learning principles (Bricker & Bricker, 1971). Since these initial approaches that were largely dependent on behavior analytic procedures, considerable change and growth have occurred. Programs have changed to reflect the influence of different philosophies, areas, and fields. Parent involvement in programs has increased as research findings have demonstrated the importance of their meaningful involvement (Bricker, 1989) and the negative effect of their maladaptive behavior on their young children (Beckwith, 1990; Sameroff, 1993). Concern has shifted from discrete behavioral responses directed by adults to appreciation of the importance of child-initiated play and social communication behavior (Linder, 1993; Ostrosky, Kaiser, & Odom, 1993). Finally, the critical nature of children's socioemotional growth and adjustment has been recognized and is increasingly becoming an intervention target (Cicchetti & Cohen, 1995).

Despite all of the change and expansion, the use of behavioral learning principles has continued to be a hallmark of quality early intervention programs. Although behavioral learning principles are fundamental to sound programming, there have been questions about the manner in which the principles have been applied (Bricker, 1989; Guess & Siegel-Causey, 1985). It is important to note that the principles used to assist children in acquiring and maintaining behaviors are not in question; rather, it is the application of these principles that has stimulated debate. This debate has led, in part, to interventionists' and investigators' developing and adopting behavior analytic approaches that incorporate and encourage child initiations and the use of everyday occurrences as primary intervention activities (Bricker & Waddell, 1996; Cripe, Slentz, & Bricker, 1993; Hancock & Kaiser, 1996; MacDonald, 1989; Rice, 1995). The integration of behavioral learning principles into functional and daily child activities has offered an exciting and significant step forward in enhancing the effectiveness of early intervention programs.

WHAT IS ACTIVITY-BASED INTERVENTION?

Activity-based intervention is an approach that uses behavioral learning principles to encourage child interactions and the participation in meaningful daily activities with the explicit purpose of assisting the child in acquiring targeted functional goals and objectives. The following three scenarios about a nature walk exemplify how activity-based intervention differs from other early intervention approaches.

An Early Childhood Approach

An early childhood approach would have children discuss what they are likely to see prior to taking the nature walk. While on the walk, the children are encouraged to explore, ask questions, and even try some "experiments." The interventionist might point out an anthill and suggest that the children watch the insects' activities. The goals are acquisition of general information, improvement of language and cognitive skills, and the encouragement of exploration and innovation by the children. It is unlikely that any child will have specific objectives to be addressed during the walk or that the interventionist will be working to develop specific response forms in any of the children. Evaluation of the activity would focus on the children's level of enjoyment and the interventionist's sense of accomplishment.

A Traditional Behavior Analytic Approach

In a traditional behavior analytic approach, each child would have a set of specific objectives, and the walk would be used to address the generalization of these skills. Prior to the walk, the children would be engaged in specific training to address these objectives. For example, children with an object-labeling goal would be exposed to specific training sessions in which the interventionist has pictures of trees, leaves, ants, or clouds. These pictures would be presented to the children repeatedly until they could readily name the picture. On the walk, the interventionist would locate examples of items and ask the children to name the objects. The number of correct and incorrect responses would be noted and later transferred to a graph to monitor child progress over time.

An Activity-Based Intervention Approach

Using an activity-based intervention approach also requires that children have goals and objectives, but the goals are written as general functional response classes rather than as specific responses. For example, an object-labeling goal might be stated as *uses words, phrases, or sentences to describe objects, people, or events,* as opposed to a more specific goal that might be stated as *child will label the object leaf, tree, bug, and path.* Prior to the walk, items that might be encountered on the excursion would be placed around the classroom. As the children use or encounter these items, the interventionist would encourage child-initiated actions such as counting the leaves, placing them on trees, naming them, or crumpling them. Once on the walk, the interventionist might encourage the children to find leaves to develop opportunities to practice targeted objectives. For example, if one child picks up a leaf, then the interventionist might draw attention to this as an opportunity to "talk" about leaves (e.g., color, texture). On returning to the classroom, the interventionist would present examples of items encountered on the walk and record the children's abilities to correctly label these items. These data would be used to systematically monitor child progress toward desired goals.

In many ways, the activity-based approach is a combination of selected strategies found in early childhood and behavior analytic approaches. Following children's leads and interests is taken from an early childhood approach, and the need for targeting objectives and monitoring child progress is adopted from the behavior analytic approach.

THE EVOLUTION OF ACTIVITY-BASED INTERVENTION

As indicated previously, activity-based intervention combines elements from a number of different perspectives. Understanding the origin of these perspectives and how they have been blended into a unified intervention approach may deepen the reader's appreciation for the foundations that underlie this approach.

We believe two lines of work are primarily responsible for spawning the activity-based intervention approach. This work includes the philosophical and practical information generated by the early childhood education field and the information generated by behavior analysts working with individuals with disabilities. Important events and people in each of these areas are highlighted in the following sections.

Early Childhood Education

Perhaps the most important catalyst for the development of early education programs was poverty. Educational leaders living in a variety of countries in the late 1800s to early 1900s saw the need to develop programs to protect young children from catastrophic effects of serious and long-term poverty (Maxim, 1980). Unfortunately, this problem has never been solved and remains a concern in the world today.

Of these early workers, Maria Montessori stands out in her concern for the health and intellectual stimulation of young children with mental retardation who were living in poverty in Rome. She developed an educational approach to assist these children in better meeting the demands of future educational environments. Montessori's approach focused on the use of activity centers that contained didactic materials specifically designed to teach children a variety of basic concepts. One aspect of the Montessori approach with particular relevance to this discussion is the insistence on the correct way materials should be handled and used. Each material is designed for a specific purpose and is to be used only for that purpose. This highly organized approach requires that children follow the dictates of the teacher and the materials.

The Montessori method became popular in the United States in the early 1900s (Maxim, 1980) and joined a larger movement to develop nursery school and child care programs to assist children living in conditions of extreme poverty (Lazerson, 1972). These programs developed slowly until the Great Depression. During this period, the federal government, with the assistance of the Work Projects Administration, provided money to develop nursery school programs in order to create jobs for unemployed teachers. Child care programs received a second opportunity for growth during World War II when women were required to enter the work force in large numbers. Again, federal support was provided for the development of child care programs. However, since the late 1940s, federal support for child care programs has been limited. This lack of support likely reflects the ambivalence of our society toward its children (Schorr & Schorr, 1989).

As nursery school and child care programs have evolved, many changes and disagreements about instructional approaches have ensued. Early programs tended to focus on children's physical and emotional needs. It may be fair to characterize nursery schools from 1920 to 1960 as helping children learn social skills and develop creativity while deemphasizing academic goals. However, early leaders such as Montessori established programs that also included intellectual stimulation in young children. Beginning in the 1960s, nursery school programs once again included preacademic activities.

In the early 1960s, the War on Poverty was initiated and with it came the advent of Head Start. Although often viewed as an educational program for children living in poverty, the goals of Head Start are much broader and include the enhancement of children's health and physical abilities, emotional and social development, and conceptual and verbal skills (Bricker, 1989). Head Start programs operate using a variety of intervention models and approaches. These approaches cover a continuum from those that are structured and emphasize academic skills to those that are experiential and emphasize socioemotional development.

During the 1970s and 1980s, early childhood programs, kindergarten programs, and child care programs adopted a variety of approaches that ranged from structured with activities that were primarily adult directed to nonstructured with activities chosen largely by children. Experts have continued to this day to debate the merits of the various approaches.

Beginning in the late 1980s and continuing through the early 1990s, early intervention/early childhood special education (EI/ECSE) programs have been increasingly affected by experientially based approaches advocated by many early childhood educators. Appreciation for children's motivation to explore, initiate, play, and learn has become fundamental to a number of approaches such as activity-based intervention that have been specifically developed for groups of children who have or who are at risk for disabilities.

Education of People with Disabilities

A widely recognized attempt to formally educate a young person with severe disabilities was conducted in the 1800s by Itard, a French physician. The focus of this study was Victor, a boy approximately 11 years of age who was found wandering in a wooded area near Paris. Victor's behavior was described as extremely primitive and unsocialized. Observations of the boy led authorities to declare him a "hopeless idiot" who could not be helped by education or training (Ball, 1971). Itard disagreed with this conclusion and undertook the task of educating Victor. The most interesting aspect of Itard's work for the purposes of this book is the carefully designed and implemented intervention program. This program began with sensory training and culminated in helping Victor understand symbol systems (Ball, 1971). Important to note is that much of the training devised by Itard was embedded in activities that occurred routinely for Victor and that were made meaningful for the boy.

Subsequently, Seguin, another French physician and student of Itard, elaborated on his mentor's work and applied his outcomes to individuals with more severe disabilities than those of Victor. Seguin translated Itard's educational philosophy into an explicit developmental program beginning at the most primitive levels of training and extending to responsible functioning in society (Ball, 1971).

Ball (1971) made some interesting comparisons between Seguin's approach and more contemporary approaches used for people with intellectual disabilities. For example,

- "To a much greater extent than most contemporary therapists, he [Seguin] used the natural consequences of actions to teach appropriate behavior" (p. 50).
- "Seguin's philosophy of development emphasized spontaneity and curiosity as the touchstones of optimal growth" (p. 51).
- "(Seguin) warned against using immediate command incessantly or repetitiously" (p. 64).

The development of the activity-based intervention approach has been greatly influenced by the early work of individuals such as Itard and Seguin, who clearly saw the value of making educational interventions relevant and functional. Considerable time has elapsed, however, between Seguin's approach and the development of activity-based intervention. In the mid-1800s, institutions were developed for people with disabilities, including people with intellectual disabilities, motor impairments, sensory impairments, and mental illness. Initially, these institutions were developed to help the "deviant" individual become "nondeviant." Only those people who were considered able to improve were sent to institutions (Wolfensberger, 1969).

> It thus appears that only some (people with mental retardation) were seen to be proper candidates for institutional education, and this education was to consist mostly of the transformation of poorly socialized, perhaps speechless, and uncontrolled children into children who could stand and walk normally, have some speech, eat in an orderly manner, and engage in some kind of meaningful work. (Wolfensberger, 1969, p. 91)

It was not until the late 1800s that the purpose of large residential institutions was shifted for use as permanent repositories for people considered to be "objectionable and unsavory" (e.g., people with mental retardation). Institutions ceased to provide treatment or educational programs and primarily offered custodial care (MacMillan, 1977; Wolfensberger, 1969). The word *school* was dropped from titles of institutions, and the words *asylum* or *hospital* were substituted (Wolfensberger, 1969). In addition, no need was seen for the development of alternative community-based programs, as people with mental retardation were seen as "noncurable menaces" from which society should be protected.

Beginning in the 1950s, institutions once again began to change. The motivation for change came from parent groups (e.g., the National Association for Retarded Children, now The Arc), legal action (e.g., *Wyatt v. Stickney,* 1972), and an evolving perspective about the constancy of the intelligence quotient and the influence of the environment on behavior (Gallagher & Ramey, 1987). Appreciation for environmental influence provided in large measure the conceptual base for many professionals to advocate for the development of intervention programs to offset or eradicate learning problems seen in people with disabilities. Adding to the conceptual base underlying intervention was an accumulating empirical base that demonstrated that even people with the most severe disabilities are able to learn (Ault, Wolery, Doyle, & Gast, 1989).

In the late 1950s to early 1960s, students and interpreters of B.F. Skinner began to apply the principles of the experimental analysis of behavior to people with intellectual disabilities and mental illness (Ayllon & Michael, 1959). Some of the early work was conducted with adults thought to be unteachable and uncontrollable. Using the principles of arranging antecedents, defining responses, and providing immediate feedback, investigators were able to demonstrate their ability to teach individuals with severe disabilities to perform a variety of functional behaviors, such as dressing and feeding (Staats, 1964).

Using these same principles, Bijou, Baer, and their colleagues, among others, began working with children (Baer, 1962). This work tended to focus on eliminating certain behaviors using structured training procedures that emphasized establishing easy-to-discriminate cues (e.g., verbal cue, "Do this," followed by an adult-modeled response to be imitated by the child) and often relying on artificial consequences or feedback (e.g., small drink of juice for correct imitation).

In addition, the training or educational intervention was conducted by "teachers" in settings and under conditions that were different from the children's meaningful daily activities. For example, instruction would occur in areas away from the child's usual environment, and instructional tasks would focus on discrete skills taken out of context, such as repeatedly asking children to stand up and sit down in a chair.

The direct translation of specific, overt cues and artificial contingencies (e.g., giving a child a drink of juice for naming a picture) to community-based programs was in some ways unfortunate (Bricker & Bricker, 1974a). Although these principles were repeatedly shown to be effective in teaching responses, often inadequate attention was given to the usefulness of responses and their generalization to nontraining environments (Hart & Rogers-Warren, 1978). Rather than using the principles in ways that were consistent with program goals (e.g., assisting young children in developing functional skills), the principles of arranging antecedents, defining responses, and delivering consequences became highly controlled so that curricular presentation in programs resembled teaching machine formats. Little concern was given to the continuity and meaningfulness—to use John Dewey's words—of intervention activities. Rather, children were exposed to a series of activities that may have been unrelated to each other or to the children's experiential base (Dyer & Peck, 1987). Often, reinforcement was offered in the form of a contingency that had little, if anything, to do with the desired response or activity (e.g., dispensing stars or tokens). Although the regimented use of these principles may be appropriate for some training targets, their large-scale application seems ill advised. It should be emphasized that the principles are not the issue but rather the way in which they are used (Bricker, 1989)—that is, the establishment of appropriate learning conditions, the defining of target responses, and the timely delivery of appropriate consequences remains essential to sound educational practice. However, the application of these principles should be contextually based to ensure meaningfulness to children.

Long before the development of the behavior analytic approach, the first special classes for children with disabilities were begun. Although these classes were started in the late 1800s, they did not become widely available for children until the 1950s (MacMillan, 1977). From the 1950s to 1975, there was an "explosion" of services for individuals with disabilities that were created by state and federal legislation and appropriations (Kirk & Gallagher, 1979). As these special education classes have become ingrained in public education, there has been a gradual shift toward offering classes to younger children, older youth, and children with more severe disabilities. As MacMillan (1977) noted, the curriculum and approach varies so much in special education classrooms and programs that it is difficult to summarize what content is covered and how it is approached. It may be because of this variability, among other reasons, that the approaches used for school-age children in special education appear to have had little effect on preschool programs for young children with disabilities.

CONTEMPORARY INTERVENTION APPROACHES

Beginning in the 1970s, investigative work focusing on the development of early sensorimotor, social, and social-communicative behaviors of young children served as a major impetus for changing intervention approaches for young children with disabilities (Bricker & Carlson, 1981). This work was inspired by cognitive theorists such as Piaget (1970), psycholinguists (Brown, 1973), and developmental psychologists (Schaffer, 1977).

From this early theoretical and investigative work, three major themes emerged. First, before learning symbolic systems (e.g., language), children must attain certain cognitive and social-communicative skills (Bruner, 1977). Second, communicative development begins at birth and strongly influences, and is influenced by, the social environment (Goldberg, 1977).

Third, infants' and young children's early communication is composed of functional and useful responses (Greenfield & Smith, 1976).

A number of investigators developing language intervention procedures for young children with disabilities attempted to integrate these themes into their programs. In particular, work by the Brickers reflected the shift in attention to early sensorimotor processes and making training procedures more appropriate to young children's developmental levels and interests (Bricker & Bricker, 1974a; Bricker & Carlson, 1981). Mahoney argued for approaches that recognize the importance of early communicative functions as well as the need to make intervention efforts fit into children's daily environmental interactions (Mahoney & Weller, 1980). MacDonald and his colleagues also developed an approach to language intervention that emphasized the importance of children's interactions with significant others in their environment (MacDonald & Horstmeier, 1978).

During the 1970s, investigators working in the behavior analytic tradition also began to explore the use of less-structured intervention strategies. Of particular importance was the work of a group of researchers at the University of Kansas, which focused on incidental and milieu language teaching. Hart and Risley defined *incidental teaching* as "the interaction between an adult and a *single* child, which arises naturally in an unstructured situation" (1975, p. 411, emphasis added). Hart and Risley emphasized that the incidental teaching situation is child selected and child initiated, with the adult responding to the child's request through a series of graded prompts. Prompts can range from no cues to employing a full range of cues.

A milieu approach to teaching language incorporates many of the features of incidental teaching but is broader in focus in order to serve "as a bridge between the training setting and the natural talking environment" (Hart & Rogers-Warren, 1978, p. 199). The milieu model requires teachers to 1) arrange the environment to promote a child's use of language, 2) assess a child's level of functioning, and 3) find ways for a child to interact with the environment. A primary way to encourage this interaction is through environmental arrangements (Hart, 1985).

By the 1980s, a number of investigators were developing training techniques focused on teaching functional language or communication skills as opposed to more didactic or academic approaches (e.g., labeling pictures out of context, being drilled on syntactic structures). These approaches, whether narrow or broad based, focused on the importance of training functional communication skills in environments that provided children with the necessary motivation for communication to occur (Oliver & Halle, 1982).

MacDonald (1985, 1989) expanded his approach into a comprehensive system that emphasizes more strongly the interactive nature of communicative development and competence. Duchan and her colleagues described an approach called *nurturant-naturalistic,* which moves away from didactic teaching routines to "nurturant interactions in which the child takes the interactive lead and to naturalistic contexts which the child is likely to encounter in everyday life" (Duchan & Weitzner-Lin, 1987, p. 49). Snyder-McLean posed an intervention strategy that relied on structuring joint action routines that are designed to assist children with language impairments in improving their functional communication skills (Snyder-McLean, Solomonson, McLean, & Sack, 1984).

Mahoney and Powell (1988) developed a Transactional Intervention Program that focuses on the quality of the interactive behavioral match between children and their primary caregivers. Successful matching requires that caregivers have three skills: 1) an understanding of their child's developmental level, 2) sensitivity to the child's interests and communicative intentions, and 3) responsiveness to the child's activities (Mahoney & Powell, 1984). In the area of autism, the Koegels and their colleagues have devised an approach that they call *natural language teaching* (Koegel & Johnson, 1989; Koegel & Koegel, 1995). This approach includes 1) capitalizing on opportunities to respond to natural reinforcers, 2) reinforcing verbal attempts to respond to tasks, 3) varying tasks, and 4) taking turns and sharing control over activities.

Since the introduction of natural language teaching, interest in incidental teaching and milieu language teaching has grown. Warren and Kaiser (1986) broadened the initial descriptions of incidental teaching to include the following elements: arranging the environment to encourage child initiations, selecting targets appropriate for children's developmental levels, asking children for elaboration, and reinforcing children's communicative attempts.

Likewise, studies of milieu language training have been broadened to examine its effectiveness with parents (Alpert & Kaiser, 1992) and siblings (Hancock & Kaiser, 1996). Warren and Bambara (1989) expanded the rubric of milieu language intervention to include several "naturalistic" training procedures.

Kaiser, Hendrickson, and Alpert (1991) and Kaiser, Yoder, and Keetz (1992) presented an extensive discussion of milieu language training and its effectiveness. Their description of milieu training delineates a number of features that the activity-based intervention approach encompasses. These features include combining developmental theory and behavior analytic learning principles, emphasizing child initiations, promoting adult contingent responding using functional reinforcers, focusing on the development of generalized responses by employing a variety of eliciting conditions and antecedents, and conducting intervention in children's everyday environments (Kaiser et al., 1991). Activity-based intervention shares these features with milieu training (and other naturalistic approaches as well); however, differences do exist. These differences include the following:

1. The focus of the activity-based intervention may be directed toward a group of children or an individual child. Individual children's objectives are recognized and coordinated within activities.

2. The activity-based intervention approach goes beyond communication and language. This comprehensive approach addresses all major curricular areas (e.g., social, adaptive, motor, cognitive, social-communication).

The National Association for the Education of Young Children (NAEYC) published a position statement in 1987 on developmentally appropriate practice (DAP) (Bredekamp, 1987). Although the NAEYC monograph has been revised (Bredekamp & Copple, 1997), the purpose has remained, in part, to counter the trend toward increased formal academic instruction for young children. To offset this trend, the 1997 NAEYC monograph offers 12 principles for guiding DAP. These principles reflect general recommended practice principles; however, Carta et al. (1991) suggested these principles may be too broad or not sufficient to ensure the delivery of effective intervention to young children with disabilities. The debate concerning the applicability of DAP for children with disabilities appears to have begun, in part, because of the increasing placement of children with disabilities into community-based programs (Wolery & Bredekamp, 1994). This change has produced a growing need for the application of DAP principles or for their sensible modification with young children with disabilities (Carta, 1994; Johnson & Johnson, 1994; Odom, 1994).

Activity-based intervention shares many theoretical and philosophical underpinnings with NAEYC's DAP principles (Novick, 1993). Both approaches cite the work of Dewey,

Piaget, and Vygotsky as the basis for designing processes and content that match the child's current developmental level. Both approaches maintain that child-initiated, child-directed play activities are preferable to adult-directed, highly structured activities. Activity-based intervention and DAP emphasize comprehensive curricula for children's development across the motor, language, social, and cognitive domains through integrated learning activities. The importance of teachers' and/or interventionists' observations of children at play to determine interests and activities is emphasized in both approaches. Neither approach advocates the use of extrinsic rewards; instead, each suggests that children learn through intrinsic rewards provided by the environment. Both approaches emphasize the role of the teacher/interventionist in using the activity to ensure that active exploration and interaction occur. Activity-based intervention and DAP describe the importance of varying activities and materials and increasing the complexity of these as children progress. The role of the teacher/interventionist is described by both approaches as a facilitator of engagement and a provider of opportunities for learning. The importance of the family, their input to activities, and their participation in decision making is described in both approaches. In addition, activity-based intervention and DAP both respect the cultures of involved children and families.

The broad similarities between DAP and activity-based intervention are important and suggest a basic congruence and compatibility between the two approaches; however, two critical differences exist. First, activity-based intervention, by definition, targets specific goals and objectives for children and embeds these targets within a variety of activities that occur throughout the child's day. Furthermore, activity-based intervention emphasizes the targeting of functional and generative goals and objectives. DAP, in contrast, targets global goals (e.g., *improve language skills*) that are applicable across a broad range of children; rarely are goals individualized for specific children. Second, in activity-based intervention, goals and objectives for individual children are identified through comprehensive and systematic assessments that are updated consistently to monitor progress. Activity-based intervention places considerable emphasis on the fundamental need for accurate and complete assessment and evaluation of children in order to ensure that selected goals and objectives are developmentally and environmentally appropriate. Although Bredekamp and Copple (1997) suggested that assessment is essential, only general assessment guidelines are offered. DAP does not require the administration of assessment/evaluation tools to select intervention goals or to monitor child progress.

Although DAP and activity-based intervention differ, the DAP guidelines can be viewed as complementary with activity-based intervention. DAP principles provide a general base for EI/ECSE recommended practices that also are conceptually and practically compatible with the activity-based intervention approach. Superimposed on this base are the more specific practices of activity-based intervention that address and link goal selection and assessment/evaluation.

RATIONALE FOR AN ACTIVITY-BASED INTERVENTION APPROACH

"Sound educational experience involves, above all, continuity and interaction between the learner and what is learned" (Hall-Quest, 1976). We know, without doubt, that the transactions between children and their social and physical environments produce change. In large measure, much of what children learn and the way they exhibit that knowledge is a social process (Vygotsky, 1978). For example, children learn to talk by initiating and responding to communications from other children and adults. Feedback from others and imitation of what children see and hear gradually shape their early communicative attempts into more complex and culturally appropriate responses.

The nature of the transactional experiences that occur between children and their environment is fundamental to what they learn and how well they learn it. As Dewey (1959) argued, education should be a continual restructuring of children's experiences if it is to be maximally useful to their learning and development. To create nonauthentic activities (i.e., those that lack meaning for children) as vehicles for learning is counter to Dewey's notions of how children learn to become thinking, productive adults. Other writers appear to share Dewey's perspective but speak of focusing on teaching children through functional activities. Functional approaches have been popular with interventionists who work with young children and who work with children with severe disabilities (Carr & Durand, 1985; Koegel & Koegel, 1997).

Not only should experiences or activities be functional and reflective of children's realities, but they should also be developmentally appropriate. That is, children should have the necessary behaviors in their repertoire to participate meaningfully in an activity. Daily experiences or activities (e.g., dressing, eating, problem solving) often meet these criteria and provide children with the opportunity to interact using functional behaviors. Planned experiences such as a walk or an art project should also be developmentally appropriate (i.e., match a child's developmental level of functioning).

It is important to emphasize that the term *developmentally appropriate* does not mean that children are asked to engage in activities that require no change or modification of their repertoires. Instead, experiences and activities should be framed to present children with moderate novelty. By introducing moderate change, children will need to expand the range and quality of their responses. Increasing environmental demands upsets the child's internal equilibrium and requires adaptation in behavior to return to a state of relative balance (Piaget, 1967). The gradual increase in environmental demands for more independence and problem solving results in richer and more sophisticated repertoires in order to meet those demands. Furthermore, *developmentally appropriate* does not mean that we are advocating for the use of age-*in*appropriate activities and materials; for example, 4-year-old children should not be given rattles for sensorimotor play. Rather, materials that are appropriate for preschoolers should be used.

The nature of experiences provided to children is fundamental to their learning. An activity-based intervention approach reflects this position by using child-initiated, routine, and planned activities that 1) emphasize environmental transactions, 2) are meaningful and functional, 3) are developmentally appropriate, and 4) are designed to produce change in repertoires.

To use child-initiated or routine activities or to design planned activities that meet the four elements listed above requires a sound and comprehensive infrastructure to guide early intervention personnel using this approach. Personnel must know children's goals and objectives, and they must know how to arrange activities to provide children with the opportunity to practice targeted skills. Sound planning and execution are necessary to successfully implement an activity-based approach. Interventionists cannot expect change to occur by simply permitting children to engage in a variety of activities that have no direction or underlying structure. Nor can personnel expect change in children's behaviors by requiring them to engage in actions or activities that have little meaning or have failed to capture the children's interest (e.g., requiring children to practice cutting out shapes for one purpose, requiring children to engage in cutting when their attention is on other events).

The nature of the learning environment is also critical to successful implementation of an activity-based approach. Whenever possible, intervention should be integrated into the daily activities of children's lives. The use of planned activities should also occur as extensions of what children like to do and not as separate, fragmented training experiences apart from their daily needs and understandings. Using daily and play activities assists greatly in helping children develop useful and generalizable responses. Stokes and Osnes (1988) identified three principles for efficient generalization: 1) take advantage of natural communities of reinforcement, 2) train diversely, and 3) incorporate functional mediators. By conducting training using daily activities, these three principles are an integral part of activity-based intervention.

SUMMARY

The purpose of this chapter has been to describe the historical underpinning of activity-based intervention. Understanding the roots of the approach and their evolution and interactions over time will ideally assist the reader in better understanding the approach. It should be clear that activity-based intervention is a synthesis of traditions and perspectives. Although these traditions have made contributions to the education of young children, they clearly have fallen short for those who have learning problems or other disabilities. Our initial efforts to educate young children with disabilities were too invasive and too structured. As we have observed young children and learned from those observations, the field has moved steadily toward developing and adopting strategies and content that capitalize on children's motivations and daily activities. The activity-based intervention approach has organized our past learning into a cohesive system designed to produce optimal growth in young children with developmental problems.

REFERENCES

Alpert, C., & Kaiser, A. (1992). Training parents as milieu language teachers. *Journal of Early Intervention, 16*(1), 31–52.
Atwater, J., Carta, J., Schwartz, I., & McConnell, S. (1994). Blending developmentally appropriate practice and early childhood special education: Redefining best practice to meet the needs of all children. In B. Mallory & R. New (Eds.), *Diver-*

sity and developmentally appropriate practices (pp. 185–201). New York: Teachers College Press.

Ault, M., Wolery, M., Doyle, P., & Gast, D. (1989). Review of comparative studies in the instruction of students with moderate to severe handicaps. *Exceptional Children, 55*(4), 346–356.

Ayllon, T., & Michael, J. (1959). The psychiatric nurse as a behavioral engineer. *Journal of the Experimental Analysis of Behavior, 2,* 323–334.

Baer, D. (1962). Laboratory control of thumbsucking by withdrawal and representation of reinforcement. *Journal of the Experimental Analysis of Behavior, 5,* 525–528.

Bagnato, S., Neisworth, J., & Munson, L. (1997). *LINKing assessment and early intervention: An authentic curriculum-based approach.* Baltimore: Paul H. Brookes Publishing Co.

Ball, T. (1971). *Itard, Seguin, and Kephart: Sensory education: A learning interpretation.* Columbus, OH: Charles E. Merrill.

Beckwith, L. (1990). Adaptive and maladaptive parenting: Implications for intervention. In S. Meisels & J. Shonkoff (Eds.), *Handbook of early childhood intervention* (pp. 53–77). New York: Cambridge University Press.

Bredekamp, S. (Ed.). (1987). *Developmentally appropriate practice in early childhood programs serving children from birth through age 8.* Washington, DC: National Association for the Education of Young Children.

Bredekamp, S., & Copple, C. (Eds.). (1997). *Developmentally appropriate practice in early childhood programs.* Washington, DC: National Association for the Education of Young Children.

Bricker, D. (1989). *Early intervention for at-risk and handicapped infants, toddlers and preschool children.* Palo Alto, CA: VORT Corp.

Bricker, D., & Bricker, W. (1971). *Toddler research and intervention project report: Year 1 (IMRID Behavioral Science Monograph No. 20).* Nashville, TN: George Peabody College, Institute on Mental Retardation and Intellectual Development.

Bricker, D., Bricker, W., Iacino, R., & Dennison, L. (1976). Intervention strategies for the severely and profoundly handicapped child. In N. Haring & L. Brown (Eds.), *Teaching the severely handicapped* (pp. 277–299). New York: Grune & Stratton.

Bricker, D., & Carlson, L. (1981). Issues in early language intervention. In R. Schiefelbusch & D. Bricker (Eds.), *Early language: Acquisition and intervention* (pp. 477–515). Baltimore: University Park Press.

Bricker, D., & Waddell, M. (Eds.). (1996). *Assessment, evaluation, and programming system for infants and children: Vol. 4. AEPS cur-*

riculum for three to six years. Baltimore: Paul H. Brookes Publishing Co.

Bricker, D., & Widerstrom, A. (Eds.). (1996). *Preparing personnel to work with infants and young children and their families: A team approach.* Baltimore: Paul H. Brookes Publishing Co.

Bricker, W., & Bricker, D. (1974a). An early language training strategy. In R. Schiefelbusch & L. Lloyd (Eds.), *Language perspective: Acquisition, retardation, and intervention* (pp. 431–468). Baltimore: University Park Press.

Bricker, W., & Bricker, D. (1974b). Mental retardation and complex human behavior. In J. Kauffman & J. Payne (Eds.), *Mental retardation* (pp. 190–224). Columbus, OH: Charles E. Merrill.

Brooks-Gunn, J., McCarton, C.M., Casey, P.H., McCormick, M.C., Bauer, C.R., Bernbaum, J.C., Tyson, J., Swanson, M., Bennett, F.C., Scott, D.T., Tonascia, J., & Meinert, C.L. (1994). Early intervention in low-birthweight premature infants: Results through age 5 years from the Infant Health Development Programs. *Journal of the American Medical Association, 272,* 1257–1262.

Brown, R. (1973). *A first language.* Cambridge, MA: Harvard University Press.

Bruner, J. (1977). Early social interaction and language acquisition. In H. Schaffer (Ed.), *Studies in mother–infant interaction* (pp. 271–289). New York: Academic Press.

Carr, E., & Durand, V.M. (1985). Reducing behavior problems through functional communication training. *Journal of Applied Behavioral Analysis, 18,* 111–126.

Carta, J. (1994). Developmentally appropriate practice: Shifting the emphasis to individual appropriateness. *Journal of Early Intervention, 18*(4), 342–343.

Carta, J. (1995). Developmentally appropriate practice: A critical analysis as applied to young children with disabilities. *Focus on Exceptional Children, 27*(6), 1–14.

Carta, J., Schwartz, I., Atwater, J., & McConnell, S. (1991). Developmentally appropriate practice: Appraising its usefulness for young children with disabilities. *Topics in Early Childhood Special Education, 11*(1), 1–20.

Cicchetti, D., & Cohen, D. (1995). Perspectives on developmental psychopathology. In D. Cicchetti & D. Cohen (Eds.), *Developmental psychopathology: Theory and method* (pp. 3–20). New York: John Wiley & Sons.

Cripe, J., Slentz, K., & Bricker, D. (Eds.). (1993). *Assessment, evaluation, and programming system for infants and children: Vol. 2. AEPS curriculum for birth to three years.* Baltimore: Paul H. Brookes Publishing Co.

Cutler, B.C. (1993). *You, your child, and special education: A guide to making the system work.* Baltimore: Paul H. Brookes Publishing Co.

Dewey, J. (1959). *Dewey on education.* New York: Columbia University, Bureau of Publications.

Duchan, J., & Weitzner-Lin, B. (1987). Nurturant-naturalistic intervention for language-impaired children. *Asha, 29*(7), 45–49.

Dyer, K., & Peck, C. (1987). Current perspectives on social/communication curricula for students with autism and severe handicaps. *Education and Treatment of Children, 10*(4), 330–351.

Gallagher, J.J., & Ramey, C.T. (1987). *The malleability of children.* Baltimore: Paul H. Brookes Publishing Co.

Goldberg, S. (1977). Social competence in infancy: A model of parent–infant interaction. *Merrill-Palmer Quarterly, 23,* 163–177.

Greenfield, P., & Smith, J. (1976). *Structuring and communication in early language development.* New York: Academic Press.

Guess, D., & Siegel-Causey, E. (1985). Behavioral control and education of severely handicapped students: Who's doing what to whom? And why? In D. Bricker & J. Filler (Eds.), *Severe mental retardation: From theory to practice* (pp. 230–244). Reston, VA: Council for Exceptional Children.

Guralnick, M.J. (1997). *The effectiveness of early intervention.* Baltimore: Paul H. Brookes Publishing Co.

Hall-Quest, A. (1976). *Editorial foreword.* John Dewey experience and education [Editorial foreword]. New York: Colliers Books.

Hancock, T., & Kaiser, A. (1996). Siblings' use of milieu teaching at home. *Topics in Early Childhood Special Education, 16*(2), 168–190.

Hart, B. (1985). Naturalistic language training techniques. In S. Warren & A. Rogers-Warren (Eds.), *Teaching functional language* (pp. 63–88). Baltimore: University Park Press.

Hart, B., & Risley, T. (1975). Incidental teaching of language in the preschool. *Journal of Applied Behavioral Analysis, 8,* 411–420.

Hart, B., & Rogers-Warren, A. (1978). A milieu approach to teaching language. In R. Schiefelbusch (Ed.), *Language intervention strategies* (pp. 193–235). Baltimore: University Park Press.

Hutinger, P. (1988). Linking screening, identification, and assessment with curriculum. In J. Jordan, J. Gallagher, P. Hutinger, & M. Karnes (Eds.), *Early childhood special education: Birth to three* (pp. 29–66). Reston, VA: Council for Exceptional Children.

Johnson, J., & Johnson, K. (1994). The applicability of developmentally appropriate practice for children with diverse abilities. *Journal of Early Intervention, 18*(4), 343–345.

Kaiser, A., Hendrickson, J., & Alpert, C. (1991). Milieu language teaching: A second look. In R. Gable (Ed.), *Advances in mental retardation and developmental disabilities* (Vol. IV, pp. 63–92). London: Jessica Kingsley Publishers.

Kaiser, A.P., Yoder, P.J., & Keetz, A. (1992). Evaluating milieu teaching. In S.F. Warren & J. Reichle (Eds.), *Communication and language intervention series: Vol. 1. Causes and effects in communication and language intervention* (pp. 9–47). Baltimore: Paul H. Brookes Publishing Co.

Kirk, S., & Gallagher, J. (1979). *Educating exceptional children* (3rd ed.). Boston: Houghton Mifflin.

Koegel, R., & Johnson, J. (1989). Motivating language use in autistic children. In G. Dawson (Ed.), *Autism* (pp. 310–325). New York: Guilford Press.

Koegel, R., & Koegel, L. (1995). *Teaching children with autism: Strategies for initiating positive interactions and improving learning opportunities.* Baltimore: Paul H. Brookes Publishing Co.

Koegel, R., & Koegel, L. (1997). *Teaching children with autism.* Baltimore: Paul H. Brookes Publishing Co.

Lazerson, M. (1972). The historical antecedents of early childhood education. *Education Digest, 38*, 20–23.

Linder, T.W. (1993). *Transdisciplinary play-based assessment: A functional approach to working with young children* (Rev. ed.). Baltimore: Paul H. Brookes Publishing Co.

MacDonald, J. (1985). Language through conversation: A model for intervention with language-delayed persons. In S. Warren & A. Rogers-Warren (Eds.), *Teaching functional language* (pp. 89–122). Baltimore: University Park Press.

MacDonald, J. (1989). *Becoming partners with children.* San Antonio, TX: Special Press, Inc.

MacDonald, J., & Horstmeier, D. (1978). *Environmental language intervention program.* Columbus, OH: Charles E. Merrill.

MacMillan, D. (1977). *Mental retardation in school and society.* Boston: Little, Brown.

Mahoney, G., & Powell, A. (1984). *The transactional intervention program.* Woodhaven, MI: Woodhaven School District.

Mahoney, G., & Powell, A. (1988). Modifying parent–child interaction: Enhancing the development of handicapped children. *Journal of Special Education, 22*(1), 82–96.

Mahoney, G., & Weller, E. (1980). An ecological approach to language intervention. In D. Bricker (Ed.), *Language resource book* (pp. 17–32). San Francisco: Jossey-Bass.

Maxim, G. (1980). *The very young.* Belmont, CA: Wadsworth Publishing.

Novick, R. (1993). Activity-based intervention and developmentally appropriate practice: Points of convergence. *Topics in Early Childhood Special Education, 13*(4), 403–417.

Odom, S. (1994). Developmentally appropriate practice, policies, and use for young children with disabilities and their families. *Journal of Early Intervention, 18*(4), 346–348.

Odom, S.L. (1988). Research in early childhood special education: Methodologies and paradigms. In S.L. Odom & M.B. Karnes (Eds.), *Early intervention for infants and children with handicaps: An empirical base* (pp. 1–21). Baltimore: Paul H. Brookes Publishing Co.

Oliver, C., & Halle, J. (1982). Language training in the everyday environment: Teaching functional sign use to a retarded child. *Journal of The Association for the Severely Handicapped, 8,* 50–62.

Ostrosky, M.M., Kaiser, A.P., & Odom, S.L. (1993). Facilitating children's social-communicative interactions through the use of peer-initiated interventions. In A.P. Kaiser & D.B. Gray (Eds.), *Communication and language intervention series: Vol. 2. Enhancing children's communication: Research foundations for intervention* (pp. 159–185). Baltimore: Paul H. Brookes Publishing Co.

Piaget, J. (1967). *Six psychological studies.* New York: Random House.

Piaget, J. (1970). Piaget's theory. In P. Mussen (Ed.), *Carmichael's manual of child psychology* (Vol. 1, pp. 703–732). New York: John Wiley & Sons.

Ramey, C., & Ramey, S. (1991). Effective early intervention. *Mental Retardation, 30,* 337–345.

Rice, M.L. (1995). The rationale and operating principles for a language-focused curriculum for preschool children. In M.L. Rice and K.A. Wilcox (Eds.), *Building a language-focused curriculum for the preschool classroom* (pp. 27–38). Baltimore: Paul H. Brookes Publishing Co.

Risley, T., & Wolf, M. (1967). Establishing functional speech in echolalia children. *Behavior Research Therapy, 5,* 73–88.

Sameroff, A. (1993). Models of development and developmental risk. In C. Zeanah (Ed.), *Handbook of infant mental health* (pp. 3–13). New York: Guilford Press.

Schaffer, H. (1977). *Studies in mother–infant interaction.* New York: Academic Press.

Schorr, E., & Schorr, D. (1989). *Within our reach.* New York: Doubleday Anchor Books.

Shearer, D., & Shearer, M. (1976). The Portage Project: A model for early childhood intervention. In T. Tjossem (Ed.), *Intervention strategies for high risk infants and young children* (pp. 335–350). Baltimore: University Park Press.

Shonkoff, J., & Meisels, S. (1990). Early childhood intervention: The evolution of a concept. In S. Meisels & J. Shonkoff (Eds.), *Handbook of early childhood intervention* (pp. 3–31). New York: Cambridge University Press.

Snyder-McLean, L., Solomonson, B., McLean, J., & Sack, S. (1984). Structuring joint action routines. *Seminars in Speech and Language, 5*(3), 213–228.

Staats, A. (1964). *Human learning.* New York: Holt, Rinehart & Winston.

Stokes, T.F., & Osnes, P.G. (1988). The developing applied technology of generalization and maintenance. In R.H. Horner, G. Dunlap, & R.L. Koegel (Eds.), *Generalization and maintenance: Life-style changes in applied settings* (pp. 5–19). Baltimore: Paul H. Brookes Publishing Co.

Vygotsky, L. (1978). *Mind in society.* Cambridge, MA: Harvard University Press.

Warren, S., & Bambara, L. (1989). An experimental analysis of milieu language intervention: Teaching the action-object form. *Journal of Speech and Hearing Disorders, 54,* 448–461.

Warren, S., & Kaiser, A. (1986). Incidental language teaching: A critical review. *Journal of Speech and Hearing Disorders, 51,* 291–299.

Warren, S.F., & Kaiser, A.P. (1988). Research in early language intervention. In S.L. Odom & M.B. Karnes (Eds.), *Early intervention for infants and children with handicaps: An empirical base* (pp. 89–108). Baltimore: Paul H. Brookes Publishing Co.

Wolery, M., & Bredekamp, S. (1994). Developmentally appropriate practice and young children with disabilities: Contextual issues in the discussion. *Journal of Early Intervention, 18*(4), 331–341.

Wolfensberger, W. (1969). The origin and nature of our institutional models. In R. Kugel & W. Wolfensberger (Eds.), *Changing patterns in residential services for the mentally retarded* (pp. 59–72). Washington, DC: President's Committee on Mental Retardation.

Wyatt v. Stickney, 344 F. Supp. 387 (1972).

Chapter 10

Conceptual Foundations
for Activity-Based Intervention

Conceptual or theoretical frameworks can offer the necessary structure for planning intervention activities for young children who have or who are at risk for disabilities in order to compensate for their developmental problems or for the risk conditions to which they have been exposed. These frameworks can also offer sound information on how to frame and deliver the targeted compensatory activities.

We believe that the study of selected theoretical positions that address learning and growth in young children can offer guidance for developing rationales, goals, and approaches for the field of early intervention/early childhood special education (EI/ECSE). We must be able to provide persuasive reasons if we expect to obtain consistent and sufficient support to develop and maintain early intervention programs. In addition to having a rationale, it is important that the field of early intervention have general goals for at least three reasons. First, goals are necessary to help establish boundaries of a field or area of study. Second, goals are essential to developing intervention content and procedures that are the focus of the field. Third, if progress is to be measured, there must be standards (i.e., goals) toward which the field is directed. These standards should also serve as evaluative benchmarks.

Without a well-articulated rationale and associated goal(s), the field of EI/ECSE lacks direction. Specifically, the selection of assessment/evaluation measures, curricular content and focus, intervention approaches, family involvement strategies, and professional staff activities may be arbitrary and inefficient.

With this in mind, the purpose of this chapter is to offer a rationale and goal for EI/ECSE. The discussion then shifts to activity-
based intervention and its conceptual foundation. The chapter
concludes with a description of authentic activities and their relevance for activity-based intervention.

RATIONALE AND GOAL OF EARLY
INTERVENTION/EARLY CHILDHOOD SPECIAL EDUCATION

The rationale underlying EI/ECSE for young children who have
or who are at risk for disabilities is built on a nested set of assumptions (Bricker & Veltman, 1990). The first set of assumptions addresses the early development of children in general
and includes the following:

1. Genetic and biological problems/deficits or risk factors can
    be overcome or attenuated.
2. Early experience is important to children's development.

The second set of assumptions underlies the specific need for
the delivery of habilitative services to children identified as
needing early intervention services and includes the following:

1. Children with disabilities require more practice opportunities
    and/or compensatory learning opportunities than do chil-
    dren without disabilities to ensure progress toward targeted
    developmental goals. Children who are at risk for disabili-
    ties may also require compensatory learning opportunities
    to counter the potential negative effects of risk conditions.
2. Formal service delivery programs staffed with trained per-
    sonnel are necessary to provide the expanded or compen-
    satory learning opportunities necessary to counter develop-
    mental disabilities or risk conditions.
3. Developmental progress is enhanced in children who have
    or who are at risk for disabilities if they participate in early
    intervention programs that deliver quality services.

The Goal for Early Intervention/Early Childhood Special Education

Based on the rationale provided here, we propose a slight re-
statement of the goal for the field of EI/ECSE proposed in
Chapter 8:

To improve children's acquisition and use of important motor, social, affective, communication, and intellectual (i.e., problem solv-

ing) behaviors that, in turn, are integrated into response repertoires that are generative, functional, and adaptable.[1]

Most early interventionists may agree with the initial part of this goal, which addresses the acquisition and use of important behaviors; but they may not have considered the second part of the goal, which focuses on the integration of learned responses into generative, functional, and adaptable repertoires. There-fore, a further elaboration of the concepts of *generative, functional,* and *adaptable* is provided.

Generative Repertoire

The term *generative* refers to a child's ability to formulate (i.e., gen-erate) a response that is relatively novel or to appropriately use or adapt an existing response to meet changing conditions. For example, if children learn to produce phrases composed of agent–action or action–object sequences and those skills be-come generative, then the children (as long as the vocabulary is available) should be able to produce or generate the phrases to fit a variety of events about which they wish to communicate (e.g., boy go, daddy sit, dog play), even if they were never specifically taught to produce these specific word sequences. If a grasping response becomes generative, then children will be able to effectively grasp a variety of objects of different sizes and shapes without direct training occurring with those objects.

Although the definition of *generative* overlaps or shares sim-ilarities with the term *generalization,* we prefer generative be-cause it suggests that the child is actively engaged in producing responses to meet environmental demands. In our opinion, the term *generalization* suggests a less-active role for the child. To consistently meet social and environmental demands and get one's needs met, it is necessary for the child to produce or "gen-erate" appropriate responses.

Functional Repertoire

The term *functional* refers to the usefulness of responses for a child. Teaching children to insert pegs into a pegboard may not be functional unless the children can generate reach, grasp, and place movements to accommodate a variety of circumstances

---

[1]We recognize that other fundamental goals exist (e.g., assisting the family in developing a sound and comfortable relationship with their child, maximizing access to community resources); however, the focus of the material contained in this book is directed toward the goal presented above.

encountered in the environment. Teaching the child to reach, grasp, and move utensils at mealtime may be more functional than teaching the same moves with blocks. Learning to open doors, climb steps, and turn faucets is likely to be more functional (i.e., increase their independent functioning) for most children than inserting puzzle pieces or walking on a balance beam.

Adaptable Repertoire

The term *adaptable* overlaps somewhat with generative but still brings a unique quality to children's repertoires. Our use of *adaptable* refers to children's abilities to modify their response repertoires to accommodate social or physical constraints or demands. For example, if a child cannot gain an adult's attention by asking a question, then he or she should be able to adapt or substitute another method (e.g., ask another adult, use a gesture) to attract attention. Adaptability or flexibility of response repertoires is critical if children are to meet the demands of the physical and social environments, which are often changing and unpredictable.

To assist children in acquiring integrated generative, functional, and adaptable response repertoires, we developed activity-based intervention. Activity-based intervention is an approach guided by, and consistent with, the goal for early intervention proposed previously in this chapter. The remainder of this chapter discusses the theoretical context for this goal and for the activity-based intervention approach. The theoretical assumptions that underlie the approach are neither new nor unique to activity-based intervention. Activity-based intervention is eclectic in that its conceptual foundations were derived from several major theories, each of which emphasizes a different aspect of human growth and learning. We have attempted to blend these various positions into a cohesive system for effective intervention that is described in detail in Chapter 2.

FOUNDATIONAL THEORY FOR ACTIVITY-BASED INTERVENTION

Failure to assist children in the development of integrated generative, functional, and adaptable repertoires is a problem that has served as an impetus for the continuing development of educational theory and practice (Brown, Collins, & Duguid, 1989). Although this problem has been noted for decades by educational theorists (e.g., Dewey, 1976), our inability to assist children in developing useful, meaningful, and effective learning strategies may be even more serious for groups of children who require long-term intervention and who, by the nature of their disabilities, are less able to compensate for poor instruction and inefficient, misguided interventions.

Activity-based intervention requires the appropriate application of learning principles (e.g., antecedent arrangements, reinforcement of desired responses) that have been identified and described by behavior analysts. The approach has also been influenced by the writings of sociohistorical theorists such as Vygotsky, cognitive theorists such as Piaget, learning theorists such as Dewey, and developmental theorists such as Cicchetti. The selected perspectives of these four theorists that have been incorporated into the conceptual framework for activity-based intervention are discussed here. Then, a discussion of behavioral learning principles that provide the intervention guidelines for activity-based intervention follows.

Sociohistorical Theory

The continuing influence of Vygotsky's writing has in no small measure been responsible for other theorists' and investigators' attention to the effect that the immediate and historical sociocultural environment has on the developing child (John-Steiner & Souberman, 1978; Moll, 1990). The dialectical approach, although admitting the influence of nature on man, asserts that man, in turn, affects nature and creates through his changes in nature new natural conditions for his existence (Vygotsky, 1978). As Vygotsky noted, learning is a profoundly social process that is affected by the history of the child and the child's culture (John-Steiner & Souberman, 1978).

Vygotsky argued that although there is a clear biological basis for development, interactions that occur between a child and the social environment affect the development of the child as well as the larger social context. This phenomenon was noted by Hart and Risley (1995) while conducting their longitudinal study of language acquisition in young children. They noted that parental responses changed as children acquired more sophisticated language, which, in turn, led to the children's producing yet more complex language. Vygotsky's interactional perspective recognized the bidirectionality of effect between children and their immediate social environment. His position also addressed sociocultural change that results from the individual's action on and reaction to the sociocultural times, which may, in turn, modify the sociocultural context for future generations. For example, the introduction of new words (e.g., cyberspace) or changes in word meaning (e.g., cool) may produce permanent cultural shifts.

Vygotsky's writings complement other interactional positions such as those described by Sameroff and Chandler (1975), which focus on child–environment interactions, or those described by Cicchetti and Cohen (1995), which focus on intra-system interactions. These interactional positions have in turn provided the impetus for significant change in approaches to EI/ECSE. Approaches such as activity-based intervention clearly reflect an appreciation for the interactional perspective between the child and environment as well as between areas of development.

Cognitive Theory

Piaget's influence on child development and EI/ECSE approaches has been profound. His theory of development postulates that children act on their environment to construct an understanding of how the world operates (Piaget, 1952). Varying interpretations of Piagetian theory have provided an important tenet underlying the activity-based intervention approach. Piagetian theory emphasizes the need for children to be actively involved in constructing knowledge of their physical environment. Children need to explore, experience, manipulate, and receive feedback from their actions on objects in order to move from the sensorimotor stage to representational and formal operations.

A critical aspect of children's active exploration of their environment is the relevant and direct feedback they receive. As infants examine objects within their reach, they find that the result of a ball being thrown is different from that of a ball being squeezed. Infants discover through systematic feedback from their actions that, for example, books are to look at, whereas hammers are better for pounding. Many professionals understand and respect the need for infants and young children to act on their environment in meaningful ways.

Although focused on examining the effects between children and their physical environment (Uzgiris, 1981), Piaget's writings have greatly enhanced our appreciation for the development of higher mental functions. Piaget pointed out the importance of children's actions on their environment and the importance of subsequent feedback to the development of increasingly more sophisticated problem-solving behavior. This position underlies the critical nature of children's active involvement with their environment. From these operations, children first derive concrete meaning that subsequently evolves into abstract thought (Piaget, 1967). Piaget suggested that both the nature of environmental feedback and children's active participation are important for meaningful learning to occur. Again, this perspective can be seen in the elements and application of activity-based intervention.

Learning Theory

Dewey's theory, like Piaget's and Vygotsky's theories, rests in part on the idea that the interaction between children and their environment is fundamental to development and learning. For Dewey, genuine education comes about through experience. "Every experience is a moving force. Its value can be judged only on the ground of what it moves toward and into" (1976, p. 38). According to Dewey (1976), it is necessary for experiences to be interactive and have continuity to move children toward meaningful change.

As Dewey (1959) noted, children by nature are active, and the question is how to capture and direct their activity. Through thoughtful organization and planning, experiences (activities) can be arranged to meet children's interests and to address sound intervention goals. A fundamental aspect of activities is that they are meaningful and functional for children and are not scattered or impulsive. "A succession of unrelated activities does not provide, of course, the opportunity or content of building up an organized subject-matter. But neither do they provide for the development of a coherent and integrated self" (Dewey, 1959, p. 122). Dewey's concept of continuity implied that the effective interventionist determines children's present levels of understanding and then arranges experiences in such a way as to move children efficiently toward a higher level of functioning.

Another aspect of Dewey's theory that is of particular relevance to the activity-based intervention approach is that children should be allowed to participate fully in activities. This may include the selection of what to do and how to do it. The interventionist's role is to guide the selection of experiences so that they become interactive and continuous. The interventionist's job, in effect, is to map relevant intervention goals onto the experiences that occur in children's lives.

In addition, as Dewey emphasized, learning occurs as a result of all experiences, not just of those designated for formal training. Effective intervention approaches use the array of activities that occur in children's lives on a daily basis. The variety of activities available to young children on a regular basis can often be used to facilitate the acquisition of important knowledge and skills. The child's desire for an object, person, or event can be used to develop and expand communication skills. Playing in a sandbox can be arranged to develop motor and social skills. Rather than routinely having children wash their hands before snacktime, this can become an activity that demands problem solving (e.g., locate the soap, reach the sink, find the towel) and that is relevant and meaningful to the children. The effective use of child-selected, routine, and unanticipated activities is a fundamental part of activity-based intervention.

Developmental Theory

Theories addressing early development have also been useful in structuring activity-based intervention. The organizational perspective on development proposed by Cicchetti and Cohen has particular relevance. The organizational perspective "focuses on the quality of integration both within and among the behavioral and biological systems of the individual . . . and specifies how development proceeds" (1995, p. 6). This theory postulates development as a series of "qualitative reorganizations" within and between biological and behavioral systems (e.g., cognitive, social, linguistic, emotional). Change occurs as earlier structures are incorporated into new levels of organization both within and across systems. For example, children acquire more advanced language skills by expanding, rearranging, or changing the syntactic rules that govern sentence production. These changes in language will likely also affect other major systems. That is, because of the interaction between developmental domains and the reciprocal impact, enhanced communication skills may also change the child's cognitive, social, and even emotional systems.

Aspects of the organizational perspective particularly applicable to intervention efforts include attention to the potential interactive effects between systems and the systematic reorganization of behavior into more complex stages of behavior. The implication is that intervention efforts should be comprehensive and take into account all major systems. For example, a delay in problem-solving abilities may also affect the child's other behavioral systems. A second implication of developmental theory is the need for accurate, ongoing, and in-depth assessment of a child's repertoire to determine appropriate intervention targets across behavioral systems. Activity-based intervention is designed to address multiple targets across behavioral domains and to incorporate comprehensive assessment of children's behavioral repertoires as prerequisites to intervention efforts.

Behavioral Learning Principles

Behavioral learning principles can be blended into the most effective intervention strategy available. No matter what one's theoretical orientation, it is essential that EI/ECSE personnel be knowledgeable about and competent users of behavioral learning principles. Interventionists have a responsibility to apply these principles in an organized and purposeful manner in order to serve the best interests of children and families and to meet program goals of quality services. The primary principles can be conceptualized as a three-part sequence known as ARC:

Antecedent → Response → Consequence

Antecedent refers to a condition, setting, or level of support that can be used to or that serves to call forth or elicit a particular response or class of responses. For example, if a child is learning to name common objects (e.g., ball, teddy bear, apple), then the interventionist may request that the child name the desired object (e.g., ball) before he or she will hand it to the child. The interventionist's asking for the object's name serves as the antecedent for a target response (e.g., naming). *Response* refers to the particular behavior (e.g., spoken object name or specific label). *Consequence,* in turn, refers to the actions that occur after responses. For example, an interventionist pours juice into a cup (the antecedent); the child points and says, "juice" (the response); and the interventionist gives the child the cup of juice (the consequence).

Antecedents, responses, and consequences work in tandem, and it is often useful to think in terms of ARC units rather than to examine individual elements. Furthermore, it is useful to think of antecedents, responses, and consequences as broad classes rather than as specific actions, events, or outcomes, as illustrated in the comparative examples below.

Individual Associations

Antecedent	Response	Consequence
Picture of a dog	Child says, "Doggie."	Teacher says, "Correct."

Classes of Associations

Antecedent	Response	Consequence
Pictures, toy exemplars, real dogs	Child says, "Doggie," to all appropriate exemplars.	Receives appropriate feedback, such as attention, verbal praise, and an object

Using ARC units to formulate specific contingencies (i.e., relationships between a specific antecedent, response, and consequence) is usually an overly narrow application of behavioral principles. Rather, caregivers and interventionists should be working to have children respond across a range of correct and relevant antecedents (e.g., events, pictures, objects, words) and to provide consequences that fit or match the child's responses (e.g., providing affirmation, giving an object or desired action). This brief section on behavioral learning principles can be supplemented through a number of published resources including Alberto and Troutman (1982), Dunlap (1997), and Zirpoli (1995).

MAJOR TENETS

From the writings of Vygotsky, Piaget, Dewey, and Cicchetti, we have extracted four tenets that underlie the conceptual framework of activity-based intervention:

1. The immediate environment and the larger sociocultural context have a significant influence on the developing child.
2. Child initiations and active involvement enhance learning.
3. Children should be engaged in functional and meaningful activities.
4. Development progresses through the integration of multiple processes.

The first tenet is derived from Piaget, Vygotsky, and Dewey's acknowledgment of the importance of the environment for learning and development. Vygotsky, in particular, recognized the effect of the larger sociocultural context that surrounds children and their immediate social environment. Although each theorist acknowledged the neurophysiological substrata (i.e., a physiological base) necessary for the development of higher-order processes, each also emphasized environmental context and feedback as fundamental to children's learning and development.

The environment that envelops the child is important in a historic, contemporary, and future sense. History shapes the contemporary status. Clearly, the evolution of intervention approaches for young children has been influenced by experience gained from previous work. The contemporary influences (for both child and program) help in turn to shape future outcomes.

The second tenet emphasizes the need for active involvement by the child if efficient learning is to occur. Passive, unmotivated, nondirected activity may do little to enrich a child's response repertoire. The environment, or experience, to use Dewey's term, must be arranged to attract and motivate children. Equally important is the need to follow children's initiatives and leads and direct them into enriching activities that ensure maximum involvement of the children.

Effective and efficient learning requires that young children be involved in the learning process. Except in unusual cases (e.g., children with significant motor impairments), children benefit from actively engaging in the learning process rather than passively receiving knowledge and skills. We believe that this is particularly true for young children whose use of language may be primitive or incompletely formed, making concrete involvement a prerequisite to gaining knowledge or skills.

A third tenet that underlies activity-based intervention is that activities or experiences should be designed to be meaningful and functional for children. As Vygotsky wrote, "If we ignore the child's needs, and the incentives which are effective in getting him to act, we will never be able to understand his advance from one developmental stage to the next" (1978, p. 92). According to Dewey, "We have to understand the significance of what we see, hear, and touch. This significance consists of the consequences that will result when what is seen is acted upon" (1976, p. 68). Cicchetti and Cohen (1995) stressed the importance of offering interventions that match a child's stage of developmental organization. These authors suggested that there may be times in a child's development when there are excellent opportunities for reorganization and change not only in individual process (e.g., communication) but also across systems (e.g., communication, social, and cognitive areas).

As stated previously, for development and learning to occur, the child should be engaged in functional and meaningful activities. Although active involvement is important to young children's learning, the nature of the involvement (e.g., the type of activities) also appears to be critical. Children must be involved in activities that use or stretch their present repertoires or provide the necessary experience to expand their repertoires.

The final tenet addresses the importance of viewing development and learning as an ongoing, integrative process that is responsive to an array of biological and environmental factors. Effective intervention approaches require a comprehensive and organized structure that permits the user to accurately determine a child's current level of functioning across major developmental domains (i.e., systems), to formulate appropriate and timely learning activities that will lead to the successive growth and reorganization of important developmental systems, and to take into account the multiple variables that can affect a child's learning. Activity-based intervention is designed to address and meet these important tenets.

AUTHENTIC ACTIVITIES

In an article entitled "Situated Cognition and the Culture of Learning," Brown and his colleagues addressed the need to change what they believed is much of the educational activity offered to children in schools:

> We suggest that, by ignoring the situated nature of cognition, education defeats its own goal of providing usable, robust knowledge. And conversely, we argue that approaches . . . that embed learning in activity and make deliberate use of the social and physical context are more in line with the understanding of learning and cognition that is emerging from research. (1989, p. 32)

By "situated nature," Brown et al. meant that learning is an integral part of the activity and situation in which it occurs. "Activity, concept, and culture are interdependent. No one can be totally understood without the other two. Learning must involve all three" (Brown et al., 1989, p. 33).

Brown et al. (1989) blended logic and data into a case for what they call "authentic activity." These writers argued that the acquisition of knowledge and learning of skills should occur under conditions that are authentic; that is, the knowledge or skill is necessary or useful to cope with real tasks or problems. This is in opposition to training or education that employs abstract, fragmented strategies that do not reflect conditions found in nontraining environments. For example, attempting to enhance children's communication skills by conducting 10-minute drill sessions is less meaningful than assisting children to expand their communication skills as needed to negotiate their daily environment.

The applicability of the Brown et al. (1989) position is apparent for young children and provides additional conceptual support for activity-based intervention. If Brown and his colleagues are correct, then developing generative, functional, and adaptable response repertoires can be made efficient and effective by embedding intervention activities in authentic situations. Authentic situations for young children should include activities that reflect the reality and demands of their daily living. Authentic activities have, from the children's perspective, a logical beginning, a sequence of events, and an ending. They either are fundamental to young children's existence (e.g., requesting help) or mirror conditions and demands the children face on a routine basis (e.g., learning to feed themselves). Authentic activities permit children to learn and practice skills that will improve their abilities to cope with the many demands offered by their physical and social environment. Children view authentic activities as relevant, as evidenced by their interest and motivation to become involved. Such activities lead children to better understand and respond to their immediate sociocultural context. Furthermore, an authentic activity meets Dewey's criteria of sound educational practice because it "supplies the child with a genuine motive; it gives him experience at first hand; it brings him into contact with reality" (1959, p. 44).

Employing authentic activities to promote children's learning is not synonymous with permitting children to engage in any type or form of activity. It also does not mean that the interventionist or caregiver abdicates responsibility for assisting children in reaching their developmental or educational goals. Rather, it means that the interventionist must develop a structure that guides and directs children's activities in useful ways. It means more intense observations of children's motivation and skills, and it means remaining flexible without losing sight of children's goals and objectives. As Dewey (1959) noted, permitting children to become actively involved in the educational process means more effort by teachers, not less.

SUMMARY

The purpose of this chapter is to provide the reader with a conceptual framework for understanding the formulation and application of activity-based intervention. The tenets distilled from the work of a variety of theorists give strength to the positions that children are greatly influenced by their social and physical environment and their cultural context, that children need to be actively involved in the construction of higher mental processes, and that the nature of the environmental activities (i.e., experiences) children encounter are fundamental to their development and learning. Given these positions, an intervention approach that uses authentic activities has great appeal.

As Dewey wrote, "There is no such thing as educational value in the abstract" (1976, p. 46). "I believe that the only true education comes through the stimulation of the child's powers by the demands of the social situation in which he finds himself" (Dewey, 1959, p. 20). The goal of activity-based intervention is to create and use authentic activities to enhance children's development and learning.

REFERENCES

Alberto, P., & Troutman, A. (1982). *Applied behavior analysis for teachers.* Columbus, OH: Charles E. Merrill.

Bricker, D., & Veltman, M. (1990). Early intervention programs: Child-focused approaches. In S. Meisels & J. Shonkoff (Eds.), *Handbook of early childhood intervention* (pp. 373–399). New York: Cambridge University Press.

Brown, J., Collins, A., & Duguid, P. (1989). Situated cognition and the culture of learning. *Educational Researcher, 17*(1), 32–42.

Cicchetti, D., & Cohen, D. (1995). Perspectives on developmental psychopathology. In D. Cicchetti & D. Cohen (Eds.), *Developmental psychopathology: Theory and methods* (pp. 3–20). New York: John Wiley & Sons.

Dewey, J. (1959). *Dewey on education.* New York: Columbia University, Bureau of Publications, Teachers College.

Dewey, J. (1976). *Experience and education.* New York: Colliers Books.

Dunlap, L. (1997). Behavior management. In L. Dunlap (Ed.), *An introduction to early childhood special education* (pp. 276–299). Needham Heights, MA: Allyn & Bacon.

Hart, B., & Risley, T. (1995). *Meaningful differences in the everyday experience of young American children.* Baltimore: Paul H. Brookes Publishing Co.

John-Steiner, V., & Souberman, E. (1978). Afterword. In M. Cole, V. John-Steiner, S. Scribner, & E. Souberman (Eds.), *L.S. Vygotsky—Mind in society* (pp. 121–133). Cambridge, MA: Harvard University Press.

Moll, L. (1990). *Vygotsky and education.* New York: Cambridge University Press.

Piaget, J. (1952). *The origins of intelligence in children.* New York: W.W. Norton.

Piaget, J. (1967). *Six psychological studies*. New York: Random House.

Sameroff, A., & Chandler, M. (1975). Reproductive risk and the continuum of caretaking casualty. In F. Horowitz, E. Hetherington, S. Scarr-Salapatek, & G. Siegel (Eds.), *Review of child development research* (Vol. 4, pp. 187–244). Chicago: University of Chicago Press.

Uzgiris, I. (1981). Experience in the social context. In R. Schiefelbusch & D. Bricker (Eds.), *Early language: Acquisition and intervention* (pp. 139–168). Baltimore: University Park Press.

Vygotsky, L. (1978). *Mind in society*. Cambridge, MA: Harvard University Press.

Zirpoli, T. (1995). *Understanding and affecting the behavior of young children*. Columbus, OH: Charles E. Merrill.

Chapter 11

Issues Associated with Activity-Based Intervention

Applying the general principles of activity-based intervention may at first appear to be simple, straightforward, and much less complicated than employing approaches that are adult directed with lessons specifically scripted. In conversations with others, however, and through observation of individuals applying the principles of activity-based intervention, several important issues have been identified. These issues include attention to areas of need, loss of control, opportunities to practice targeted skills, applicability to children with severe disabilities, use in community-based programs, evaluation of child progress, and effectiveness of the approach. Each of these issues is discussed in the following sections.

ATTENTION TO AREAS OF NEED

Capitalizing on activities that are of interest to children is an important element of activity-based intervention. Following child initiations or using activities that children find inherently motivating keeps interest high and usually alleviates the need for extrinsic reinforcement. Nonetheless, it raises an issue of whether children will direct their initiations or interests to activities that will necessarily address their particular cognitive, social, communicative, adaptive, or motor deficits. It may be unrealistic to expect children, especially those with challenging physical, mental, emotional, or a combination of needs, to consistently select activities that would enhance or expand their current repertoires. For example, a child with a serious articula-

239

tion problem may find it both unproductive and unrewarding to ask for desired objects. The child who walks slowly with difficulty may not be inclined to engage in actions that require walking. The quiet child with few social skills may not seek out peers even when opportunities present themselves. These examples make it evident that team members cannot always wait for children to initiate activities that will necessarily lead to practicing targeted skills in areas of need.

Successful application of activity-based intervention requires that child-initiated and child-directed activities be balanced with the embedding of priority goals and objectives into routine and planned activities. The balancing of these elements is essential. Children are encouraged to initiate and direct activities; however, the activities should incorporate their major training needs and not only be ones they prefer. For example, children may indicate the desire to sing the same songs at group time. The interventionist may be able to adapt the children's requests by adding new target words or actions to the songs, to introduce new songs, or to intersperse other activities between songs into which target goals can be embedded.

Successful application of activity-based intervention also requires the careful scrutiny of child initiations to ensure that practice on targeted skills is occurring, and if it is not occurring, to shape child-initiated activities so that they do incorporate target goals. For example, Keith has a significant motor impairment that requires the use of a walker. A priority goal for Keith is to increase his use of the walker and to increase the speed with which he can move from place to place. Not surprising, this 6-year-old child would rather play board games with his friends than practice walking with his walker. The teacher arranges the situation so that Keith is required to use his walker to get to the toy shelves to retrieve games and walk to the table where his friends wait. This arrangement has capitalized on Keith's interest, playing board games, to practice the targeted skill of using his walker. With thought and planning, embedding goals that may appear incompatible with high-interest activities can be accomplished while still respecting children's choices and reinforcing their initiations.

Efficient child change will not occur unless children's needs are frequently and systematically addressed. Children's needs should be reflected in their individualized education program/individualized family service plan (IEP/IFSP) goals and objectives, which, in turn, should guide and direct intervention efforts. If caregivers and interventionists are aware of the children's educational and therapeutic goals and objectives, then activities that are routine, planned, and child initiated can be directed toward the acquisition of the skills specified in the goals and objectives. Using IEP/IFSP goals and objectives to guide intervention efforts ensures that activity-based intervention is directed by the developmental needs of children while attending to their unique interests.

To reiterate, activity-based intervention is not a laissez-faire approach that is directed totally by children and their interests. The approach is designed, when possible, to use the activities initiated and enjoyed by children. However, the use of child initiations does not preclude the introduction of planned activities or the use of routine activities, nor does it preclude the redirection of child-initiated activities. It is a balance among child-initiated, routine, and planned activities that ensures children's important developmental targets and needs are systematically addressed.

LOSS OF CONTROL

Direct service delivery personnel, consultants, and caregivers who have typically scripted and directed children's activities have reported feeling a significant loss of control when first employing child-directed approaches such as activity-based intervention. Team members who traditionally have chosen each activity and child response may be uncomfortable using an approach that responds to and encourages child initiations. The training that many professionals have experienced—particularly those working with individuals who have disabilities—has taught them the importance of structure and the need to occupy children with productive tasks. Although no one disagrees with such goals, it is the nature of the structure and the type of task that differentiates programs that are primarily adult directed from those that encourage child initiations.

Interventionists may sense the loss of some control when children are permitted to reshape an activity or introduce an unanticipated action; however, if that activity is directed toward the children's goals and objectives, then the lack of predictability for the interventionist or adult orchestration is likely not important. It is essential that children have frequent and meaningful opportunities to practice targeted skills, and it is likely that planned, routine, and child-initiated activities provide such opportunities. Rather than losing control, activity-based intervention offers team members additional ways of encouraging children's learning of important targeted skills. The appropriate application of activity-based intervention does not permit children to engage in nonproductive or inappropriate actions. Rather, the approach provides an underlying structure that we believe enhances children's learning of priority goals and objectives.

Some professionals have also voiced concern that following children's leads or initiations may result in children's engagement in nonproductive activities or in moving from activity to activity without sustained interest or involvement. Most professionals have encountered children whose attention span is short and who, if permitted, cycle quickly through many training activities apparently without learning new skills. Is activity-based intervention appropriate for such children? Does this approach encourage and intensify their inabilities to focus and sustain attention? If team members are following children's leads and encouraging self-initiated activities, then is it likely that children will learn they can control the situation and shift activities at the expense of learning new skills or expanding their behavioral repertoires? What about 3-year-old Sabrina? She typically looks at a book for a few minutes and then discards the book to grab a toy, which quickly is relinquished in order to take another toy from a peer. This lack of sustained attention is neither appropriate for Sabrina nor does it represent the appropriate application of activity-based intervention.

Use of activity-based intervention does not require that interventionists or caregivers follow child initiations when they do not lead to productive outcomes. *Productive outcome* refers to improvement in children's IEP/IFSP goals and objectives. Fundamental to the appropriate use of activity-based intervention is the development of functional goals and objectives for each child. The selection of meaningful intervention targets provides the necessary guidance for selecting activities and for monitoring change over time. Routine, planned, and child-initiated activities should always be directed toward the acquisition of children's goals and objectives. If goals for Sabrina include increasing her vocabulary and increasing her attention span, then the interventionist would instigate activities or support child-initiated activities that provided opportunities to work on these goals. The interventionist could use a variety of strategies to discourage rapid discarding of books, for example, by adding puppets or actions to the story.

Underlying this discussion of control is the need for structure to guide and direct the actions of children and team members. The structure for activity-based intervention is provided by the selection of functional and meaningful goals that guide intervention efforts. This structure is described in Chapters 5 and 6.

OPPORTUNITIES TO PRACTICE TARGETED SKILLS

Providing an adequate number of opportunities to practice targeted goals and objectives is a challenge for activity-based intervention as well as for other approaches. Data (e.g., Bricker & Pretti-Frontczak, 1997; Pretti-Frontczak, 1996; Schwartz, Carta, & Grant, 1996), along with our observations of many classrooms, tend to verify the finding that interventionists do not consistently use a variety of recommended practices to ensure that children have opportunities to practice targeted skills. Clearly, use of a skill is necessary if it is to be learned and become functional for a child. This is particularly true for children with disabilities.

During child-initiated, routine, and planned activities, sufficient numbers and types of opportunities should be offered to ensure that children learn targeted skills. Offering adequate opportunities, however, will not occur without careful planning. The team must give thought to the type of activities that are necessary to provide appropriate opportunities and how to introduce opportunities into child-initiated and routine activities. For skills to generalize, children need practice opportunities that vary in relevant ways. For example, if a child is learning the names of common objects, then he or she can work on labeling objects many times throughout the day. The caregiver or interventionist should examine the child's daily schedule and estimate the number of times the child could potentially practice targeted object names. If the number of opportunities appears insufficient to improve the child's performance, then the team should add activities or create ways to expand opportunities in routine or child-initiated activities. For example, at bathtime, a variety of objects could be introduced. As the child reaches and grasps the object, the caregiver can ask, "What did you find?" Three or four objects could be introduced at each bathtime to provide many opportunities for the child to label objects resulting in additional practice opportunities to supplement other child-initiated, routine, or planned activities that might also target object labeling. (For a more detailed discussion, see Chapter 8.)

Another element of activity-based intervention that helps ensure that children have sufficient opportunities to practice targeted skills is the attention given to the acquisition of functional and generative responses. Critical response classes that encourage independent functioning should be targets for all children. Such response classes include problem solving, communication, manipulation of objects, mobility, dressing and feeding, and social interaction skills. Targeting the response class of mobility does not mean that all children will learn to walk, but it does mean that independent mobility should be a goal for most children, whether mobility is accomplished by foot or with a walker, wheelchair, or other adapted system. The comprehensive and pervasive nature of response classes provides thoughtful and innovative caregivers and interventionists numerous opportunities to use child initiations or to embed such response class goals into routine and planned activities.

Team members who employ activity-based intervention need to be spontaneous, flexible, and generative in order to provide multiple opportunities for infants, toddlers, and young children to practice targeted skills. If blowing bubbles is a favorite activity but blowing is not a target, then this activity potentially can be used to provide opportunities to practice a variety of important skills including communication (e.g., requesting bubbles; following directions; using words such as blow, pop, more, all gone), social interaction (e.g., taking turns, playing with peers), and motor skills (e.g., visually tracking the bubbles, chasing and popping bubbles, opening and closing the lid on the bubble jar).

It is apparent that children will not acquire new information or skills unless provided with multiple opportunities to practice the target. Such opportunities do not necessarily arise or occur spontaneously. Therefore, a major responsibility of the team is to ensure that each child is provided with as many opportunities to practice a skill as can be reasonably and meaningfully embedded in child-initiated, routine, and planned activities.

APPLICABILITY TO CHILDREN WITH SEVERE DISABILITIES

Another important issue is the applicability of activity-based intervention to infants, toddlers, and young children with moderate to severe disabilities. Typically developing children and those who have or who are at risk for mild disabilities tend to engage in many more diverse activities than do children with more severe disabilities. In addition, children with less severe disabilities are often more easily engaged, and their attention may be maintained longer. Children with less severe disabilities tend to initiate action and respond more frequently than do children with more severe disabilities. In fact, a major characteristic of many people with severe disabilities is the lack of appropriate self-initiated activity (Koegel, Koegel, Frea, & Smith, 1995).

An important question is whether the lack of initiation—or at least appropriate initiation—in individuals with severe disabilities is physiologically based or is systematically fostered by their being ignored or punished by the social environment (Guess & Siegel-Causey, 1985). We believe that the low frequency of useful initiations by children with severe disabilities stems from a combination of biological problems and training. As Drasgow, Halle, Ostrosky, and Harbers (1996) pointed out, many young children with severe disabilities have a number of subtle or idiosyncratic behaviors that could be used or shaped into useful responses. Our experience suggests, however, that often these responses are ignored and training is directed toward adult imposition of the response to be performed by the child.

For children without disabilities, play and self-initiated activities provide essential vehicles for learning increasingly more complex social, communicative, cognitive, and motor skills. We believe that play and child initiations are equally important ways for children with severe disabilities to learn new skills. Activity-based intervention supports this form of learning by emphasizing the importance of child-initiated interactions within daily caregiving routines, play, and child initiations. Caregivers and interventionists need to carefully observe and respond to children's signals and actions, however minimal and idiosyncratic, as they occur, and they need to build on these responses or redirect them into more useful and meaningful response forms.

We believe that increased attention to enhancing appropriate child-initiated and child-directed activity (not self-destructive or stereotypical behavior) may enhance the ability of children with severe disabilities to show caregivers and interventionists what they like and what interests them. In fact, some treatment by level of development analyses (i.e., aptitude) find that younger children who have fewer skills profit more from child-driven interventions than from adult-driven approaches (Cole, Dale, & Mills, 1991; Yoder, Kaiser, & Alpert, 1991; Yoder et al., 1995). These findings, however, do not negate the need for structure and careful programming for children with severe disabilities.

The adequacy of training across areas of need requires coordination and joint planning by team members involved in a child's intervention program. This coordination and planning is especially important for children with severe disabilities if they are to develop functional and generalizable skills that, as indicated previously, have consistently been identified as serious problems for this population (Drasgow et al., 1996; Horner, Dunlap, & Koegel, 1988).

Activity-based intervention uses the behavior analytic techniques known to be successful in helping individuals with severe disabilities acquire useful and meaningful skills. The approach incorporates the people and places important to children by intervening in daily routines, and it emphasizes skills with immediate utility by providing something helpful or desirable for children as needs arise (e.g., getting the child a cup of juice when he or she vocalizes and points to the juice pitcher). Intervention targets are embedded in various activities to ensure that learning opportunities occur under different conditions to increase the generalizability of skills.

Activity-based intervention does not preclude, nor is it incompatible with, the use of adult-directed activities or a massed-trial format (i.e., asking the child to repeat the same response across several sequential trials). The magnitude and number of problems presented by children with severe disabilities will likely require team members to employ a variety of training strategies if they are to ensure systematic child progress. The successful use of activity-based intervention requires the thoughtful balancing of planned activities with child initiations and the balancing of training opportunities dispersed across activities with multitrial practice opportunities.

USE IN COMMUNITY-BASED PROGRAMS

Increasing numbers of children with disabilities are being placed in community-based child care, educational, and recreational programs (Wolery et al., 1993). Most of these programs were designed to accommodate typically developing children and their families. Furthermore, the staff of these programs generally have training and experience focused on children and families who do not have serious disabilities. Thus, the placement of children with disabilities into community-based programs often is unsatisfactory for the children and their families as well as problematic for program staff for two important reasons. First, staff are often not prepared to offer children with disabilities specialized training or to manage the children's behavior successfully. Second, many community-based programs operate with limited budgets, which do not permit individualized attention to participating children. The outcome will likely result in limited child progress, the development of inappropriate behavior, parent dissatisfaction, and staff frustration. The use of activity-based intervention cannot solve these two important problems. The approach's reliance on routine activities and child initiations, however, makes it compatible with how most community-based programs function and, therefore, applicable for use in these programs.

The compatibility between activity-based intervention and the philosophy and operation of many community-based programs occurs because activity-based intervention's foundation evolved, in part, from the child development and early education literature and practice rather than exclusively from special education. Encouraging child initiations and child-directed actions within the context of routine and play activities is familiar to most child care workers and early childhood teachers.

In addition, activity-based intervention is compatible with developmentally appropriate practice (DAP) that guides quality child care and early education programs. Both activity-based intervention and DAP encourage child exploration and initiation, embed consequences into child activity, target tasks that are developmentally appropriate for children, and view adults as supporters of children's actions and interests.

Activity-based intervention encourages the physical, social, and instructional inclusion of children with disabilities in all activities rather than relocating children into isolated settings for specific instruction. The activity-based approach emphasizes the use of antecedents and consequences that can be provided in child-initiated as well as teacher-directed activities. These emphases blend well with most approaches used in community-based programs; however, the application of activity-based intervention in community-based settings will likely require modifications in the approach.

The successful use of activity-based intervention in community-based programs will require that mechanisms be developed to ensure that children with disabilities are assessed, appropriate IEP/IFSP goals are developed, ample opportunities to practice targeted skills are provided, and progress is monitored. Most child care workers and early education personnel are not prepared to conduct these activities. Consequently, the use of activity-based intervention will likely require that training and support be provided to the staff of community-based programs. The philosophical congruence between activity-based

intervention and DAP, however, as well as the compatibility between activity-based intervention and the previous experiences
of early childhood workers should enhance the understanding
and acceptability of this training.

EVALUATION OF CHILD PROGRESS

Evaluation of child progress is an issue of importance to the
field of early intervention/early childhood special education
(EI/ECSE). Without objective documentation of change, one
cannot be sure that team members' time and efforts are producing desired outcomes. Unfortunately, the monitoring of child
progress is done poorly and infrequently in most programs because it is difficult and costly to do. The difficulty stems from
finding evaluation strategies that capture children's response
classes in ways that generate useful feedback (e.g., measuring
effective social interaction between peers). Then, too, measuring change in complex processes (e.g., problem solving) can be
expensive because many evaluation systems require the collection of frequent and extensive data to determine effectiveness.
Nevertheless, it is imperative that child change be monitored if
the effectiveness of intervention efforts are to be determined.

The activity-based intervention format makes the evaluation of child change both mandatory and challenging. Across
priority goals, monitoring change in frequency, quality, or duration of skills in child-initiated, routine, and planned activities
for many children can severely tax the resources of team members. Only through systematic documentation of change, however, can team members be assured that the intervention being
offered to children is effective.

Because we believe the evaluation of child change over
time is mandatory for those using activity-based intervention as
well as other approaches, the issue is not *whether* to but *how* to
monitor change. The approach that we have found to be most
practical and yet provide adequate information for making
sound educational decisions is the use of evaluation "probes."
Probes can be thought of as "mini" tests of a child's ability to use
a targeted skill. Rather than conducting a lengthy and comprehensive evaluation of the child's performance daily or weekly,
the probe is designed to quickly capture feedback on how
closely the child meets the stated criteria for the targeted skill.
For example, during snacktime the caregiver may assess
(i.e., probe) a child's targeted skill of reach and grasp by hand-
ing the child a cup.

To use a probe system for evaluation, children's program plans need to be formulated and their goals and associated objectives must be written in measurable terms (e.g., specify the child's response). Accompanying each goal and objective should be a list of antecedents that can be embedded in routine, planned, and child-initiated activities. In addition, a variety of activities need to be suggested that could be used to elicit or practice the skill(s) targeted in the goal/objective. Finally, a data collection plan needs to be specified. In most cases, the data collection can be accomplished by administering probes to children once or twice a week. To do this, certain times or activities can be designated for collecting probe data for each goal/objective (e.g., asking the child for a target behavior when an activity is completed). Then during the specified time or activity, the assigned team member provides the child an opportunity to perform the targeted skill.

The relatively spontaneous and flexible format of activity-based intervention requires monitoring child progress toward selected goals and objectives. In addition, when using an approach such as activity-based intervention, it often becomes necessary to accurately monitor the number of opportunities children are given to practice new skills as well as the rate of acquisition and maintenance of targeted skills.

As indicated previously, evaluation of child progress is a vitally important issue for EI/ECSE. The need for monitoring child progress is essential for all intervention approaches, and activity-based intervention is no exception. To address the challenges of evaluating child progress in an approach that embeds training in ongoing daily activities, a detailed description of an integrated evaluation plan that permits monitoring training opportunities and child progress is offered in Chapter 7.

EFFECTIVENESS OF THE APPROACH

Determining the effects of intervention is hampered by insufficient funds, pragmatic and clinical challenges, and methodological constraints (Bricker, 1989). In addition, sorting through the complex array of interactive program features and child/family variables is inordinately difficult (Baer, 1981) and, until the 1990s, generally was not addressed in early intervention efficacy research (Guralnick, 1997). Although replete with confounds, the first generation of research designed to examine the impact of early intervention "supports the generally held opinion that early intervention programs are indeed effective" (Guralnick, 1997, p. 11).

Our attempts to study the effectiveness of activity-based intervention have faced each of the problems noted previously. In particular, we have been challenged by attempting to find legitimate control or comparison groups against which we can evaluate the effects of activity-based intervention. Even when locating contrast groups, their comparability as well as the comparability of other intervention approaches is often not established nor can it be (Baer, 1981). For example, think about the potential number of variables that can affect child outcomes and how one would match children or groups on all of these variables. Although confronted by these realities, the developers of activity-based intervention have collected information on child progress, parent satisfaction, and the general effectiveness of the approach since the early 1980s. Much of this information was formative and used internally to refine the approach; however, a series of outcome studies have been published. These studies are reviewed here with an eye toward evaluating the effectiveness of activity-based intervention. Participants in these studies included typically developing young children and those who have or who are at risk for disabilities and who attended the University of Oregon's Early Intervention Program. The approach used in this program was activity-based intervention.

The first published study examining the effectiveness of activity-based intervention presented 2 years of program evaluation data on more than 100 children who ranged in age from 6 months to 5 years and who spanned the continuum from children without disabilities to children with severe disabilities (Bricker & Sheehan, 1981). Standardized and criterion-referenced tests were administered at the beginning and end of each school year. During both years, almost all pre- and posttest comparisons indicated that children's performances were significantly better at posttest than at pretest and that all changes from pre- to posttest were educationally significant (i.e., change exceeded 1 standard deviation).

Bricker, Bruder, and Bailey (1982) reported the impact of activity-based intervention on a group of 41 young children. This study also used standardized and criterion-referenced measures and a pre- and posttest design. The findings indicated that statistically and educationally significant gains from pre- to posttest were made on the criterion-referenced tests and on the standardized test with one exception (i.e., no significant shift in the general cognitive index for one classroom).

In another study, the effect of activity-based intervention was examined on more than 80 children from infancy to 3 years of age with a range of disabilities (Bailey & Bricker, 1985). An analysis of pre- and posttest comparison found significant gains for all children on the criterion-referenced measure, significant differences using maturity scores on the standardized test, and no differences when using developmental quotients.

Bricker and Gumerlock (1988) reported 2 years of data collection on 46 infants and toddlers. The effect of activity-based intervention was also measured using a pre- and posttest comparison of scores on criterion-referenced and standardized measures. The analysis showed, in general, that the children's performance improved significantly from pre- to posttest on the standardized and criterion-referenced measures.

In a study reported by Losardo and Bricker (1994), an alternating treatment design was used to compare the effect of direct instruction with activity-based intervention on vocabulary acquisition and generalization. The outcomes of this well-controlled study found that acquisition occurred more quickly with direct instruction but that generalization was significantly better when activity-based intervention was used. In addition, subsequent maintenance of the gains was significantly greater for the activity-based condition than for the direct instruction condition.

Except for the Losardo and Bricker (1994) study, these investigations described are representative of first-generation early intervention efficacy work (Guralnick & Bennett, 1987). That is, the outcomes from such studies produced global outcomes that indicated early intervention, or, in this case, activity-based intervention, is effective in producing change in children. The Losardo and Bricker (1994) study moves closer to what Guralnick (1997) has termed *second-generation studies*. A major goal of future research is to identify specific program features and determine their effect or their interactive effect on child outcomes. Although such research is more sophisticated and likely more challenging, such work is necessary in order to move the field forward.

We believe the general efficacy of activity-based intervention has been demonstrated. The next step is to move to a second-generation paradigm that permits the examination of the specific features of activity-based intervention and to document their effects on child outcomes (Bricker & Pretti-Frontczak, 1997).

SUMMARY

The development and application of approaches such as activity-based intervention have raised a number of issues. We have discussed what we believe to be the most critical concerns that have been raised in regard to activity-based intervention. Nonetheless, some readers may remain uneasy about adopting the approach for at least two reasons.

First, the issues raised in this chapter are important and represent some of the more serious challenges facing the field of early intervention. For example, finding effective strategies to be used with groups of children with severe disabilities has and will continue to be a significant problem for many years. We believe the activity-based intervention approach can be successfully employed with children with severe disabilities, but that does not mean that these children will be able to function without substantial assistance from their caregivers. There are not, at this time, perhaps there will never be, techniques that will completely eliminate or compensate for the limitations experienced by individuals with severe disabilities. Professionals who hold expectations of normalcy for this population will surely be disappointed with activity-based intervention as well as other intervention strategies available.

Second, maintaining a familiar approach is less difficult and threatening than instituting change. Professionals who resist exploring alternatives should, we believe, weigh the trauma of change, which is real, against the potential for improved outcomes. In most EI/ECSE programs, there is considerable room for improvement. Empirical findings suggest that early intervention makes a positive difference, but often the differences are minimal or fade over time (Brooks-Gunn et al., 1994). Until we are producing maximum outcomes for children and families, continued exploration of and change in intervention approaches will be necessary. Used by well-trained and sensitive interventionists, we believe activity-based intervention and similar approaches hold considerable promise for moving the field forward; however, verification of this belief awaits second generation research focused on determining the effectiveness of the elements that compose activity-based intervention.

REFERENCES

Baer, D. (1981). The nature of intervention research. In R. Schiefelbusch & D. Bricker (Eds.), *Early language: Acquisition and intervention* (pp. 559–573). Baltimore: University Park Press.

Bailey, E., & Bricker, D. (1985). Evaluation of a three-year early intervention demonstration project. *Topics in Early Childhood Special Education, 5*(2), 52–65.

Bricker, D. (1989). *Early intervention for at-risk and handicapped infants, toddlers, and preschool children.* Palo Alto, CA: VORT Corp.

Bricker, D., Bruder, M., & Bailey, E. (1982). Developmental integration of preschool children. *Analysis and Intervention in Developmental Disabilities, 2,* 207–222.

Bricker, D., & Gumerlock, S. (1988). Application of a three-level evaluation plan for monitoring child progress and program effects. *Journal of Special Education, 22*(1), 66–81.

Bricker, D., & Pretti-Frontczak, K. (1997, November 21). *Examining treatment validity: A critical and often overlooked construct in evaluating assessment instruments.* Paper presented at the International Conference for the Division for Early Childhood, New Orleans.

Bricker, D., & Sheehan, R. (1981). Effectiveness of an early intervention program as indexed by child change. *Journal of the Division for Early Childhood, 4,* 11–27.

Brooks-Gunn, J., McCarton, C., Casey, P., McCormick, M., Bauer, C., Bernbaum, J., Tyson, J., Swanson, M., Bennett, F., Scott, D., Tonascia, J., & Meinert, C. (1994). Early intervention in low-birth-weight premature infants. *Journal of the American Medical Association, 272*(16), 1257–1262.

Cole, K., Dale, P., & Mills, P. (1991). Individual differences in language delayed children's responses to direct and interactive preschool instruction. *Topics in Early Childhood Special Education, 11*(1), 99–124.

Drasgow, E., Halle, J., Ostrosky, M., & Harbers, H. (1996). Using behavioral indication and functional communication training to establish an initial sign repertoire with a young child with severe disabilities. *Topics in Early Childhood Special Education, 16*(4), 500–521.

Guess, D., & Siegel-Causey, E. (1985). Behavioral control and education of severely handicapped students: Who's doing what to whom? And why? In D. Bricker & J. Filler (Eds.), *Severe mental retardation: From theory to practice* (pp. 230–244). Reston, VA: Council for Exceptional Children.

Guralnick, M., & Bennett, F. (1987). *The effectiveness of early intervention for at-risk and handicapped children.* New York: Academic Press.

Guralnick, M.J. (1997). Second-generation research in the field of early intervention. In M.J. Guralnick (Ed.), *The effectiveness of early intervention* (pp. 3–20). Baltimore: Paul H. Brookes Publishing Co.

Horner, R.H., Dunlap, G., & Koegel, R.L. (Eds.). (1988). *Generalization and maintenance: Life-style changes in applied settings.* Baltimore: Paul H. Brookes Publishing Co.

Koegel, R.L., Koegel, L.K., Frea, W.D., & Smith, A.E. (1995). Emerging interventions for children with autism: Longitudinal and lifestyle implications. In R.L. Koegel & L.K. Koegel (Eds.), *Teaching children with autism: Strategies for initiating positive interactions and improving learning opportunities* (pp. 1–15). Baltimore: Paul H. Brookes Publishing Co.

Losardo, A., & Bricker, D. (1994). A comparison study: Activity-based intervention and direct instruction. *American Journal on Mental Retardation, 98*(6), 744–765.

Pretti-Frontczak, K. (1996). *Examining the efficacy of embedding young children's goals and objectives into daily activities.* Unpublished doctoral dissertation, University of Oregon, Eugene.

Schwartz, I., Carta, J., & Grant, S. (1996). Examining the use of recommended language intervention practices in early childhood special education classrooms. *Topics in Early Childhood Special Education, 16*(2), 251–272.

Wolery, M., Holcombe-Ligon, A., Brookfield, J., Huffman, K., Schroeder, C., Martin, C., Venn, M., Werts, M., & Fleming, L. (1993). The extent and nature of preschool mainstreaming: A survey of general early educators. *Journal of Special Education, 27*(2), 222–234.

Yoder, P., Kaiser, A., & Alpert, C. (1991). An exploratory study of the interaction between language teaching methods and child characteristics. *Journal of Speech and Hearing Research, 34,* 155–167.

Yoder, P., Kaiser, A., Goldstein, H., Alpert, C., Mousetis, L., Kaczmarek, L., & Fisher, R. (1995). An exploratory comparison of milieu teaching and responsive interaction in classroom applications. *Journal of Early Intervention, 19*(3), 218–242.

Chapter 12

Into the Future

If the past is a predictor of the future, and many contend it is the very best predictor, then the United States should see a steady growth in the number of programs and services available to young children who have or who are at risk for disabilities and their families. In part, this growth is fueled by the national resurgence in the belief that early intervention has both preventive and curative powers that can offset the myriad of ills that beset today's young children and their families. Although those of us who are associated with early intervention/early childhood special education (EI/ECSE) and early childhood education (ECE) believe that intervention provided early in children's lives can be effective, we are aware that the problem is considerably more complicated than the delivery of services to young children and families. Providing poorly organized, off-target programs, however early they are begun, will not produce the protective and curative outcomes politicians and voters are being led to expect from the investment of resources into early education programs. These national "cure-all" expectations for early intervention place considerable pressure on us as a field to improve the quality of programs to ensure, to the extent possible, that children enter public schools with the necessary foundation for optimal learning. Indeed, expectations have expanded from preparing young children to learn to also preparing young children to have an emotionally and physically balanced life. Preparing children with disabilities and children who come from poor environments to learn effectively and to be emotionally well adjusted is a tall order for those of us associated with EI/ECSE and ECE. Meeting such challenges will require that we move forward in the exploration of methods to enhance early development, adjustment, and learning.

We believe that the ensuing growth in early intervention programs will be paralleled by an increasing number of programs that adopt child-directed approaches such as activity-based intervention. The success of these programs in meeting national expectations for young children will be determined in part by our ability to describe and teach the principles that make these approaches effective. Since completion of the first edition of this book, we have engaged in extensive training of personnel to use the approach; delivered many presentations on its application; written a number of documents designed to further elucidate the approach; and, most important, participated in many discussions that have led to the exploration of better ways to explain and present the approach. These activities, although often humbling, have assisted us significantly in expanding the description and explanation of activity-based intervention contained in this volume.

Our teachings, writings, and discussions focused on activity-based intervention have led to important insights. Two of these insights have had a significant impact on our thinking and on how we will proceed in the future. One insight is that program personnel do not tend to adopt an entire model or approach (Bricker, McComas, Pretti-Frontczak, Leve, & Stieber, 1997). Rather, individuals appear to choose parts, elements, or pieces of an approach. It appears that pieces are selected because 1) they match an individual's personal belief about how to teach or intervene, 2) they are compatible with an individual's present style or approach, or 3) they can be managed or integrated into an individual's present approach. Pieces or elements of an approach that do not fit personal beliefs, are not compatible with present approaches, or simply cannot be managed because of time and resources appear to be discarded and not adopted. The outcome, then, is anything but the straightforward application of an approach.

A second significant insight is the finding that interventionists require a considerable amount of time (e.g., months) to consistently integrate a new element (e.g., embedding) into their repertoires (Bricker & Pretti-Frontczak, 1997). We have found after training and conscientious follow-up that direct service delivery personnel experience considerable difficulty in increasing the frequency with which they embed children's goals and objectives into routine, play, and planned activities (Bricker & Pretti-Frontczak, 1997). We believe these phenomena (i.e., piecemeal application of an approach and long latencies to improve intervention techniques) are not peculiar to activity-based intervention but rather reflect programmatic and personal realities that make change slow and arduous.

These observations on the willingness and ability of personnel to instigate change raise serious questions. The first set of questions is in regard to how to assist program personnel in learning about and adopting an approach or elements of an approach: How can training and follow-up consistently improve the services delivered to young children and their families? The second set of questions raises more difficult issues surrounding the integrity of the approach and measuring program effectiveness. For example, if an interventionist chooses to employ only two elements of activity-based intervention, then is he or she using activity-based intervention? Then too, how does one address the impact or effectiveness of an approach if personnel employ only bits and pieces of the approach? Part of the answer lies in the careful delineation of program features as we discuss in Chapter 8 and as suggested by Guralnick (1997) in his proposal for second-generation research on program effectiveness. Another part of the answer appears to lie in our concepts or expectations about adopting models or approaches. The adoption of an entire approach or model is not a realistic expectation given what we know about human behavior. We will likely accomplish more if we change our expectations to asking personnel to consider the implementation of recommended practice features. The manner and way of implementation can be varied in order to address the realities of specific settings, children, families, and direct service delivery personnel.

We expect activity-based intervention to be applied with thoughtful modification. We do not expect that all consultants, family members, and direct service personnel will understand, interpret, or apply the elements of the approach in the same way. We expect and value variation. We do hope, however, that the fundamental recommended practice features that underlie activity-based intervention are employed by all early interventionists. We further hope that the articulation of the approach in this book will assist personnel in that application. As we move into the future, feedback from the field of EI/ECSE and ECE will tell us how well this hope has been realized.

REFERENCES

Bricker, D., McComas, N., Pretti-Frontczak, K., Leve, C., & Stieber, S. (1997). *Activity-based collaboration project: Final report*. Eugene: University of Oregon, College of Education, Early Intervention Program.

Bricker, D., & Pretti-Frontczak, K. (1997, November 21). *A study of the psychometric properties of the Assessment, Evaluation, and Programming Test for 3 to 6 Years.* Paper presented at the International Conference of the Division for Early Childhood, New Orleans.

Guralnick, M.J. (Ed.). (1997). *The effectiveness of early intervention.* Baltimore: Paul H. Brookes Publishing Co.

Index

Page references followed by *f* or *t* indicate figures or tables, respectively.